DID YOU KNOW ...

- The rating *A-1,* meaning excellent, originated with ships ... not sauce?
- The true, horrific history of *arena* may give you a chill each time you encounter the word?
- The innocent-sounding *round robin* is linked with acts of political defiance and rebellion?
- That to call a glass a *tumbler* is ignoring hundreds of years of technology?
- In what way *aboveboard, room and board,* and *board of directors* are all related?
- Why you'd never guess the lowly roots of being *all balled up*?

From ancient Rome to the Wild West, the English language has adopted colorful, varied words and phrases for expressing our ideas and feelings. Morton S. Freeman's lively scholarship makes our complex, wide-ranging language heritage accessible and great fun to discover. Every thinking person will find this superb collection a valuable reference and a source for hours of enjoyment.

MORTON S. FREEMAN is the former director of publications of the American Law Institute–American Bar Association. He writes the popular syndicated column "Word Watcher," which can be read in the *Philadelphia Inquirer, St. Louis Post-Dispatch, Buffalo News, San Diego Union-Tribune,* and other newspapers. He is the author of *Hue and Cry and Humble Pie* (Plume) *Words to the Wise* (Meridian), and *The One-Minute Grammarian* (Signet), among other books. He lives in Wynnewood, Pennsylvania, and Boca Raton, Florida.

Other Books by Morton S. Freeman

Hue and Cry and Humble Pie
The One-Minute Grammarian
Words to the Wise
The Grammatical Lawyer
A Handbook of Problem Words & Phrases

Even-Steven
and
Fair and Square

More Stories
Behind the Words

Morton S. Freeman

Foreword by Leo Rosten

A PLUME BOOK

PLUME
Published by the Penguin Group
Penguin Books USA Inc., 375 Hudson Street,
New York, New York 10014, U.S.A.
Penguin Books Ltd, 27 Wrights Lane,
London W8 5TZ, England
Penguin Books Australia Ltd, Ringwood,
Victoria, Australia
Penguin Books Canada Ltd, 10 Alcorn Avenue,
Toronto, Ontario, Canada M4V 3B2
Penguin Books (N.Z.) Ltd, 182–190 Wairau Road,
Auckland 10, New Zealand

Penguin Books Ltd, Registered Offices:
Harmondsworth, Middlesex, England

First published by Plume, an imprint of New American Library,
a division of Penguin Books USA Inc.

First Printing, August, 1993
10 9 8 7 6 5 4 3 2 1

Copyright © Morton S. Freeman, 1993
Foreword copyright © Leo Rosten, 1993
All rights reserved

 REGISTERED TRADEMARK—MARCA REGISTRADA

LIBRARY OF CONGRESS CATALOGING-IN-PUBLICATION DATA

Freeman, Morton S.
    Even-Steven and fair and square : more stories behind the words / Morton S. Freeman;
  foreword by Leo Rosten.
      p.   cm.
    ISBN 0-452-27067-7
    1. English language—Etymology—Dictionaries.   2. English language—Terms and
phrases.   I. Title.
PE1580.F73   1993
422′.03—dc20   92-44484
                                                                             CIP

Printed in the United States of America
Set in Times Roman
Designed by Leonard Telesca

BOOKS ARE AVAILABLE AT QUANTITY DISCOUNTS WHEN USED TO PROMOTE PRODUCTS OR SERVICES. FOR
INFORMATION PLEASE WRITE TO PREMIUM MARKETING DIVISION, PENGUIN BOOKS USA INC., 375 HUDSON
STREET, NEW YORK, NEW YORK 10014.

To Herman F. Kerner,
a friend to whom I am
indebted in many ways.

Foreword

Of all the marvelous (nay, miraculous!) inventions of the human race, none is more astounding than language. Words, I have written elsewhere, are what separate us from the rest of the animal kingdom. It is words that we live by: Love, Truth, God. It is words that we fight for: Freedom, Country, Fame. And it is words for which we die: Liberty, Honor, Glory. Those who have most profoundly shaped our history are those who used words with clarity, grandeur and passion: Socrates, Jesus, Luther, Lincoln, Churchill.

Words were our first, boundless feat of magic. They liberated us from ignorance and a life of barbarism. Words sing. They teach. They hurt. And they sanctify.

To those who yammer that a picture is worth a thousand words I say, "Really? Then draw me a picture of the Gettysburg Address."

As Mario Pei tartly put it, if you scoff at those who so highly estimate language, how—except in terms of language—can you scoff? Without words, from "Mama" to "infinity," we would have no science, no Bible, no poetry, no medicine, no astronomy, no physics, no recipes for everything from *crêpes-suzettes* to apple pie ... And beyond all this, every word, said Emerson, was once a poem.

Which brings me to Morton Freeman. I do not know him; I have never met him. But I have dipped into his *Even-Steven and Fair and Square*—and pulled linguistic pearls out of it.

I have been hooked on words ever since I can remember, and their stories—where they came from, how they took on different meanings, what nuances they acquired—never cease to beguile me.

Take the picturesque phrase, "to steal one's thunder," and savor the way Mr. Freeman expatiates upon it:

The interesting thing about this expression is that basically it is true—in one sense someone's thunder was stolen. It all started in 1709 when a play written by John Dennis, called *Appius and Virginia,* was produced at the Drury Lane Theatre in London. Dennis introduced a device to simulate thunder, which turned out to be more realistic than any that had been heard before on stage. Dennis's play was a tragedy, and the critics thought it a tragedy in other ways as well. The play was a financial flop, and the theater's manager soon withdrew it. Dennis later attended a performance of *Macbeth.* When the witches' scene came on with thunder and lightning, Dennis recognized that his invention to produce the sound of thunder was being used. He rose and shouted, "That's my thunder, by God! The villains will not play my play, and yet they steal my thunder!"

Or consider the marvelous story that explains the odd phrase "That gets my goat." Mr. Freeman enlightens (and delights) us this way:

It was the practice some years ago to provide a high-strung race-horse with a companion, a docile animal, one that would stay close whenever the horse was in its stall. A stablemate tended to quiet the thoroughbred so that it didn't become restive. Since thoroughbred horses, especially stallions, become competitive when near each other, and since a mare might excite them, a goat was used instead. The continued presence of the goat as a companion put the horse at ease. Then the bright but nefarious idea arose that if someone would get the goat, that is, steal it before a major race, the horse might become nervous and lose its composure and, in all likelihood, the race, too. Sure enough, once a thief got a horse's goat, the horse became upset and irritable, which is exactly how a person feels when someone unfelicitously gets his goat.

A language, I must remind you, is an extremely complicated *country:* it has frontiers, dimensions, laws, curves, and curses and curlicues all of its own. A language is, in fact, an entire *Weltanschauung*—and please note that one must resort to German to capture the exact reach and overtones.

The more one reads, down the years, the more exhilaration one finds in words that once seemed ordinary enough but sprouted subtle changes in meaning and implications and overtones. Popular phrases emphatically testify to particular sensibilities—and *values.* Any language, any dialect, any tribe or sect or nation reflects its own special and historically embroidered attributes: admiration or scorn, affection or contempt, the quirky ideas of special outrage. I like to drive this point home to skeptics by reminding them that *conscience* in English means something quite different in French—"conscientiousness" (or consciousness); or that Germans had no demotic word for "bully" until the twentieth century(!) and that, even more significantly, it was not until the twentieth century that Germans began to use "fair *spielen*" when they mean what Anglo-Saxons had for centuries known as "fair play."

We must make an effort to believe—*really* believe—that each culture teaches people through language what to feel and how to respond to it. We are forever children to the concepts that language offers us. Take so simple a matter as the written symbols used to express certain universal experiences; for example, how to write—that is to create the visual aspect of hearing—the sound of a scissors snipping: A Chinese writes the scissors sound as *su-su,* but an Italian denotes it as *kri-kri,* and a Spaniard resorts to *ri-ri!*

And so the charming tales presented to us by Mr. Freeman are noteworthy not only for their brightness but as sharp reminders of how languages grow and how they steal and embellish and add new embroidery of nuance.

I started out by emphasizing the extraordinary capacity of a language to take root and grow and expand and establish its own identity, overtones—and *singularity.* The science of today has demanded new words, phrases, significations, symbolic exactitudes. It is extraordinary how even "simple" languages respond to so enormous a challenge. Everyday words are being added to English, like *neutron, fission, black hole, quarks,* and so on. For languages, which, as the Bible says, preceded man, will always grow with him in trying to instill old language in an ever new, momentarily changing universe.

Need I go on? *Even-Steven and Fair and Square* is a delicious book to browse in, refer to, quote. Or, as the current vernacular diction would encourage me to say: Enjoy! Enjoy!

Leo Rosten

Read This First

Learning the history of words can be a fascinating and educational experience. The precursor to this book, *Hue and Cry and Humble Pie,* attempted to open a door to the intriguing development and evolution of words. My hope is that this first book has whetted the reader's desire sufficiently to pursue the subject further.

While the parents of some words are merely obscure, others are completely unknown. Still others have no story behind them to justify inclusion in a book of this nature. But to those of us who enjoy the quest, whose interest has been piqued, the thing to do is to keep probing, and perhaps our intellectual curiosity will lead to new and satisfying answers.

Although the essays in most instances tell a positive story about the word or phrase under discussion, it is interesting to see how many of our words have checkered origins. For example, Spanish invaders saw a strange-looking animal in South America. They asked the Indians, in Spanish naturally, what it was called— *"¿Como se llama?"* After repeating *llama* several times, the natives responded in kind—*llama,* which the invaders took to be the name of the animal. And so to this day we call this furry animal *llama.* A similar story can be told about the naming of the kangaroo. Captain James Cook, in 1770, asked the native Australian aborigines for the name of the two-legged marsupials that were jumping all over the area. He was told *kangaroo,* which name he noted in his log. What he failed to realize was that in the Australian native language *kangaroo* meant "I don't know."

In 1780, Pierre Sonnerat, while exploring the interior of Madagascar, heard his guide call him, then point to a lemur and shout, *"Indri! Indri!"* Sonnerat thought his guide was telling him the name of the animal, but what he was saying was, "Look! Look!" The name *indri,* like *kangaroo,* has stayed with us in both French and English.

And then there is the naming of Canada, our northern neighbor. One belief (rooted in folklore) is that a Spaniard, while exploring North America, reached a point south of the Canadian border. He climbed a tree to see what lay to the north. His companion down below hollered to him, *"¿Que ve usted?"* ("What do you see?") The reply was, *"Aca nada"* ("Nothing's there"). The *a* was swept away by the wind, leaving *ca nada,* which was anglicized, caught on, and has remained. Another story about the naming of Canada involves the explorer Jacques Cartier, who asked the Indian chief whom he was visiting for the name of the village. The chief swept his hand in a northward swing and said, *"Kana' da."* Cartier thought he was referring to the entire region, and so an Indian word for *village* has become the name of the second largest country in the world.

One more: Alaska's large city, Nome, had not been given a name when it was founded, but the theories behind the name dubbed on this westernmost city in the continental United States can fill a page. Here are a few: A cartographer, seeing that no name had been inserted in a map being prepared for the area, wrote "Name," meaning that one was needed. The draftsman in error accidentally changed the *a* to *o,* and so we have *Nome.* Then again, it is claimed by some wordsmiths that *Nome* is simply a shortened form of the Innuit *ka-no-me,* which in their native language means "I don't know." That was the response the explorers got to the question "What is this place called?"

In view of all the "I don't knows," it might be rewarding for the reader to garner some "I knows" in the game of words. That reader will soon discover that he or she can be the life of the party, as the saying goes, as many people are delighted to hear these tales of long ago that remain the foundation of much of our present incredibly rich English language.

"I have here only made a nosegay of culled flowers, and have brought nothing of my own but the string that ties them."

—Michel de Montaigne

A

ABET

To *abet* is to incite, encourage, or instigate, especially in wrong-doing. But it also means, though less usually, "to assist or support in the achievement of a purpose," as, for example, "The writer was abetted by his skillful copyeditor." It is often seen as a paired word—"to aid and abet." When bear baiting was a common form of entertainment, dogs were encouraged to keep attacking. The spectators were said to abet them. The immediate ancestor of *abet* is the Old French *abeter,* a combining of *a,* to, plus *beter,* to bait, which is of Teutonic origin. *Beter,* in turn, was derived from the Old Norse *beita,* from which emerged two senses: one, "to cause to bite" (as in "to bait a bear") and two, "food" (as in "to bait a fishhook with a worm"). In the first the hounds are being urged to bite the bear; in the second, fish are being enticed to eat the worm. An etymology punster might say, "He's so sure the bear will lose and the worm will be eaten that he's willing to take *a bet* on it."

ABORIGINES

Aborigines are the earliest known inhabitants of an area. The term is also used to distinguish members of the native race, indigenous inhabitants, from invaders or colonists. *Aborigines,* in Latin meaning "ancestors" and spelled with a capital *A,* was the name of the primeval Romans. But the term came to be applied to all first inhabitants, such as the American Indians, the Eskimos, and the original Australians. The odd etymological development of this word is that it derives from the Latin *ab,* from, plus *origine* (ablative of *origo,* origin), which gives the sense "from the beginning." The noun *aborigines* therefore consists of a preposition, its governed case (an ablative form), and a modern pluralizing final *s.*

ABOVEBOARD

> All his dealings are square, and above the board.
> —Joseph Hall, *Virtues and Vices*

Aboveboard is a common expression to suggest that which is honest, open, and straightforward. The word, a combination of *above* and *board* (meaning "table"), can be traced to the days of early conjurers, who prepared their tricks under the table and out of the view of the audience. Later they showed their tricks above the table while performing. Hence *aboveboard* became the equivalent of "open sight, without tricks or concealment."

Dr. Johnson, in his *Dictionary of the English Language,* attributed the expression to gamblers. He called it "A figurative expression borrowed from gamesters, who, when they put their hands under the table, changed their cards." According to the OED, the term has been in print since 1616, the year of Shakespeare's death. Its second half, *board,* still means "table," as in "room and board," a table on which food will be served, and "board of directors," a table around which a meeting is held.

The opposite of *aboveboard* is *underhand,* meaning "secret." Brewer offers this quotation: "Let there be no under-hand work, but let us see everything." That'll keep it, if you'll excuse a common redundancy, *honest* and *aboveboard.*

ABSURD

> Fye, 'tis a fault to Heaven,
> A fault against the Dead, a fault to nature,
> To reason most absurd.
> —Shakespeare, *Hamlet*

The current meaning of *absurd* is "foolish" or "ridiculous beyond all reason." That which is *absurd* is "plainly not true, logical, or sensible, so contrary to reason that it is laughable." Yet a person who says, "I refuse to listen to absurdities," is, in a way, being redundant, as will be shown shortly.

The ultimate ancestor of *absurd* was the Latin *surdus,* meaning "deaf," which later also came to mean "silent, mute." With time, *ab-,* meaning "away from," was prefixed to *surdus,* its sense being something audible but out of tune. The word then became a musical term to mean "out of harmony." Still later, the term left the field of music and acoustics and, through a more immediate forebear, the French *absurde,* came to mean "out of harmony with reason." And so today *absurd* is used to describe something that is "ridiculously incongruous or unreasonable," and has become a synonym for plain silly.

ACCORDING TO HOYLE

Although card-playing was a favorite indoor sport among the wealthy for many generations, it was not until the seventeenth century that the manufacture of inexpensive decks of cards enabled the masses to enjoy this activity, which soon became the rage throughout Europe. The game that held an irresistible attraction for the English was whist, the forerunner of modern-day bridge.

Whist could be played according to many systems (actually dozens of them), which led Edmund Hoyle, an Irish barrister (1672–1769), to recognize the need for systematizing the game. To this end, he prepared a set of rules, wrote a book called *A Short Treatise on the Game of Whist*—and eventually became the accepted authority on the playing of the game. He subsequently wrote on other popular card games and was regarded as the authority on them, too.

Ever since Hoyle assumed jurisdiction over the correct play of a game, many players have consulted one of his books to see whether the procedure being followed had his approval. If the play followed the rules set forth by Hoyle, its correctness was beyond dispute. Because of the frequent and widespread reference to Hoyle, whenever someone wished to indicate that everything was in order—that it was being handled properly—whether or not card-playing was involved, it became proverbial to say, "It was *according to Hoyle.*"

Incidentally, Hoyle must have lived his life according to the rules—according to Hoyle—because he laid down his last trump at the age of ninety-seven.

ADULT

It is agreed that an *adult* once was an *adolescent.* And just as an adult has come through *adolescence,* so has the word *adult.*

It all started with an Indo-European ancestor from which was derived the Latin word *alere,* meaning "to nourish," and subsequently the word *alescere,* "to grow." To this latter word was affixed the Latin *ad-,* meaning "to" or "at," which gave the Romans the word *adolescere,* "to grow up." An *adolescent,* a designation of a person during the period of puberty to maturity, is, according to its literal meaning, one who is growing up. A person who has reached full physical development, who has now grown up, is an *adult.* That word came from the past participle of *adolescere— adultus.* But be not beguiled by the Latin masculine ending into thinking that its feminine counterpart is *adultress,* a nounal English feminine ending; it's not, it's *adulta.*

AEGEAN SEA

Some names of places designate happy occasions; others, tragic circumstances. Consider the naming of the *Aegean Sea,* an arm of the Mediterranean Sea located between Turkey and Greece.

Aegeus was a mythological king of Athens. Under an agreement with Minos, king of Crete, seven men and seven women were to be sent each year to be devoured by a monster, the *minotaur.*

One year, Theseus, the son of Aegeus, volunteered to be fed to the monster. However, he told his father that he intended to slay the monster and that, to give him good news promptly, on his return from Crete his ship would use white sails. Previously all the ships returning from Crete used black sails to signify mourning. Theseus did slay the minotaur and joyfully returned to Greece, with wife in hand. But, for whatever reason, Theseus forgot to use white sails. When his ship approached the harbor sailing along with black sails, old Aegeus was heartstruck with despair at the presumed death of his son. And so he leaped from a rock to his death in the sea. From that day until now, that body of water has been named after him—the *Aegean Sea.*

AESOP

One who says that something is as unlikely as an Aesop fable alludes to the kind of story that made Aesop, the most renowned weaver of tales in classical antiquity, a legendary figure among storytellers. Aesop's fables centered on animals, but they pointed up human foibles. Aesop used his own fables with striking effect when debating the vicissitudes of real life. Further, they were his favorite ploy to defend himself against criminal accusations. It is said that during a trial for stealing a goblet from Apollo's temple, he saved his life by reciting the fable of the eagle and the beetle. On another occasion he successfully defended a politician on trial for embezzlement by telling a fable about a sly fox.

Although Aesop's fables have survived for over two thousand years, and many of them have been read and reread by untold numbers, little is known about Aesop's personal life, and what is believed true is unverifiable. Historians agree that Aesop was a slave during most of his life and that he was associated with Solon and the Seven Wise Men of Greece. After obtaining his freedom, he reputedly was employed by Croesus, king of Lydia, but this fact has not been substantiated.

Addendum: While Socrates was imprisoned, he recorded Aesop's fables and made note of Aesop's physical ugliness and deformity. Aesop was put to death in a "fabulous" manner by the citizens of Delphi, whom he had offended: they threw him over a precipice—and that was his downfall.

ALADDIN'S LAMP

None of the tales of *The Arabian Nights* is better known than that of "Aladdin," especially since possessing his lamp is almost everyone's fondest dream. Metaphorically, an *Aladdin's lamp* is a fount of wealth and good fortune, a talisman that can gratify any desire.

> When I was a beggarly boy
> And lived in a cellar damp,
> I had not a friend nor a toy,
> But I had Aladdin's lamp.
> —J. R. Lowell, *Aladdin*

Aladdin was that fortunate man. A wicked magician hired him to go into a cave and bring out a magic lamp. Aladdin got it but decided to keep it for himself. When he rubbed the lamp, a *genie* was released who granted Aladdin's every wish. Aladdin immediately became wealthy, married the daughter of the Sultan of China, and built a magnificent palace. The magician later tricked Aladdin's wife into surrendering the lamp. He then had Aladdin's palace transported to Africa. Aladdin searched for the magician, found him, and killed him—and regained the lamp. Whereupon the genie carried everyone and everything—Aladdin, his wife, the palace—back to China.

The lamp retained its potency only as long as it was well cared for. Aladdin foolishly allowed it to become rusty, and its magical charm disappeared. The moral of all this may be "Take care of a good thing, especially if it's the light of your life."

ALCOVE

Today an *alcove* is understood to be a recess or a partly enclosed extension of a room. But that would not have been an accurate description as the word was making its way into English. The forebear of *alcove* is the Arabic *al,* the, and *qubbah,* vault. An *alcove* originally was a more impressive area because it was vaulted. The Spanish picked up the word and the concept during the occupation of the Moors, but called it *alcoba,* a slight phonetic change. The French spelled it *alcôve,* and so did the English, but without the circumflex. However, these stylish-minded people used the word to designate a recessed area in which a bed had a vaulted ceiling or draperies that resembled one.

One can readily see the word *cove* in *alcove,* yet these words are not etymological cognates. *Cove* was derived from the Old English *cofa,* a closet or a small room, entered Middle English having the same meaning, but came to be applied to an indented coastline, an inlet. So today a *cove* is "a small room" to protect small boats.

ALL BALLED UP

This widely used slang expression means "confused" or "botched." Something that went wrong, or is baffling, or is in a helpless condition, may be said to be *all balled up.* The sense of "ball," the kind one throws or bounces, does not seem inherent in that idiom. And yet it's there.

It may be, and it is, according to the belief of some, that the allusion is to a snarled ball of yarn. Certainly if the cat got to Grandma's knitting kit, the yarn would undoubtedly be *all balled up.* But more likely the genesis of this phrase can be attributed to the problem encountered by horses during snowy weather. If snow or ice formed on a horse's hooves, usually rounded into balls, the horse would have difficulty walking. Sometimes the horse would slip; sometimes flounder about; sometimes fall entirely. If this last happened, one could imagine the state of confusion that followed. It was very exasperating to have a horse lying on the road, and all because its hooves were *all balled up.* From that hazard of early transportation in all probability came the general use of that expression, even though it may chagrin a confused person to think he's being likened to horses' hooves.

ALL OVER BUT THE SHOUTING, IT'S

When victory is about to be assured, one might say, "It is all over but the shouting." The expression is often applied to a sports contest about to end with a lopsided score or to an election in which the political polls show that the outcome is not in doubt.

Many years ago, before the days of the printed ballot, it was customary, under English common law, to submit local issues to a voice vote. The assembled citizens would simply shout their approval. With time, when there was no doubt about the result of an impending vote, it was not unusual to hear someone say, even in a whisper, "It's all over but the shouting."

ALMIGHTY DOLLAR, THE

Many people worship the Almighty God, but, who really knows, perhaps they and others avariciously worship even more the *Almighty Dollar.* That our economic life and many, many aspects that stem from it are founded on financial strength need no proof.

The expressive term—*the almighty dollar*—was coined by Washington Irving in 1836. It first appeared in print in the *Knickerbocker* magazine in his sketch "Wolfert's Roost, Creole Village." Irving wrote: "The almighty dollar, that great object of universal devotion throughout our land. . . ." The term was subsequently used by Dickens, a friend of Irving's, in his *Martin Chuzzlewit.*

It is believed that two hundred years earlier an expression of Ben Jonson's was paralleled, in essence, by Irving, which led to his memorable saying. Jonson, in his *Epistle to Elizabeth, Countess of Rutland,* wrote: "That for which all virtue now is sold, and almost every vice—almightie gold."

Irving's term pointed, and still does, to the all-powerful dollar and to the influence of crass materialism in the lives of people. Perhaps in the light of today's inflation, we should speak of the almighty sawbuck instead.

ANECDOTE

A short narration delivered interestingly or humorously of a biographical incident is called an *anecdote.* For example, a person returning from a pleasure trip through the Orient may recount some amusing stories or hair-raising experiences. These stories, or anecdotes, are bound to enliven and brighten the conversation.

But that is not what the word *anecdote* meant in A.D. 562 when it appeared in the title, *Anekdota,* of a work by Procopius. That Greek word consists of *an,* not, and *ekdotos,* given out, or, in today's language, "not previously published." The accounts written under this cloak of confidentiality were usually of matters that could warrant the writer's execution, and hence better published posthumously. For example, Procopius's unpublished work took the emperor Justinian to task, attacking him for his corrupt regime and his many cruel misdeeds. Procopius also wore no diplomatic gloves regarding Theodora, Justinian's wife, whose father kept and trained bears for a Constantinople circus. Theodora was an actress and a courtesan before Justinian succumbed to her charms.

Although at first *anecdota* was accepted into English, it had a short life. It disappeared in the eighteenth century, but then surfaced as *anecdotes,* from the French, with its current meaning, "the narration of an incident to illustrate a point."

ANSWER

A person who answers a question propounded by someone is, in current usage, simply replying. But many years ago, when Anglo-Saxon law predominated, the verb *to answer* had a much stronger connotation than it does today. Its forebear was Anglo-Saxon *andswerian,* meaning "to swear in opposition to," from *and,* against (akin to Latin *anti*) plus *swerian,* to answer. An *answer* was a solemn statement, a swearing in refutation of a charge. Today it may be used similarly in "to answer the charge," but generally it is no longer considered a serious reply. Sometimes it is only a fresh one, like, "No, Mom, I'm playing now. I'll straighten my room later."

A-ONE/A-1

A person who says that something is *A-1* means it's excellent, perfect, top-notch, perhaps the very best. No doubt it is first-rate. But what that person may not know is that the rating *A-1* originally applied only to ships. Lloyds, the famous English insurance company, maintained a register in which was listed essential information on the seaworthiness of ships, since any ship owner might call upon the company for insurance. The register classified the ships' hulls by letters and the condition of their anchors, cables, and general equipment by numbers. A ship top-rated, excellent in all categories, was marked "A-1." "A-2" meant the hull was first-rate but the equipment was second-rate, and so on. And so from this source has come the general designation for first class in anything—*A-1*. When a man looks at a woman and says she looks A-1, he means her "hull" and "equipment" are perfect.

APPLE-PIE ORDER, IN

Cleanliness may be next to godliness, but neatness is not far behind. That which is neat, everything just so, is orderly, as might be said, *in apple-pie order.* This graphic expression took hold in England in the nineteenth century, but how it originated and what relation apple pie had to orderliness has never been determined. Most philologists have simply given up on this one.

Among the conjectures favored by some word sleuths as a source for this phrase is *cap-à-pie,* which in French means "from head to foot," as is said of a knight in complete armor. Saying *cap-à-pie* quickly does sound somewhat like "apple pie." But since it contains no inherent suggestion of orderliness, any relationship to *apple-pie order* remains obscure. Those looking to Greek *alphabeta* as the source, implying that the phrase represents the orderliness of the letters of an alphabet, are unconvincing. Also farfetched is the theory that the expression emerged from the French phrase *nappes pliées* (folded lines), of which *apple-pie bed* is an English corruption. This bed was made in such a way, as a trick by college students, that one lying in it could not straighten out. The tucked-in sheets were said to resemble the crust of a pie.

Perhaps word historians have not accepted any of these theories or origins because the evidence submitted was not, to borrow a phrase, in apple-pie order.

ARCTIC

One might never guess that the water-repellant overshoes called *arctics* and the word *bear* have something in common. The overshoes (properly pronounced *arhk-tick,* not *ar-tick),* as can be imagined, are associated with the regions around the world's two poles—Arctic, the area that surrounds the North Pole, and Antarctic, the area that surrounds the South Pole. The overshoes came by their name quite naturally; they obviously were designed to be worn for the kind of climate one would expect to find at the pole— hence *arctics*. But the poles had gotten their names from a completely unrelated source—a constellation that revolves around the North Star, the Great Bear (its scientific name is *Ursa Major*; in Latin, *ursa* means "bear"). In Greek, the word for *bear* is *arktos*. From that Grecian source the polar regions came to be called *Arctic* and, to distinguish the South from the North, *Antarctic* (*anti*— against). What has turned out to be serendipitous is that in that region live the mammoth white polar bears.

ARENA

> First Odius falls and bites the bloody sand.
> —Homer, *The Iliad*

Spectators of this generation go to an *arena* to watch a contest or a spectacle. Everything is well ordered and the players or actors are well dressed. When the performance is over, the audience applauds as the entertainers bow and leave for their dressing room. The only things marring the beauty of the arena are some discarded programs. But this was not so when the greatest arena during the splendor of Rome was the Roman Colosseum. In Latin, *harena* means "sand," and that was the stuff strewn on the amphitheater floor to absorb the blood of the slain gladiators and animals (the *h*, which was weakly articulated, was dropped). The philosopher Seneca expressed his revulsion at the grisly deaths designed to entertain the butchery-loving Romans:

> I happened to drop in upon the midday entertainment of the Arena in hope of some milder diversions, a spice of comedy, a touch of the relief in which men's eyes may find rest after a glut of human blood. No, no: far from it. All the previous fighting was mere softness of heart. . . . Now for butchery pure and simple! . . . Kill! Flog! Burn! Why does he jib at cold steel? Why

boggle at killing? Why die so squeamishly? Cut a few throats to keep things going!

From that gory use, *arena* has come to mean a modern building or stadium in which sporting events are held and in which the spectators may never see blood or sand. They may shout with glee or in anger, and, with tongue in cheek, cry "Kill the umpire," but not the death-dealing Roman shouts of "Kill! Flog! Burn!"

ARGENTINA

Argentina, second in size to Brazil among South American countries, can thank Latin for its name, *argentum,* which means "silver." It is said that llamas, while grazing on Mt. Potsi in 1545, dug up some shrubs, which revealed a vein of silver. That the Spanish who settled in that territory had expected to find silver was evident by the name given the largest river in the region—Rio de la Plata; in Spanish *plata* means "silver." When in 1816 it came time to name the country, the Latin form was adopted. The country was named *La Republica Argentina,* "The Silver Republic."

ASBESTOS

It is a lexical error to define *asbestos* as "an inextinguishable substance." The fact is that asbestos is incombustible, which, of course, means that it cannot burn. Clearly, therefore, *inextinguishable,* which means "unquenchable," is not applicable, since asbestos could not have been ignited in the first place.

But the Greeks are not to blame for this erroneous use of the word *asbestos.* They called unslaked lime *amiantos lithos,* undefiled stone. The Roman naturalist Pliny (A.D. 23–79) in his work *Historia Naturalis* mistakenly named this mineral, combining *a,* not, and *sbestos,* to quench. According to Dr. Johnson, Pliny had seen napkins made of this material which, to be cleaned, were thrown into the fire and were scoured better than if they had been washed in water. No one thought to correct Pliny, and the name *asbestos* has continued to this very day.

ASSAY/ESSAY

Commonly an *essay* is known as a literary composition on a particular subject, such as the one you're now reading; an *assay* is the analysis of an ore or alloy to find out the quantity of gold, silver, or other metal in it. These words had the same ancestor—the Old French *essai,* meaning a try or an attempt.

Everyone will recognize in the word *assay* a trial, a testing, in that it suggests an examination to determine quantity or genuineness. But not so with *essay.* Yet that in essence is what *essay* meant for many generations—to taste food or drink set before a monarch to see whether it was poisoned. To take the assay or essay was to serve as a royal taster. Whereas *assay*'s sense today applies only to testing, *essay* has developed several meanings: "to attempt"; "a trial or test of the value or nature of a thing"; "a literary composition."

A French Renaissance writer, Michel de Montaigne, first applied the word *essai* (but spelled with an *i*) to his informal experiments with written conversations. Later, but still during early times, a work sent to a publisher might modestly be called by the author an *essay* to indicate that it was not on such a high level as a treatise. Francis Bacon composed the first works in English named *Essays,* a collection of writings of worldly wisdom. In 1597, he wrote: "Certain brief notes . . . I have called *Essays.*" Incidentally, the word *essayist* (a person who writes essays) is a hybrid coined from the noun *essay* and a suffix of Greek origin, *-ist.*

ASSET

An *asset* (a singular noun) is an item of value or a useful quality. *Assets* (a plural noun) is defined as "things of value." The strange thing about all this is that until the nineteenth century, English had no word spelled *asset,* only *assets.* The term *assets* was a singular noun, derived from the Old French *asez* or *asetz* (pronounced *asets*), meaning "enough" (to satisfy creditors). (In today's French the word for "enough" is *assez.*) The ancestor of these words was the Latin *ad satis,* "in sufficiency" (from *ad,* to, and *satis,* enough). The original of the English use, according to the *Oxford English Dictionary,* is to be found in the Anglo-French law phrase *aver assetz,* to have sufficient; namely, to meet certain claims, through which *assets* passed as a technical term into the vernacular. Although *assets* is a singular, it mistakenly came to be treated as a plural because of its final *s* and its collective sense. Then, through a process of back formation, English created a singular companion: *asset.*

ATLANTIC OCEAN

If those visiting the casinos on the New Jersey shore would pause to view the crashing waves of the Atlantic Ocean, some of them might wonder how that body of water got its name. No explorer named this ocean, the way Magellan, for instance, named the Strait of Magellan. In fact the two words in its name—Atlantic Ocean— came from different sources, both mythological. The second came first.

The Greeks imagined that the land where they lived was encircled by a large river. They knew that the expanse of the Mediterranean Sea, which they frequently sailed on, and the waters beyond that point (the Strait of Gibraltar) were greater than the eye could see or the mind could imagine. It was believed that in those waters lived *Oceanus,* the god of the great primeval water, the Greek god of the sea before Poseidon. Oceanus was a Titan whose power and importance ended when Zeus defeated the Titans and became the ruler of the Olympians. But his former position was not forgotten. The vast body of salt water to the west (and of course all such large seas) became his memorial. Such extensive stretches of water we now call *ocean,* which, in original Greek, meant "the great stream or river."

The *Atlantic* half comes from a group of nymphs called *Atlantides.* They were fathered by *Atlas,* a Titan who, like Oceanus, fought on the losing side in the battle for power between Zeus and the Titans. Atlas was condemned to hold up the heavens. The nymphs (*nymph* is a Greek word for "young girl") were associated with the sea. Their name was given to the waters west of Greece because they were supposed to be dwelling there. Hence this vast body of water was called *Atlantic,* but sometimes *Oceanus.* Evidently the words were run in tandem and the waters called *Atlantic*

Ocean. And so it has remained—*Atlantic* now a proper name and *ocean* a generic term.

As a footnote, the mythic continent that disappeared into the ocean after an earthquake was an imaginary story of the great Plato. He called the continent *Atlantis.* No geography book lists the name *Atlantis,* and no scientist believes that such a continent ever existed. But then again, who knows?

AUTOMOBILES, NAMES OF

Automobiles have been named from many sources. Some cars were named for their inventors—the Ford, for example, or the Stutz (Stutz Bearcat). Some were named after animals—the Cougar, the Mustang; and some were named after places—Seville.

One popular car, the Mercedes-Benz, was named in a more unusual way. The Benz part came about through regular channels, the name of the Benz company with which the Daimler firm was merged in 1926. The Daimler automobile works had been manufacturing a car called Mercedes, one of many cars that bore that name. Why was the name used on different cars, and what made the name important? An Austrian at the turn of the century, Emil Jellinek, had a daughter whom he adored so much that he named his cars after her. The Daimler company built a car for Jellinek, which too was named after his daughter—her name, Mercedes. The name Mercedes-Benz has been continued by the present manufacturer.

AVERAGE

Those who study baseball averages might never guess that the first use of the word *average,* which was around 1500, was as a maritime term. About that time the sea lanes became filled with ships transporting cargo between Europe and the Levant. As might be expected, shipowners incurred a great deal of expense (port taxes) and often suffered heavy losses (damaged merchandise). To assure an equitable financial responsibility for these expenses, a method was devised whereby the owners of the ship and the owners of the cargo (or the insurers) shared the costs proportionally. This was called an *average* (from French *avarie,* meaning "damage to ship or cargo") and was a figure arrived at by an *average-adjuster.* English altered the spelling of *avarie* to conform with the spelling of other English words such as *pilotage* and *towage.*

From this notion of an equal division of loss among a number of persons evolved the idea of a mathematical average—an arithmetical mean. Then, with time, *average* spawned synonyms that were unrelated to the middle figure that *average* implied, such words as *typical, usual,* and *ordinary.*

AX TO GRIND, AN

This expression refers to a person who has a particular objective, a personal interest at stake. Who originated the term has been a matter of dispute among authorities. Some credit Benjamin Franklin; others, Charles Miner. The weight, however, seems to be in favor of the latter by reason of an article he published in 1811 in the *Wilkes-Barre* (Pennsylvania) *Gleaner.*

The story given by all authorities, no matter to whom they attribute the source, is basically the same, that a man approached a boy, and in flattering terms asked whether he could use a grindstone that he spotted in the boy's yard. The boy, influenced by the flattery, agreed, and then the man, even more flatteringly, asked to see how the machine would grind his ax. The boy demonstrated by grinding the ax, but, since the man kept praising him, the boy continued until the job was finished. Whereupon the man left without so much as a "thank you" or, according to Miner, said, "Now, you little rascal, you've played the truant; scud to school or you'll rue it." It may be that a person who engages in flattery or is obsequious when asking a favor has a selfish motive; he has, it might be said, an ax to grind.

Miner later published a series of essays under the title *Essays from the Desk of Poor Robert the Scribe.* Some people apparently confused that title with Benjamin Franklin's *Poor Richard's Almanac,* and so mistakenly attributed the expression *an ax to grind* to Dr. Franklin.

BACTERIA

The term *bacterium* was coined by Christian Gottfried Ehrenberg in 1838; its plural form is *bacteria*. *Bacteria* come in three basic shapes. One is rod-shaped, named after the Latin *bacillus*, little rod (its parent word is *baculus*, stick). The second, which is ball-shaped, is called *coccus*, after "berry." The third, the *spirillum*, meaning "spiral," is twisted like a corkscrew.

An *antibiotic* is a drug that destroys bacteria (Greek *bios*, life, and *anti*, against). Hence an antibiotic is "against life"—but only the kind that would destroy the life of others. This medical term originated in 1941 with Dr. Selman Abraham Waksman, the discoverer of streptomycin.

BADGER

The verb *badger* as used today means "to persistently annoy, worry, or torment." Its sense comes not from the name of the animal, however, but from the name of a sport, badger-baiting. For the entertainment of certain "sports"-minded people, a badger was released from a barrel and hounds then set on it. The badger was the one being tormented, of course, not the dogs or the sportsmen.

A badger, originally called *gray, brock,* or *brawson,* bears a white mark on its forehead. Those who believe that the animal's name derived from that "white badge" are engaging in folk etymology. Though there is no certainty, the word *badger* may have come from the Late Latin *bladger* (*bladum*, corn), a dealer in corn and butter. With time, the *l* was dropped and the shortened *badger* was applied to this kind of dealer, although the more usual name was *hawker* or *huckster.*

A theory espoused by some word historians, and this was not a corny story, is that the practice of hoarding corn by commodity dealers in anticipation of price increases was likened to that of this burrowing animal which hoards corn, as well as wheat, thriving on the labor of others. The practice became so prevalent that during the reign of Edward VI, son of Henry VIII, badgers (the name given these business agents in Middle English) had to be officially licensed.

This court taking notice of the great prices of corn and butter . . . , it was ordered that from henceforth no badger whatsoever be licensed but in open court.
—*Somerset Quarter Sessions Record* (1630)

BARK UP THE WRONG TREE, TO

The gist of this expression is that what is being done is wrong, that energy is being wasted, or, considering the origin of the phrase, that a wrong scent is being followed. It all started with raccoon hunting, which usually takes place after dark because raccoons are primarily nocturnal animals. The hunt begins with the release of dogs to seek and find the raccoons through their scent. When the dogs think they have cornered their quarry hiding in a tree, they bay at the foot of the tree until their master arrives. However, in the dark dogs sometimes make mistakes and howl at the base of the wrong tree. Davy Crockett in *Sketches and Eccentricities* wrote, in 1833: "I told him . . . that he reminded me of the meanest thing on God's earth, an old coon dog, barking up the wrong tree." And so we say that a person on the wrong track is like a dog barking up the wrong tree.

Coon hunting has given us another common expression: *up a tree.* A person said to be "up a tree" is having difficulty; he's in a quandary. Like the coon that sought refuge, he is confused and helpless.

BARKIS IS WILLIN'

A person signifying that he is ready, that he's willing to abide by someone else's idea, may express agreement by simply saying, *"Barkis is willin'."*

No one at first might think so, but that quotation originally was a romantic utterance, a proposal of marriage. In Charles Dickens's *David Copperfield* (1850), Barkis announced his matrimonial intentions to Clara Peggotty in just those words. Probably no proposal has ever been more direct or demanding, certainly according to Barkis, who said, "When a man says he's willin', it's as much as to say, that man's a-waitin' for a answer."

BARNACLE

According to a dictionary definition, *barnacles* are "small salt-water animals that attach themselves to something under water." They are often seen on jetties and rocks when the tide is low. And, of course, they adhere to the bottom of ships.

When the word *barnacle* first appeared, in the fifteenth century, it was applied to a wild goose—the barnacle goose—allied to the Brent goose. Centuries later the sea animal, a crustacean called *Cirripedes,* acquired the popular name of *barnacle.* In terms of etymological development, therefore, the goose beat that underwater shellfish, so to speak, by a long neck.

In medieval times it was believed that this species of goose was born in a barnacle, where it was nurtured and grew, fed by the heat of the sun. Perhaps this notion was based on the appearance of the *goose barnacle,* so-called because it was thought to look like the head and neck of a goose. But all this notion did was lead etymologists on a wild goose chase. The fact is that the bird spent its summer in the Arctic, and its breeding habits were unknown.

The current figurative sense of *barnacle* is a person who, like the shell animal, clings tenaciously to someone, refusing to be shaken off. He might be called a hanger-on.

BASSINET

Question: What does a baby's crib and a knight's protective mask have in common? They both have the same ancestor, a *basin*. The word for *basin* dates back to Roman times, when its Latin form was *bachinus,* an eating bowl. During the reign of Charlemagne knights wore a basin-shaped protective headgear with movable visors that resembled the kitchen utensil. From the Old French *bacinet* the helmet was called *bacin*. The protective idea spread to England, where the soldiers of Edward I used it in the thirteenth century during their conquest of Wales, anglicizing the name of the gear to *basin*. With time the multiribboned baby's crib came to be called a *bassinet* (with a diminutive ending appended) because this wicker basket was shaped like the knight's facial protector. The word is still with us, even though the crib may no longer be beribboned nor made of wicker.

BAYONET

This lethal weapon used by soldiers was named after a prominent French town. At least some sources believe that the weapon was first conceived in the seventeenth century in Bayonne, France, where steel blades and daggers were manufactured. Others say that *bayonet* is a diminutive form of *bayon,* the shaft of a crossbow. Still others say its origin has never been established.

The chief weapons of a foot soldier at one time were the spear and the pike. With the arrival of firearms, the use of the older weapons quickly diminished. One problem with the musket was that when it had to be reloaded, the infantryman was virtually an unprotected target against cavalry. Mixing soldiers carrying pikes with those carrying firearms was a big help. But eventually the bayonet was affixed to the muzzle of the musket, so that the soldier on foot always had at the ready some weapon.

This new weapon, according to legend, surfaced during the siege of Bayonne. The defenders had expended all their munitions. In desperation they attacked their foe with long-handled knives. One ingenious soldier thrust the handle of his knife into his musket to give him a wider range. Other soldiers followed suit, and so the *bayonet,* as the story goes, was born—named after the place where it was first used.

William Ralph Inge made the most pointed remark about bayonets, as reported in *Wit and Wisdom of Dean Inge:* "A man may build a throne of bayonets, but he can't sit on it."

BEARD THE LION, TO

This is a proverbial statement meaning to confront a dangerous opponent with utter boldness or to take on a dangerous mission, as one would, so to speak, seize a lion by the beard. In the story of David and Goliath in the Old Testament, Saul expressed misgivings because David was a mere youth and Goliath a giant skilled in warfare. But David reassured Saul, saying, "Your servant used to keep sheep for his father; and when there came a lion, or a bear, and took a lamb from the flock, I went after him, and smote him and delivered it out of his mouth; and if he arose against me, I caught him by his beard, and smote him and killed him." To the expression *to beard the lion* was added the words *in his den* to acknowledge the story in which Daniel was thrown into a den of lions, but survived. He explained that God had sent an angel who closed the lions' mouths. This metaphor caught on so well that it was quoted by Horace and Martial and later by Erasmus, in a story about a timid hare that disdainfully plucked a dead lion's beard. But Scott made the saying proverbial in his *Marmion:*

> ... And dar'st thou then
> To beard the lion in his den,
> The Douglas in his hall?
> And hop'st thou thence
> unscathed to go?
> No, by St. Bryde of Bothwell, no!

A quipster might ask whether one, in a dangerous spot or in a dilemma, should prefer to beard a lion in his den or, to use another old idiom, to grab a bear by the tail? Fine choice!

BEAT AROUND THE BUSH, TO

> 'Twas I that beat the bush,
> The bird to others flew.
> —George Wither, "A Love Sonnet"

This cliché figuratively means that a person is approaching an objective indirectly or is hemming and hawing; that is, speaking in a roundabout way. He is being so cautious that he's not getting to the point of the matter at hand. The phrase originally, and for many years thereafter, was *to beat the bush,* which was the practice of hunters in flushing out game birds that might be lurking there. John Heywood, in 1546, said it this way in his *Proverbs:* "And while I at length debate and beat the bush, /There shall step in other men and catch the birds." It is said that Henry V uttered this expression, slightly altered, at the siege of Orléans: "Shall I beat the bush and another take the bird?" The addition of *around* to the phrase—"to beat around the bush"—has given us the current sense of evading a matter, of coming to it indirectly, of shilly-shallying. Its antonymous cliché is *to call a spade a spade*—to speak explicitly, to talk plainly, to tell it like it is.

BEAT THE RAP, TO

A person asked what the word *rap* means to him or her may come up with many unrelated answers, some curious. A *rap* is certainly a sharp knock by the knuckles on a door or on a desk. Or if the knuckles themselves are given a sharp blow, the answer may be "a rap on the knuckles." The younger generation speaks of *rap sessions,* and *to rap* is taken to mean "to speak with one another, to converse." On the other hand, journalists use *rap* as a shorter and more forceful word for "censure or criticize" ("The teacher was *rapped* for her brusque manner"). A person given a criminal sentence, especially if taken to save someone else, is said *to take the rap.*

None of these *raps* applies to the cliché *beat the rap.* That idiom means "to escape punishment, to go free." How this notion came about is not entirely clear, but it is the thought of some wordsmiths that the *rap* referred to was a rapping of a judge's gavel to sound the court's adjournment. Until the gavel is rapped on the judge's desk, there is still a chance to avoid a penalty.

We must conclude by saying that those dubious about the etymology of *rap* may, if they wish, throw up their hands in despair and say, "This whole thing is not worth a rap," *rap* in this sense being a worthless coin.

BEE IN ONE'S BONNET, TO HAVE A

> Her lips were red, and one was thin,
> Compared with that was next her chin,
> Some bee had stung it newly,
> —Sir John Suckling, *Fragmenta Aurea*

One can live a lifetime without hearing that someone has had a bee trapped in his bonnet or his hat. But it is easy to imagine that if such were the case—a bee was actually trapped inside someone's hat—that person would be greatly distressed. The idiom, therefore, has come to mean that a person is crotchety or even crazed on some point and often refers to someone obsessed with an idea which that person refuses to stop talking about. It has become an eccentric fixation. At one time there was a belief that bees and the soul were somehow connected. Mohammed welcomed bees to Paradise. Coming to more recent times, in 1648 the following appeared in Robert Herrick's "Mad Maid's Song:"

> Ah, woe is mee, woe, woe is mee,
> Alack and well-a-day! For pitty, sire, find out that bee,
> Which bore my love away. I'le seek him in your bonnet brave.

And in 1845, in *Coleridege and Opium,* by De Quincey: "John Hunter, notwithstanding he had a bee in his bonnet, was really a great man."

BEEF, TO

To beef is to voice a complaint or to express discontent. A person with a *beef* is dissatisfied with what was done or what was not done. This slang phrase arose during Western cowpunching days when herds were driven for long periods over all kinds of terrain and in all kinds of weather to railroad points for shipment to the East. Extreme heat and scarcity of fodder along the way caused the cattle to suffer torment. The only thing they could do to relieve themselves was to bellow. And this they did. When a herd was approaching its destination, everyone there knew for a long while what was coming, for the bellowing of the cattle could be heard miles away. The cattlemen would say, "Here comes 'the beef.' " Today a person who complains, whether bellowing or not, is said to have a beef.

BEFORE YOU CAN SAY JACK ROBINSON

Not uncommonly a person intending to do something at once is heard to say, "I'll do it before you can say Jack Robinson." Why *Jack Robinson*? No one really knows, but there have been some conjectures. If the origin of this name is ever convincingly established, we may learn that, of itself, it has nothing to do with immediacy and that it consists of nothing more than meaningless words.

One surmise, based on a book written in 1875 by Francis Grose, the *Classical Dictionary of the Vulgar Tongue*, attributes the origin of the phrase to a peripatetic person known for brief stops: "Before one could say Jack Robinson is a saying to express a short time, originating from a very volatile gentleman who would call on his neighbors and be gone before his name could be announced." Brewer mentions as a possible source Halliwell's *Archaic Dictionary* (1846), in which the following lines from "an old play" are elsewhere given as the original phrase—

A worke it ys as easie to be done
As tys to says Jacke! robyson.

A more interesting background, but also unattested, is a byplay that took place in the English Parliament during the course of a debate between Fox and Sheridan over the India bill. A charge was made of bribery. The M.P.'s began shouting, "Name him. Name him," to which Sheridan responded by looking directly at John

Jack Robinson. What he implied by staring at Robinson was clear, and it presumably fathered the current idiom meaning "with no loss in time."

BELL, BOOK, AND CANDLE

> Bell, book, and candle shall not drive me back.
> —Shakespeare, *King John*

Sleuths of English expressions disagree on the proper sequence in the saying *bell, book, and candle*. As given, the order has a pleasant musical sound, but the order does not agree with the steps taken by the Roman Catholic Church when performing an act of excommunication. After a priest's pronouncement that a communicant may no longer participate in the sacraments of the church, the priest closes the book, quenches the candle, and then tolls the bell. These symbolic actions of the cleric follow logically, in that the ringing of the bell, a symbol of death, concludes the ceremony; hence *book, candle, and bell*. But the popular expression remains otherwise: *bell, book, and candle*.

Not everyone, of course, is concerned with excommunication. Such a person might express his lack of interest by saying he'll do or say what he wants to "in spite of bell, book, and candle," even though the bell tolls for him.

BELL THE CAT, WHO WILL

When one asks, "Who will bell the cat?" the question in figurative language asks, Who will assume personal risks for the benefit of others? If a teacher regularly holds up the class after the bell has rung, naturally to the displeasure of the students, a student volunteering to tell the teacher to dismiss the class promptly would in effect be *belling the cat*. The allusion is to a fable by Aesop, *The Rat and the Cat*, in which a conference was held by mice to determine how to stop a cat from killing so many of their numbers. After a prolonged mulling over the problem, it was decided that the thing to do was to hang a bell around the cat's neck so that as the cat moved the bell would tinkle and warn of the cat's approach. All agreed that that would solve the problem, and they smiled at each other with pleasure over this ingenious idea. But just as the mice settled back in self-satisfaction, one sage stepped up and, with one question, dismayed the entire group. He asked, "Who will bell the cat?"

BEHIND THE SCENES

This self-explanatory expression refers to something done outside the public view. Of particular interest to those concerned with the origin of such an ordinary and obvious-meaning phrase is its historical development.

During the early days of the English theater, backdrops for stage settings were unknown. The plays were performed before an ordinary, plain curtain that had no beauty and no relationship to the theme of the play. In the mid-sixteenth century, in the reign of James I and continuing with Charles I (both of these men were followers of the arts), backdrops were painted with colorful views of landscapes to enliven the stage and make the setting more attractive. Logically, these scenic settings came to be called *scenes*.

Sordid crimes, torture, and executions were not shown on stage but were just hinted at as having taken place between the acts. The theatergoers, amused by this chicanery, would joke that the important action, the salivating histrionics, which were hidden from their view, took place *behind the scenes*. The expression has stayed with us, shifting the drama of the stage to somewhat common, and sometimes nefarious, deeds in everyday life.

BILLIARDS

Let's to billiards.
—Shakespeare, *Antony and Cleopatra*

When the game of *billiards* originated is unknown. One belief is that the ancient Greeks played a game that resembled it, but its name has escaped history. The term *billiards* is traceable to the

French *billard,* which first meant a bent stick and then a stick to push balls (a *playing cue* in its modern sense), from *bille,* log. Spenser in the sixteenth century called the game *balliards.* Perhaps he was being humorous. True, the game is played with balls, but the name of the game is *billiards.*

The story that has made the rounds is that a pawnbroker named William Kew, to safekeep the three balls hanging outside, the symbol of his trade, would nightly take them into his store. On one occasion, to amuse himself, he struck the balls with a yardstick, driving them into the stalls. Kew then got the idea of a board with side pockets on which a game could be played. The game was named *billyard* because *Bill* had used his *yard*-measurer. The name of the stick was later changed to *kew* (Bill's surname) and still later to *cue* (same pronunciation). But beware, this delightful fable has no authoritative support, for, logical though it seems, it has never been attested, and we may be following the wrong cue.

BIRD IN THE HAND, A

> He is a fool who leaves things close at hand
> to follow what is out of reach.
> —Plutarch, *Of Garrulity*

Although the sense of the phrase, which completely stated is "a bird in the hand is worth two in the bush," is obvious—that it is better to possess than to expect—its origin is far from certain. One story that has made the rounds is that Lord Surrey gave a beautifully plumaged bird to the jester of Henry VIII, Will Sommers. Lord Northampton admired the bird so much that he sent Sommers a message which said, in part, that he would give Sommers two birds one day in exchange for the one bird given him by Lord Surrey. Sommers's answer was, "I am much obliged for your liberal offer of two birds for one, but I prefer one bird in hand to two birds in the bush."

John Heywood in his *Proverbs,* in 1546, put it a little differently: "One bird in the hand is worth two in the wood."

The idea is embraced in idioms of several languages. The French say, *"Un tiens vaut, ce dit-on, mieux que deux tu l'auras"*

("One you have is worth two you will have"). The Italian phrase reads: *"E meglio aver oggi uovo, che domani una gallina"* ("It is better to have an egg today than a chicken tomorrow"). In any language it is wiser to hold on to what you've got.

BITE OFF MORE THAN YOU CAN CHEW, TO

The expression *Don't bite off more than you can chew* means that you should not undertake more than you can handle, not to be too ambitious, and not to be too greedy. It is not uncommon for a mother to say to a child who goes to a restaurant and wants to order everything: "Your eyes are bigger than your stomach."

The expression came into vogue when tobacco chewing was a common practice. It became a part of spittoon culture. It was polite to offer those nearby a bite from the plug, as one offers a cigarette from a pack today. But since no one wanted to lose his plug in one bite, it was prudent to say, as though facetiously, "Don't bite off more than you can chew." Bergen Evans points out that the usual word during that period was *chaw,* not *chew,* and he remarks on Mark Twain's counter to that jest whereby the donor, seeing how little of the plug has been left, says, "Here, gimme the *chaw,* and you take the *plug."* The Chinese spoke even more diplomatically: *"Tan to chuch pu tan"*—"If you bite off too much, you can't chew it thoroughly."

Perhaps this brief essay will give you something to chew on.

BITE THE BULLET, TO

A common expression, but of obscure origin, is *bite the bullet.* In current usage it means "to face come what may" or, to put it in popular language, "to face the music," as one does who confronts an unpleasant situation. Many years ago, however, before anesthesia was invented, the phrase had another purpose. To ease the pain of soldiers undergoing surgery, doctors had their patients bite on a lead bullet. A bullet, of course, is not an analgesic, but biting on it tended to distract the soldier's attention from the agony of the crude operation. Rudyard Kipling used it in *The Light That Failed:*

"Bite on the bullet, old man, and don't let them think you're afraid."

BITE THE DUST, TO

This term, meaning "to be vanquished, to be slain in battle," comes from a distinguished classical background, although the wording was somewhat different. The metaphor appeared in Homer's *Iliad:* "First Odius falls and bites the bloody sand." William Cowper (1838) translated Homer as ". . . bite the ground." William Cullen Bryant (1870) put it: ". . . and bite the dust." But the phrase became popular through Western lingo with Indian-killing scorekeepers who relished mouthing the words, "Another redskin bit the dust."

BLACK BOOK, IN ONE'S

Should one feel proud that his or her name has been noted in someone's *black book*? It depends. Today a black book is considered a personal address book, and if the property of a prominent person, an indication of the addressee's importance. This would seem flattering. But in yesteryear, when the term first appeared, it was quite the opposite, signifying that the addressee was out of favor and in disgrace. In the sixteenth century, the deputies of Henry VIII inscribed in a black book the names of monasteries that were "sinful." Henry compiled the list to support his case with Parliament, to justify his actions against the Roman Catholic Church. Evans mentions Almhurst and his *Terrae Filius, or the Secret History of the University of Oxford* (1726), a black book containing the names of those proscribed from proceeding to degrees. Edmund Spenser (1595) wrote: "Al her faultes in thy black booke enroll."

The change in the significance of a listing in someone's black book, from one of disgrace to one of pride, is supposedly credited to Fred Astaire, who in a musical with Ginger Rogers displayed his "black book" to Ginger in order to show her how many beautiful women treasured him, and thus to arouse Ginger's jealousy. Since

Astaire was the epitome of sophistication in the eyes of many Americans, the term *black book,* from a term of perjoration, became one of admiration.

BLACKSMITH

> Under a spreading chestnut tree
> The village smithy stands.
> The smith, a mighty man is he,
> With large and sinewy hands;
> And the muscles of his brawny arms
> Are strong as iron bands.
> —Henry Wadsworth Longfellow,
> "The Village Blacksmith"

Almost all educated people are familiar with this poem. If a survey were made, however, to learn what these people believe the word *smithy* stands for, the overwhelming response would be "blacksmith." In their minds it is the man with brawny arms who was standing under the spreading chestnut tree. But the response would be wrong. A *smithy* (sometimes mispronounced *smitty*) is a blacksmith's shop, the workshop of a *smith.* Even though clearly stating "The smith, a mighty man is he," the poem nevertheless, because of its opening line, is responsible for the misconception of the meaning of *smithy.* Incidentally, the blacksmith shop that inspired this poem was situated on Brattle Street, Cambridge, Massachusetts.

For those who wonder why this smith was called a *blacksmith,* the answer is that he worked in black metal. A blacksmith who only shoes horses is called a *farrier,* a word derived from the Old French *ferrier,* blacksmith, and ultimately from the Latin *ferrum,* iron.

BLOCKHEAD

> Nay, your wit will not so soon out as
> another man's will—'tis strongly wedged
> up in a blockhead.
> —Shakespeare, *Coriolanus*

A *blockhead* is a simpleton, a dunce. The expression has been with us for generations, at least since the days of Henry VIII. But its groundwork was laid as early as the fourteenth century, when hats generally replaced hoods. As hats became more stylish, more workmen were enlisted to make hats, which were made on blocks of wood. These "block heads" shaped the hat being made. And since they were dummy heads, people who seemed "dumb" came to be called *blockhead*, a synonymous expression for *dullard* or *dumbhead*. One might suppose that a boy hearing his father called a blockhead would not like to be known as a chip off the old block.

BLOODY BUT UNBOWED

This phrase speaks of a person who has uncomplainingly suffered the vicissitudes of life. No matter what problems have beset him, despite his many and varied wounds, he is holding his head up high, undaunted. In today's usage, there's no shedding of blood. But in times past, when soldiers fought with crude weapons, a soldier could indeed be bloodied but continue his stand, refusing to accept defeat. His head, literally, would be *bloody but unbowed*. In 1888, William Ernest Hensley, while in a tuberculosis hospital, composed a work called *Invictus,* which is Latin for "unconquered." It contained this stanza:

> In the fell clutch of circumstance,
> I have not winced nor cried aloud;
> Under the bludgeonings of chance
> My head is bloody, but unbowed.

BODICE

For many years a *bodice,* the close-fitting upper part of a dress, sometimes stiffened with whalebone, served as a corset. During medieval times it consisted of a pair of bodies. And that was what a *bodice* was—a pair of bodies—a plural word with a specialized use, the plural of *body.* The plural *bodice,* however, came to be interpreted as a singular form because it sounded like one. And so it has remained. This process of assuming that a word is singular simply because it seems like one has had its effect on other English words. Take, for example, *chintz.* Its Hindi singular form was *chint,* its plural *chints.* But with time, *chint* disappeared from the language and its plural form, with its final letter changed from *s* to *z,* became a singular word.

Returning to *bodice,* this waistcoat (as Dr. Johnson termed it) corseted a woman's body. (The word *corset* does not appear in Dr. Johnson's *Dictionary,* but *corselet,* "a light armor for the forepart of the body," does.) The origin of *corset* can be found in Old French, in which *cors* stood for body. When the undergarment designed to shape the hips became popular, the name given it was *corset,* a little body, a diminutive form of *cors.* True it is that a narrow bodice or a tight corset will make for a slimmer body.

BOGUS

Something *bogus* is a fake. It might be a copy of a Rembrandt or, more likely, counterfeit money. According to most authorities, anyone claiming to know the origin of the word *bogus* is making a bogus claim. As yet no one has come forth. But conjectures abound. Did it derive, one word historian wonders, from a Scotch gypsy word for counterfeit—*boghus*? Mencken surmised that *bogus* might be of French origin, possibly coming from *bagasse* or *bogue.* The *OED* reports that in 1827 a counterfeiting machine in Ohio was called a *bogus.* Other opinions have been offered, including one that appeared in the *Boston Daily Courier* on June 12, 1857:

The word *bogus,* we believe, is a corruption of the name of one Borghese, a very corrupt individual, who, twenty years ago, did a tremendous business in the way of supplying the great west, and portions of the southwest with a vast amount of counterfeit bills, and bills of fictitious banks, which never had an existence out of the forgetive brain of him, the said Borghese. The western people who are rather rapid in their talk, when excited, soon fell into the habit of shortening the Norman name of Borghese to the more handy one of *Bogus,* and his bills and all other bills of like character were universally styled *bogus* currency.

It might be that among these surmises is the real thing—the genuine *bogus.*

BOLT FROM THE BLUE, A

A sudden and completely unexpected event. A disaster, for instance, may be called *a bolt from the blue,* like a bolt of lightning from a clear, azure sky—a "thunderbolt" that strikes without warning. The assassination of President Kennedy was such a bolt. The *Oxford English Dictionary* of 1888 contained an entry of this phrase, but it was undated. The assumption must be that it was in common usage for many years earlier. According to Holt, the phrase appeared in Thomas Carlyle's *French Revolution* in 1837: "Arrestment, sudden really as a bolt out of the blue, has hit strange victims."

B. F. J. Schonland pointed out in *Flight of Thunderbolts* that people in a valley might see lightning and hear thunder from a distance, and the lightning might strike in the valley, even though the skies above are blue. This author knows of two cases in which baseball teams were practicing under azure skies and an outfielder chasing a fly ball was in turn chased and struck by a bolt of lightning and killed. One was at the author's alma mater, Pennsylvania State University.

BOOMERANG

A *boomerang* is an angular missile that can be thrown so as to return near or behind the thrower. No one knows for certain who invented this weapon, for it had been used both in ancient Egypt and in Ethiopia. It attained prominence when explorers found Australian aborigines using it as an instrument to kill birds and small animals. Hopi Indians also were adept with the boomerang. But all this does not explain what the word *boomerang* stands for. It is a combination of sounds uttered by the aborigines in Australia, recorded as *womurang, bumarin,* and *boomerang,* but the last survived. The surmise is that in the native language the word explains the unique ability of this wooden missile to come back to the area from which it was thrown. But since no one can pinpoint the place where the *boomerang* originated, and since no one knows what its name means, or even how to spell it, its origin must be considered obscure. Nevertheless, *boomerang* has been accepted into the English language to represent the curved stick that children now play with as a toy. In figurative usage, *boomerang* has received widespread recognition as a scheme or proposal that backfires on the originator.

BOOT

If one gets *the boot* (peremptory dismissal) for sabotaging someone's machinery (destroying it with a wooden shoe), the Medieval English *bote,* which was borrowed into Old French, sees double service. A *bote* (later English *boot*) is a foot covering, and it also appears in the second syllable of the French *sabot,* footwear commonly worn by peasants.

That which is *bootless* is not necessarily unshod. *Bootless* refers to something of no benefit or profit; it is a useless gesture or thing to do, as in Shakespeare's "Doth not Brutus bootless kneel?" It is also the expressed sense of the Duke of Venice in *Othello:* "He robs himself that spends a bootless grief"; or in *Sonnet 29:* "And trouble deaf heaven with my bootless cries."

BOOTLEGGER

Bootlegger is an odd name for a booze peddler. The name originally was applied to those who trafficked in illegal liquor by smuggling, especially among the Indians, flasks of firewater in the legs of their boots, a practice designed to conceal the illicit merchandise from government agents. With time, the term *bootlegger* came to be applied to distributors of illegal booze, whether delivered by hand or by truck or even left at a convenient place. No longer did a bootlegger operate through his boots. Remember the story of the station master who, during Prohibition, called up the Greek professor and said: "Professor, you'd better get down to the station fast because your package of books is leaking all over the platform."

BOSS

One word in the English language that disgusts many people is *boss.* Everyone knows what a *boss* is, and some regretfully. But the word in America that preceded the use of *boss* for the person in charge was *master.* That word, with its imperious ring, was completely unacceptable. The Dutch word for *master,* which is *baas,* was used by early Dutch settlers. Other groups, to avoid the sound of the undemocratic word *master,* adopted the Dutch term, which, as anglicized, was pronounced *boss* and then spelled that way. And so if you're in Dutch with your boss, remember that it is a natural etymological development. After all, someone must be the boss.

BOULEVARD

Many inner-city roadways of distinction are called *boulevards.* They are usually broad streets, lined with trees and sprinkled with foliage. In today's life one may expect to see boutiques and other stores that specialize in better-grade and expensive merchandise abutting these walkways. And yet, curiously, the progenitor of *boulevard* was completely unrelated to the meaning and use of *boulevard* today.

Years ago cities protected themselves against attacks from ene-mies by erecting thick walls about their cities. These walls were of-ten made of tree trunks, and since it was hard work to install them, a Dutch term was given them—*bolwerc,* made up of *bole,* plank, and *werc,* work. One can readily see in that compound the English word *bulwark.* The French borrowed the word, converted it into *boulevard* and used it, originally, to represent their ramparts of for-tification. As the usefulness of city walls disappeared, these ele-vated bulwarks were converted into promenades and made into pleasant walkways. The English liked the sound of the word and what it represented, and hence they adopted it to mean any wide street, sometimes with a grassy area in the middle, that need not be elevated. The boulevard is now on solid ground.

BRAILLE

The universally accepted reading system used by blind persons was named after its inventor, Louis Braille, a Parisian who spent most of his life in France. Braille, unfortunately, was blinded in an accident at the age of three.

In 1826, after Braille became a professor at the Institution Nationale des Jeunes Aveugles, he learned that the army was using a system of reading based on touch, and not on sight, a system de-vised by Captain Charles Barbier for nighttime communications. The military messages were in raised dots that were read by pass-ing the fingers lightly over them. Braille refined the system by us-ing a six-dot "cell," consisting of raised dots in an oblong, with the horizontal line containing two dots and the vertical, three. The dots were symbols. One dot is A, one dot on top of another is B, and two dots side by side are C. The sixty-three possible combinations can form not only the alphabet (with punctuation and contractions) but also a system of musical notations. Braille himself was an ac-complished organist and a composer of music, and he used the dot system to compose several musical writings.

BRAZIL

On April 22, 1500, Pedro Alvarez Cabral, a Portuguese explorer, discovered an area in South America which came to be called *Brazil*. It had originally been called *terra de brasil,* or "the land of the red dyewood," since the territory abounded in a red wood used by natives in dyeing. The ultimate ancestor of the name *Brazil* can be found in Low Latin *brasilium,* which means "a red dyewood from the East." Old French called it *bresil* and the Spanish and Portuguese *brasil,* but the name popularly given the treasured red wood was *brasilwood.* When the territory that is now known as *Brazil* became a country and needed a name, the one chosen, logically enough, recognized the country's most thriving industry, the basis of which was the pigment-yielding wood *brasil.* Hence, with a slight orthographical change, *Brazil.*

BREAD

The nursery still lisps out in all they utter—
Besides, they always smell of bread and butter
—Beppo

What we must remember when the word *bread* is being discussed is that it has several unrelated meanings. The usual meaning of *bread* is "a leavened staple food made from a flour or meal mixture that is shaped into loaves and baked." It is a most important comestible, as witness a seventeenth-century proverb: "Bread is the staff of life." But in today's slang *bread* means "money." When a desperado is looking for bread, he's not heading for a bakery— more likely for a bank. In Old English the word for *bread* was *hlaf,* which now means "loaf." The word *bread,* used only in northern dialects, meant "crumb" or "fragment." All of which makes us wonder whether during these days of rising prices our money, our "bread," is now just a crumb.

BREAK THE ICE, TO

This expression comes from the practice of freeing icebound ships during the winter months. Before the invention of power tools, boatmen would chop the ice with hatchets. The expression entered general usage with a number of unrelated meanings. One is "to prepare the way," an idiom invented by Shakespeare. In *The Taming of the Shrew,* Petruchio pointed out that an older sister must first be wed before a younger could enter matrimony. Trianio, agreeing, thought that Petruchio was the man to perform this act of liberation. He said:

> If it be so, sir, that you are the man
> Must stead us all, and me amongst the rest,
> And if you break the ice, and do this feat,
> Achieve the elder, set the younger free
> For our access.

Another is to create an atmosphere of cordiality, to break through the reserve of a cold person, to establish friendly relations, to make a social situation easier. But possibly more often the expression is used to indicate the overcoming of obstacles that would hinder the launching of an enterprise. These are all happy uses of this figure of speech. One unhappy one that sometimes surfaces is to be the bearer of unpleasant or distressing news that must be given as tactfully as possible. "To break the ice" in such an instance is far from a heartwarming job.

BRICK

> A fellow like nobody else, and in fine, a brick.
> —George Eliot, *Daniel Deronda*

Calling a person a *brick* is a compliment. It means that he's a good fellow. He has the qualities you approve of. A brick is solid; it's four-square. It has strength, it's dependable, as is a person likened to a brick. Of course, the expression is colloquial, but it has, according to Plutarch, a historical basis.

An episode appears in the *Life of Lycurgus,* in which a visiting ambassador from Epirus expressed surprise at seeing no walls around the city of Sparta. "But we have walls," replied King Lycurgus. Whereupon the king led the ambassador to the army exercise field, which was just outside the city. "There," exclaimed the king, proudly pointing to the soldiers, "are Sparta's walls; and every man is a brick."

BRING HOME THE BACON, TO

This expression means to prove yourself successful or to bring home the spoils. Or it may mean to bring home the money to support the family. In this last, the phrase is the equivalent of "breadwinner." Both *bacon* and *bread* are symbols of the food put on the table.

Various theories have been advanced as to the source of this expression, but none has been established. One idea was that the phrase grew out of the practice at country fairs of greasing a pig and letting blindfolded players try to catch it. The successful one kept the pig and, in a sense, brought home the bacon. Another was to relate it to the phrase "to eat Dunmow bacon," which referred to a couple whose conjugal life was free of discord. According to legend, an offer was made during the twelfth or thirteenth century by a noblewoman named Juga or the monks of the Dunmow priory or a certain Lord Robert de Fitzwalter, one of the barons of Magna Carta (take your pick; no one really knows who made the offer) to get a side of bacon by meeting the conditions of the following edict:

Any person from any part of England going to Dunmow, in Essex, and humbly kneeling on the stones at the church door, may claim a gammon or flitch of bacon, if he can swear that for twelve months and a day he has never had a household brawl or wished himself unmarried.

A man whose marital bliss and equanimity qualified him could "bring home the bacon." Records indicate only eight claimants.

Phrase sleuths who contest these conjectures say that none of them is kosher.

Brewer sets out the doggerel form of oath to be taken by all claimants:

> You will swear by the custom of our confession,
> That you have never made any nuptial transgression
> Since you were married man and wife,
> By household brawls or contentious strife;
> Or since the parish clerk said *Amen,*
> Wished yourselves unmarried again;
> Or in a twelvemonth and a day,
> Repented not in thought any way.
> If to these terms, without all fear,
> Of your own accord you will freely swear,
> A gammon of bacon you shall receive,
> And bear it hence with our good leave.
> For this is our custom at Dunmow well known—
> The sport is ours, but the bacon your own.

BROUHAHA

A *brouhaha* is an uproar, a disorder, a hubbub. If, after a victorious college football game, the excited shouts of players and fans in the locker room are so tumultuous that one can't make himself understood, the loud, confused noise may rightly be called a *brouhaha.* However, its sense today is most often applied to a "fuss" or "argument."

What is interesting about this word is that no one knows where it came from or when it arrived. And no one knows what it really means, despite the sense presently ascribed to it of hubbub, fuss, or noisy wrangle. What is on record is a fifteenth-century French play in which a priest, dressed to look like a devil, exclaimed, "Brou brou brou ha ha, brou ha ha!" But, here again, the priest did not explain its meaning and it has never been determined. Of course, it might simply be onomatopoeic, since it sounded like noise, as the word *hubbub* does. Or it might have come from the Hebrew Psalm 118, *barukh habba:* "Blessed be he who enters in the name of the Lord!" This latter theory sounds more logical, but who knows? It certainly is not associated with disorder. Perhaps it's best not to raise a fuss and avoid an etymological brouhaha.

BROWN AS A BERRY

Some clichés have become so ingrained that no one bothers to learn what they actually mean, whether they have substance, or even whether they make sense. Because everyone understands them, they are bandied about as though they make clear points or specific comparisons.

Take *brown as a berry* as an example. The origin of this simile is as unknown as the date when it was first used. But it must have been a long time ago, for Chaucer used it. He wrote: "His palfrey was as brown as is a berye." All of which raises a question: What berry is brown? None that most people know of. Certainly not a fruit berry. Many conjectures have been made, including the possibility that a coffee berry was meant. But that is disproved by the fact that Chaucer's statement was made hundreds of years before the discovery of coffee. The truth is that no one knows what berry was meant. The only berry that everyone is sure does not apply is the "razz berry."

BROWN STUDY, IN A

This expression is not used much anymore, but it does appear in some of the works of yesteryear. It means "absentminded, preoccupied, daydreaming." A person in a deep or somewhat purposeless thought is said to be in a *brown study.* But why brown? No one really knows, and conjectures are pointless. It might be that the term had often been used to mean "gloomy" and that it was more applicable than "daydreaming." *A Manifest Detection of the Most Vyle and Detestable Use of Dice-play,* a sixteenth-century work, had this to say: "Lack of company will soon lead a man into a brown study." There *brown study* represents "gloom." In the same century John Lyly wrote in *Euphues:* "It seems to me that you are in a brown study." Brewer guesses that a French phrase explains it—*rêverie sombre. Rêverie* means "a dream." *Sombre* means "sad, melancholy, gloomy, glum," as does *brun.* But *brun* also means "brown" as well as "somber." In present-day French *brun* has taken on a deeper, darker hue—it means "dark brown." And so we might learn of a tie-in after all, if philologists would only snap out of their daydreaming and leave their brown study.

BROWSE

One might never think that when he enters a bookstore and sees a sign reading PLEASE BROWSE that, in the original meaning, he was being invited to nibble. The story behind *browse* may be found in the lives of early settlers who, when fodder became scarce, turned their cattle out to pasture so that they could browse—that is, nibble and then move about in search of more or better food. The word *browse* was said to have come from the French *broust,* young shoot, which evolved from Old French, *brost* or *brouz,* bud. The noun was used of twigs and other small edibles that animals could feed on. The verb *to browse* was later applied to persons who read casually in a bookstore or a library, those who seemed to nibble on one book and then another, and so on. Sporadic reading came to be called *browsing* and the reader a *browser.* Still later, the word *browser* was applied not only to one who reads here and there but also to one who glances here and there. Considering the etymology of *browse,* a purist might say that a sign on a doorway saying COME IN AND BROWSE BUT EAT OUTSIDE is contradictory.

BUCKLE

One may speak of the *buccal* region of his face—referring to his cheeks and to his mouth cavity. *Buccal,* of course, is a fancy word, but its ancestor, the Latin *bucca,* which means "cheek," sired the ordinary word *buckle.*

One may sensibly ask what connection might there be between a buckle and a cheek. The answer is that centuries ago a warrior's helmet was held together securely by a strap that fastened along the cheek. Since the strap rested on the cheek, the fastener came to be called *buccala,* the diminutive form of *bucca.* The term descended into Old French as *boucle,* referring to the boss on a shield because its protuberance resembled the cheeks of a herald when blowing on a trumpet. Middle English adopted the French word as *bocle,* a belt fastener, from which came the modern *buckle,* the kind used on a belt around the waist. An early use of *buckle,* as set out in the *Oxford English Dictionary,* is in *Ayenbite of Inwyt* (1340): "That chastete ssel bi straytliche y-loked . . . be abstinence . . . that is the bocle of the gerdle" (Chastity shall be straitly locked . . . by abstinence . . . that is the buckle of the girdle). But the inventor of the chastity belt apparently had another idea—take no chances.

BUG

> Warwick was a bug that feare'd us all.
> —Shakespeare, *Henry VI*

The word *bug* almost instantly arouses in some people a feeling of discomfort, perhaps even of fear. In its original sense, it was the source of even greater fright. Coming from Welsh *bwg,* a bug was an imaginary, haunting spirit—a sprite or a ghost. The *Oxford English Dictionary* quotes Wycliffe's *Baruch* (1388): "As a bugge, a man of rags in a place where gourdes wexen." (The word for "a man of rags," *scarecrow,* first appeared in print in 1611.) Although the word *bug* no longer conjures up a picture of a goblin or sprite, it survives in a few English words that connote a sense of scare. One is *bugbear,* meaning "a scarecrow or a sort of mischievous sprite," which in the form of a bear was said to eat up bad children. Another is *bugaboo,* a sound often used to frighten. Nowadays a *bugaboo* is thought of as any imaginary (or real) thing that causes fear or worry. It might, for example, be a particular teacher of yours or your supervisor at work. Both *bugbear* and *bugaboo* have been attributed, but deviously, by some authorities to Cornish *buccaboo,* "the devil."

The common word for an *insect* (from Latin *animal insectum,* literally "divided animal," from the segmentation of its body) is *bug.* But the original source of the word *bug,* as used in this sense, is unknown. And no evidence has been advanced to explain why a sense of terror should be transformed into a crawling insect and become its generic name. Perhaps a state of fright from which some people suffer when they see a beetle or other crawling insect has been analogized to Wycliffe's *bugge.* Yet everyone was willing to ride a "horse and buggy." In any event, no one seems to like bugs except one kind: the lovebug.

BULL IN A CHINA SHOP, LIKE A

Since a bull rampaging in a china shop, considering the fragility of china, would wreak much damage, no doubt its entry would be barred. Yet the simile *like a bull in a china shop,* meaning a clumsy or reckless manner or a disregard for the personal feelings of anyone, has been with us for at least a hundred years without anyone discovering who invented it, where it was invented, or even whether a bull had ever been in a china shop. The earliest record of the phrase can be found in *Jacob Faithful,* a novel written in 1834 by Frederick Marryat, who referred to porcelainware that we call *china,* which was made in China and sold by a Chinese merchant. But word historians have surmised that the phrase's genesis was occasioned by a disruption of trade between China and John Bull (England) which occurred during the year that Marryat wrote his novel. The probabilities, nevertheless, are that the phrase had been around long before then—possibly ever since a bull first wandered into a china shop.

BULLS AND BEARS

Even those who don't play the market probably have heard of the *bulls* and the *bears.* These nonplayers must wonder what these animals are doing in a financial arena. And well they might. Of course, the names of these animals are merely designations of two kinds of investors. The one, *bulls,* became a contrast to the other, *bears.* But to start at the beginning.

Bears are investors who profit from a falling market. Anticipating a drop in market prices, they sell stock they do not own, which is called *selling short.* If the stock drops in value before the delivery date, they pay a lowered price and net a handsome return. Most authorities ascribe the origin of the term *bears,* as used in the stock market since about 1700, to the fable about the man who sold a bearskin before he caught the bear.

Investors who buy stock expecting a rise in value (said to be buying long, the reverse of those who buy short) came to be called *bulls,* which made the alliterative *bears and bulls* a felicitous combination. How the term *bull* came to be applied to the bear's opposite has not been attested, but philologists generally believe that its basis is a bull's habit of tossing its head upward and in so doing tossing upward anything speared by its horns. Investors who are *bullish* believe that the value of their stock will go upward, just the way something would that got in front of a bull's horns.

BURNING EARS

It is common today to say to a person who has been talked about in his absence, "Your ears must have been burning." Many centuries ago it was believed that if your ears itched or burned, it actually meant that you were being talked about. The Roman Pliny said: "When our ears do glow and tingle, some do talk of us in our absence." In *Much Ado About Nothing,* Shakespeare had Beatrice say, when she learned that Ursula and Hero had been talking about her, "What fire is in mine ears." This older phraseology has given way to the current one, mentioned in the first sentence, "Your ears must have been burning." But if you learn that the remarks were critical, more than merely your ears, you might, to borrow another cliché, "be all burned up."

BURN THE CANDLE AT BOTH ENDS, TO

The history of this saying can be traced all the way back into the English language through Cotgrave's French-English dictionary *(brusler la chandelle par les deux bouts),* written in the seventeenth century. Its original sense referred to a spendthrift wasting material wealth. Today's use, however, is broader and not necessarily condemning: to exhaust one's energies and resources, which, despite the physical strain, might be for a worthwhile cause. The idiom is used also of someone who works excessively long hours or, in a more critical sense, one who works too long during the day and plays too long at night, thus squandering his or her energies.

The expression was known as early as 1592, when Francis Bacon said in his *Promus of Formularies and Elegancies:* "To waste that realm as a candle which is lighted at both ends." The notion that one cannot consume his energies in one way and yet reserve them for another unimpaired was documented in 1857 by Charles Kingsley in *Two Years Ago:* "By sitting up till two in the morning, and rising again at six ... Frank Headley burnt the candle of life at both ends." Edna St. Vincent Millay in her *First Fig* (1920) used the idiom in poetic diction—beautifully:

> My candle burns at both ends;
> It will not last the night;
> But ah, my foes, and oh, my friends—
> It gives a lovely light.

BURY THE HATCHET, TO

It has become proverbial since Europeans inhabited this land to mark a cessation of hostilities or an agreement to kiss and make up to say, "Let's bury the hatchet." Of course, no hatchet is involved. And yet this phrase arose because real hatchets—tomahawks— were actually buried by Northeastern Indians as proof of their intention to be at peace with the white man. This face was recorded as early as 1680 by Samuel Sewall: "Meeting with the Sachem [Indian chiefs] they came to an agreement and buried two axes in the ground, which ceremony to them was more significant and binding than all the Articles of Peace because the hatchet was their principal weapon." Longfellow in *The Song of Hiawatha* wrote:

> Buried was the bloody hatchet,
> Buried was the dreadful war club.
> Buried were all warlike weapons,
> And the war-cry was forgotten.
> There was peace among the nations.

And so today it is said, when a person willingly ends a controversy, letting bygones be bygones, that even though he has never seen a tomahawk, he has buried the hatchet.

BUSHED

An expression meaning "exhausted," "worn out," or "all in" that came from the hinterland but is more often heard nowadays in urban areas is "I'm bushed." It's probably a bit of slang, but frequent and widespread repetition is elevating it to the rank of accepted idiom. And yet without some background the expression makes no sense. Why *bushed*? How about *treed*, or *foliaged*?

A bush is a low-growing shrub, although some grow as high as moderately high trees. The word originally spelled *busch* by the Dutch, whose duty it was to clear this form of vegetation, has been anglicized to *bush*. These chores were not only exceedingly tiring but backbreaking. Coming home from a shrub-clearing day, an exhausted workman might say, "I'm all bushed," a form of bush-clearing jargon. Even wayfarers who had to trek through bushes might find themselves worn out—*bushed*. And so this colorful term spread to mountain climbers and adventurers and sportsmen whose activities were physically demanding. Today when the strain of any activity—physical or mental—becomes so great that it's getting the better of a person, you might hear: "I'm bushed." It is doubtful, however, that any political party would use this expression if its nominee was named Bush.

BUSMAN'S HOLIDAY, A

Someone who in his free time engages in the same or a similar activity for which he is regularly paid is said to be on *a busman's holiday*. For example, a carpenter who builds a fence in his backyard in his spare time, a mailman who on his day off takes a long walk, a professional singer who sings with a church choir are said to be taking a busman's holiday. But why a busman's holiday? A story that has made the rounds is that during the days of horse-drawn buses, a busman was known, on his free day, to accompany his relief driver to make sure that he treated the horses right. Another version, to the same effect, is that the busman surreptitiously rode with the passengers so that he could observe the driver's actions without being known. Of course, that busman truly had no holiday.

BUST

What surprises people learning English as a second language is that a word can have so many unrelated meanings. Take the word *bust* as an example. As a verb, it means "to smash or break, especially forcefully," "to financially destroy," "to reduce the rank of," as well as some colloquial uses. As a noun, it means "a human chest," "a woman's bosom," and "a piece of sculpture representing the head, shoulders, and upper chest." As with many another English word, one can determine the word's meaning only in context. But what is interesting is that the genesis of *bust* had no relationship to any of the foregoing.

The noun *bust* lends itself to a somewhat intriguing story. The Latin word *bustum* meant "place of burning and burial," its sense being "surrounded by fire," a place for cremation, and eventually simply the resting place of the dead, whether buried or cremated. The custom of the Romans was to place statues of the likeness of the deceased on the tomb. Because of this custom of remembrance, the place of burial and later the statues themselves—the sepulchral monuments carved of the head, shoulders, and bust—came to be called *bustum,* passing from Italian into English as the word *bust* for a human head and torso.

BUTTER WOULDN'T MELT IN HER MOUTH

Through the years the expression *butter wouldn't melt in her mouth* has been given different, but somewhat related, meanings. The meaning most often attributed to it is of a woman so demure— that is, prim and cool—that even butter wouldn't melt in her mouth. Of course, the inference is that she is a sham; she is actually not the kind of person she appears to be. No one knows when this saying first came on stream, but it must have been centuries ago, probably long before its 1546 publication in John Heywood's *Proverbs.* With time, the expression came to signify the suspicion an overamiable or a seemingly innocent person creates, since such a person is unlikely to be just as he or she appears. Prudence dictates that despite the apparent harmlessness, one should move cautiously so as not to be misled. From its first use until more modern times, the mouth in which the butter wouldn't melt was a woman's. This is no longer so. Today a man's mouth is just as applicable. If he seems too good to be true, the saying fits.

BUXOM

> So buxom, blithe, and debonair.
> —Milton, *L'Allegro*

For many generations man has relished a *buxom* woman. That is not to say that he wanted her generously endowed, full-bosomed. What he wanted, at least before the seventeenth century, was an obedient wife. In Old English the word *bugan* meant "buxom." Its sense was "yielding or tractable," as would be a dutiful person. It is so used in *Piers Plowman*—"buxom to the law," meaning obedient to it. A bride at a marriage ceremony promised to be *buxom,* which later, but before the days of women's liberation, became "honor and obey."

In addition to this primary sense, *buxom* developed two others. One was "blithe or lively," as expressed in Shakespeare's *Henry V,* in which Bardolphus is described as "a soldier firm and sound of heart, and of buxom valor." The other was "pleasingly plump," a person good to look upon, the fullness implied in its present-day meaning—a woman who is, so to speak, robust in the bust.

BUY FOR A SONG

The implication is that something was bought cheaply, for a low price, a bargain. In fact, it might not even have been paid for, but given to one who sang a song, entertained. However, the expression meant something entirely different the first time it was spoken, quite oppositely—that too much was paid. The original reference was not to an object one usually buys, but to a poem. According to a story that was bandied about during Queen Elizabeth I's reign (there are several versions), Queen Elizabeth decided to give Edmund Spenser, the author of *The Faerie Queen,* one hundred pounds sterling for a poem. This sum, during those days, was a small fortune. When Lord Burghley, the Lord High Treasurer, was instructed to make the payment, he protested, but politely so, considering the position of the donor. "What," he asked, "so much for a song?" "Yes," replied the Queen, "all this for a song." Later, according to one version, the Queen, heeding the Treasurer's protest, modified her instruction. She told the Treasurer to give Spenser "what is reason." However, no payment was made. So Spenser sent the Queen this petition:

> I was promis'd on a time,
> To have reason for my rhyme;
> From that time unto this season,
> I have receiv'd nor rhyme nor reason.

The story ended happily. The Queen commanded that Spenser be paid; the Treasurer was bereft of reason; and Spenser got a reward for his rhyme.

BY HOOK OR BY CROOK

When a person says he will do it or get it "by hook or by crook," he means that one way or another, by fair means or foul, he'll be successful. The *hook* part seems to indicate that he will put a hook around something and pull it to him; the *crook* part, that he will purloin it if need be.

The phrase was a common one during the time of Geoffrey Chaucer. A contemporary, John Wycliffe, the theologian, in 1380 used it in his writings according to the sense of today. Yet the belief of many word historians is that the phrase, when it originated, bore no relationship to unfair devious tactics but was related, instead, to a legitimate practice of peasants who sought firewood. Old forest laws prescribed that all forests and woodlands belonged to the king and forbade the unlawful removal of live branches from trees. Peasants could enter these wooded areas only to remove dead branches, those lying on the ground or those in the trees that had not yet fallen. To bring down those branches, the peasants would use a reaper's hook or a shepherd's crook. Logical as all this seems, some authorities scorn it, labeling it pure folk etymology.

And they may be right. In the opinion of these authorities, the original meaning of *by hook and by crook* has been lost. Dictionaries list its origin as unknown because they have been unable—by hook or by crook—to establish its ancestry.

BY THE SKIN OF ONE'S TEETH

This expression appears in the Book of Job (19:20), but not in those exact words. The complete quotation reads: "My bone cleaveth to my skin and to my flesh and I am escaped *with* the skin of my teeth." In common speech the italicized excerpt is rendered *"by* the skin of my teeth," its sense being "just barely," "by a narrow margin," or "with nothing to spare." However, the quotation, as might be observed, is *"with* the skin of my teeth," not *"by* the skin of my teeth." It has therefore been suggested that the biblical meaning is "just escaped, and that is all—having lost everything." Purists who argue that Job's metaphor makes no sense because teeth, certainly human teeth, have no skin deserve plaques.

C

CAESAR

Caesar in ancient Rome meant "leader." The term spread to Russia as *czar* and to Germany as *kaiser,* all having the same meaning.

One who crosses the Rubicon has made an irrevocable decision. In 49 B.C., Julius Caesar did just that when he led his armies across the Rubicon (a river separating Roman Italy from Cisalpine Gaul) because he knew that this invasion of the Roman Republic would precipitate a civil war. It did. But Caesar crushed all opposition and emerged the ruler of the Roman world. It was after his defeat of Pharnaces, king of Pontus in Asia Minor, that he sent to the senate the tersest communiqué ever dispatched by a victorious commander—*"Veni, vidi, vici"* ("I came, I saw, I conquered").

Caesar had three wives. His second, Pompeia, was accused of having an affair with Clodius, who had been pursuing her ardently. Caesar did not believe these allegations. Unfortunately, however, at a festival in honor of the goddess of virtue, to which only women were invited, Clodius clandestinely attended, dressed in female garb. He was unmasked and Caesar concluded that he must divorce Pompeia, for "Caesar's wife must be above suspicion."

The surgical operation that removes a fetus by cutting through the abdominal wall to reach the womb (*a caeso matris utere,* "from the incised womb of the mother") is named *Caesarean section* after Julius Caesar, who it is said was so delivered. Good beginnings, however, can have bad endings. Caesar was assassinated on March 15 in 44 B.C. after having been warned by a soothsayer, according to Shakespeare's *Julius Caesar,* to be watchful during the ides of March: "Remember March, the ides of March remember."

CALCULATE

The Romans were slow to devise a simple, accurate method of counting. Working with Roman numerals is cumbersome, as anyone who has tried to add up a column of those figures knows. Until the invention of the decimal system by the Arabs, the Romans used stones or pebbles, called *calculi,* as counters. The singular form of this word—*calculus*—became the name of a complicated method of mathematics developed by Leibnitz and Newton. And from the same word we get *calculate,* in the sense of "counting and computing," and *calculating,* meaning "performing calculations" as well as "shrewd and coldly scheming."

Although young Romans were taught to count by pebbles on an abacus, taxicabs had a simpler device for computing fares, a hodometer, a contraption that released a pebble into a receptacle every time the axle turned. At the end of the trip, the pebbles—or *calculi*—were counted to add up the fare. Not sophisticated, but quick—a stone's throw, so to speak, to the tally.

CALL A SPADE A SPADE, TO

This term means to talk plainly and frankly and not to beat around the bush. A thing to be named should be named, directly and without mincing words. In other words, "tell it like it is." Although the originator of the phrase is unknown, its forebear presumably lay in Greek classics. Writers of that era expressed the same thought except that they preferred *fig* to *spade,* "to call a fig a fig." The Greek writer Lucian in the second century wrote in his native language, "To call a fig a fig, and a skiff a skiff," which Erasmus centuries later translated into Latin *"Ficum vocamus ficum, et scapham scapham."* (The Greek words for *spade*—the garden utensil—and for *boat*—a skiff—were very similar. Perhaps "a boat a boat" would have been better than "a spade a spade.") But Plutarch in *Apothegms, Philip of Macedon* used the expression current today: "The Macedonians are a rude and clownish people that call a spade a spade." Moving into more modern times, in the fifteenth century Robert Burton said, "I drink no wine at all which so much improves our modern wits; a loose, plain, rude writer, I call a spade a spade." John Taylor, who died in 1653, in *Kicksey Winsey* versified: "I think it good plain English, without fraud,/To call a spade a spade, a bawd a bawd." To which a wit with a wry sense of humor might remark, "That's a bawd thing to say."

CANDLES

> Hope, like the gleaming taper's light,
> Adorns and cheers our way.
> —Oliver Goldsmith, *The Captivity*

Candles were man's chief source of light for many centuries. Before the Common Era candles were made of fats wrapped in husks or moss, which were the wick. With time, the wick was placed inside the candle mold.

In the ritual observances of many religions, candles, bestowed with various significations, have played an important part in their own right while offering decorative lighting at the same time. When candles (Latin *candela,* from *candere,* to shine, glow, burn) came to be made of beeswax, and hand dipped, they were given an elongated, graceful shape, a tapering in that they became smaller in degrees, from the base to the wick. Hence the name—*tapers.* (*Taper* is from the Old English *tapor,* which came from the Latin *papyrus.* Klein points out that for the development of meaning it should be borne in mind that the pit of the papyrus was used in Rome as a wick.) The burning of the taper, a gradual consuming of the wick, has given rise to a colorful expression connoting an effect resembling the gradual diminishing of that to which it was being compared. A slowdown, a gradual lessening of activity, came to be called a *tapering off.* Nowadays a person reducing weight steadily or curtailing the number of daily cigarettes smoked is said to be *tapering off.*

> Much reading is an oppression of the mind, and extinguishes the natural candle, which is the reason of so many senseless scholars in this world.
> —William Penn, *Advice to His Children*

CASANOVA, LOTHARIO: LOVER BOYS

A *casanova* is a womanizer. Not only does he like women, but they like him.

The term derives directly from the name of Giacomo Jacopo Casanova (de Seingalt), who in the late eighteenth century flitted about the capitals of Europe, involving himself in erotic intrigues. He acquired a reputation for his many escapades with women. His racy memoirs, published after his death, reveal exploits of licentiousness mixed with braggadocio. His name has come to typify a promiscuous, irresistible man, a lecher.

Another lover boy, a character in Nicolas Rowe's 1703 play *The Fair Penitent,* was a rake named Lothario. After being introduced as the "haughty, gallant, gay Lothario," he then proceeded to seduce Calista, the fair penitent. (The play has no happy or gay outcome, however—Calista, after being seduced, stabs herself.)

> Oh 'twas great.
> I found the Fond, Believing, Love-sick Maid,
> Loose, unattir'd, warm, tender, full of Wishes;
> Fierceness and Pride, the Guardians of her Honour,
> Were charm'd to Rest, and Love alone was waking ...
> I snatch'd the glorious, golden Opportunity,
> And with prevailing, youthful Ardour prest her,
> 'Till with short Sighs, and murmuring Reluctance,
> The yielding Fair one gave me perfect Happiness.

CASSIOPEA

Although the Big Dipper, which resembles a question mark, points to the Pole Star, another way of finding that reference point is through a constellation called *Cassiopea,* which is in the opposite direction to the Dipper from the Pole Star and looks like the letter *W* or the outline of a chair.

In Greek mythology, Cassiopea was the wife of Cepheus, king of Ethiopia, by whom she became the mother of Andromeda. Fascinated by the comeliness of her daughter, Cassiopea extolled her beauty as being above that of the Nereids, the marine nymphs of the Mediterranean. These sea maidens, widely known for their pulchritude, were affronted. Thereupon Cassiopea was removed from earth, changed into a constellation ("the lady in the chair"), and placed among the stars.

> That starred Ethiop queen that strove
> To set her beauty's praise above
> The sea-nymphs and their powers offended.
> —Milton, *Il Penseroso*

CATCH-22

> "That's some catch, that catch-22," Yossarian observed.
> "It's the best there is," Doc Daneeka agreed.
> —Joseph Heller, *Catch-22*

The expression *catch-22* comes from the title of Joseph Heller's widely read novel in which, during World War II, an American pilot claimed to be insane and therefore deserving of release from service. The catch is a dilemma because a pilot could be released from duty in one of two ways—by proving he's mad or by being killed in flight. The argument against discharge is that only a sane person could prove he's insane.

In a similar vein, an ancient story concerned Ulysses, who was summoned to join the war against the Trojans. Ulysses didn't want to leave his young son Telemachus, so he feigned insanity, since insanity would release him from military service. A prince was sent to check on Ulysses to determine whether he was faking or making a valid claim. The prince found Ulysses plowing up a sandy beach, which of course made no sense. The prince went to Ulysses' house and returned with Telemachus in his arms. He then laid the boy on the ground where the plough would cut deeply. Ulysses stopped ploughing and thus disproved his insanity. Ulysses, of course, through his Trojan horse, an idea he had conceived, went on to capture the city of Troy.

CAT'S PAW, TO BE MADE A

A person duped into performing an unpleasant task for the advantage of another is said *to be made a cat's paw*. The allusion is to a crafty monkey that wanted some chestnuts being roasted on a hearth. The monkey approached the hearth, but was repelled by the extreme heat. After scratching its head, wondering how to extricate the chestnuts, the monkey spied a cat sleeping nearby. The monkey stole quietly to it, pounced on it, and dragged it to the fire. The monkey, although the cat kept screaming, used the cat's paw to draw out the chestnuts one by one. Which means that the monkey got the chestnuts and the cat a singed paw.

CATTYCORNERED

When you come to think about it, the word *catercornered* or *cattycornered,* meaning "diagonal," makes no sense. The term became an English word after the first element was borrowed from the French *quatre,* four, referring to the four spots on dice or cards. In the sixteenth century the pronunciation was anglicized to sound like "cater" and later like "catta," so that today *cattycornered* is its commonest pronunciation (some people prefer *kitty-cornered*). But certainly any feline allusion is obscure (even though in Late Latin *catta* means "cat"), and the change in meaning of four spots, which might have represented four corners of an intersection, to mean "crosswise"—that is, diagonally across a square—is not explainable. If anything, *cattycornered* should mean "four corners," not "diagonal." But perhaps the good people responsible for folk etymology were biased or, to borrow a phrase, were being catty.

CHARACTER

Everyone likes to project himself or herself as a person of good *character* because such a person is usually trusted, respected, and welcomed. But precisely what is character? It is hard to say, since the word is an abstract and cannot be finitely defined. Dictionaries say that *character* is "the combination of emotional, intellectual, and moral qualities distinguishing one person or group from another." During the Middle Ages, *character* had one clear meaning, and no one was likely to be confused by it. A *character* was a distinctive mark, or impression, which it still is; for example, the impression of a horse on the forehead of a bondslave. That a mark was originally meant by the word *character* can be seen from its Greek ancestor, *charakter,* to engrave. Marks, or characters, were branded on criminals convicted of adultery by burning the letter "A" on the forehead, and for murderers sentenced to servitude the letter "M." The *character* of these persons could be told at a glance, but that kind of character consisted of an obvious mark.

Later the word came to represent "an aggregate of distinctive qualities" that need not apply only to a person. For example, an organization or a community might have acquired features or attributes that set it apart from others, characteristics that give it "character." And thus the word has become generalized. Still later an odd person came to be conceived of as a character, as in Oliver Goldsmith's *She Stoops to Conquer:* "A very impudent fellow this; but he's a character, and I'll humour him a little."

One last thought. The words *character* and *reputation* are often intertwined. However, precisely speaking, *character* is what you are and *reputation* is what people think you are. A person who enjoys a good reputation may be one of poor character, his reputation for honesty, for instance, being completely misplaced. When Thomas Jefferson said: "These debts must be paid, or our character stained with infamy," he might have used the word *reputation* instead, but character goes to the inner core of our emotional beings.

CHARLEY HORSE

A *charley horse* is a popular name for stiffness in a leg that has been strained. It is a muscular cramp. But why *charley horse* and not, say, *billy horse* or *tommie horse*? No one knows for certain how this term originated, although theories have been advanced. What is generally agreed upon is that during the eighteenth century night watchmen were called *charleys*. These watchmen chiefly were disabled veterans who hobbled about their rounds. They were named *charleys* because the night watch was organized by Charles I.

This name, however, disappeared in 1829 when the police force in London was organized. Another theory is that a lamed racehorse named Charley was used to pull a roller about in the White Sox ballpark in Chicago. It did not take long before the condition of a ballplayer with a stiff leg came to be called after the horse. He had a *charley horse.* If this latter theory is true, then that old racehorse, now a dray horse, has been immortalized.

CHEAPSKATE

> I hold your dainties cheap, sir, and your welcom deer.
> —Shakespeare, *The Comedy of Errors*

A fellow who acts like a *cheapskate* with his girlfriend may be skating on thin ice. That fellow, however, is not skating, as the previous sentence suggests. In fact, the *skate* in *cheapskate* (but note that *cheapskate* arrived in two steps) has nothing to do with ice skates or roller skates. It comes directly from *skate,* a fish (from Old Norse *skata,* which also means "magpie"). The allusion of *skate* in *cheapskate* may be to the fish's odd ability to inflate itself like a blowfish. During Revolutionary War days a popular word for a person who inflated himself, who talked too much, was *blatherskate,* which occurred in a song of the day, "Maudie Lauder." The *blather* part came from an archaic word for *bladder,* a windbag. Just as *blatherskate* was a term of contempt for a gabby person, so did its progeny *cheapskate* become a term of derision for a tightwad. *Skate* was borrowed from *blatherskate* after *cheap* acquired its scornful sense. Originally *cheap* meant "trade" and may have been related to Latin *caupo,* trader, from which came Old English *ceapian,* to buy. *Cheap* is the place for buying and selling. In London it was called Cheapside, the main marketplace. From the idea of trading came the sense of a good trade, a bargain, and then that the merchandise was worth more than the price—hence its present sense of "cheap." Of course, *cheap* has developed other vernacular meanings, such as "trashy" or "of poor quality," but those senses are not being considered here.

CHEW THE RAG, TO

It is surprising that so simple a combination of words should give rise to several interpretations and be of controversial origin. Most Americans would take it to mean "to chat, to converse," but more likely "to talk at great length," akin to another phrase meaning a talkfest, "to chew the fat." In Great Britain its sense was "complaining or grumbling," "to argue." J. B. Patterson, in *Life in the Ranks* (1885), elucidates the meaning: "Persisting to argue the point, or 'chew the rag,' as it is termed in rank and file phraseology, with some extra intelligent noncommissioned officer." The question is, What kind of rag was meant? Was it a piece of cloth? Sulky children are known to chew on their collar or sleeve or any piece of rag. Or is it the "rag" that means "bullying"?

Some word sleuths have pointed to a connection between chewing tobacco and chewing on a rag. The theory is that sailors landing in the New World found natives chewing on dried leaves, the forerunner of the unprocessed tobacco leaf. The sailors followed suit, and became habituated. But when they sailed back to their homeland, they never seemed to have enough of the leaves. When their supply of leaves was exhausted, they took up chewing on a rag as a substitute. Not many word historians have bought this "rag."

CHICKEN FEED

Chicken feed is, of course, food for chickens. But the phrase has become a synonym for an insignificant amount of money. Although no one source is given credit for this expression, several sources seem plausible. The one to which most authorities subscribe is that chickens were fed food unfit for human consumption, food of inferior grain. The label *chicken feed,* in this sense, was given impetus by westward migrants who brought chickens with them and then fed them with swill good for no other purpose. Another source came through with this idea: chicken feed must be small if it is to be eaten by chickens—hence trivial amounts of money, primarily small change, are logically called *chicken feed.* If all this is not worth your time, if it sounds trivial, consider it chicken feed—and ignore it.

CHIFFON

Chiffon is a lovely, very thin fabric used especially in the manufacture of blouses, veils, lawn-party dresses, and evening gowns. Made of silk, nylon, or rayon, it is not only good to look at but also good to feel. All of which makes it hard to believe that its ancestor was a rag. Not really, of course, but yet the word that gave birth to this sheer, attractive, lightweight fabric called *chiffon* was *chiffe,* rag, an odd piece of cloth used as an adornment. *Chiffon* is a French diminutive of *chiffe.* (It may be that *chiffe* came from the Arabic *shiff,* used of a light, transparent garment.) In any event, the French "rag," which came to be called *glad rags,* eventually found itself on the shelves of the hautes couturiers of the world.

"Rags" need to be stored. And so a high chest of drawers was fashioned to hold them. Appropriately, this piece of bedroom furniture was called a *chiffonier,* a word borrowed whole from the French. But, and who can imagine this, a meaning of *chiffonier*—the name of this set of drawers (in French sometimes spelled *chiffonnier*)—was "ragpicker."

CHINAMAN'S CHANCE, NOT A

The expression *a Chinaman's chance* or, as more often said, *not a Chinaman's chance* or *he hasn't even a Chinaman's chance* has been with us since the Gold Rush days of 1849. During that period thousands of Chinese came to the United States, most remaining in California, many working in gold camps or on the railroads. The Chinese were industrious; they worked harder and spent longer hours at work than most Americans, and were generally underpaid. The wonderful attributes of the Chinese, however, did not endear them to their fellow American workers, who, in fact, despised them. If a Chinaman had a problem, if, for instance, something was stolen from him and he complained, he would find no one willing to listen or help. He could expect no justice from the frontier courts, no redress—nothing but inequity. He simply had no chance. And that is what the expression has come to mean when applied to anyone whose opportunity for success is less than slim. If he hasn't even a Chinaman's chance, he has none at all.

Incidentally, a man whose ancestry is Chinese is properly called a *Chinese,* not a Chinaman. Nevertheless, it is interesting to note that though the term *Chinaman* is considered offensive, there's nothing disparaging in *Frenchman, Welshman,* or *Irishman.*

CHIP OFF THE OLD BLOCK, A

> How well dost thou now appeare
> to be a Chip of the old block.
> —Milton, *An Apology*
> *against . . . Smectymmus*

A chip of (or *off*) *the old block* is a pleasing, homely way of saying that a son resembles his father. It may be a physical likeness or, more likely, characteristics, traits, or abilities. The allusion, of course, is that a chip from a block of stone is similar to the larger portion. This expression is ancient, going back many centuries. In 1626, in the play *Dick of Devonshire,* the expression appeared in print somewhat differently: "Why may not I be a Chipp of the same blocke out of which you two were cut?" But it was popularized in 1781 by the redoubtable statesman and writer Edmund Burke, who, after listening to a speech delivered by William Pitt the Younger before the House of Parliament, joyously exclaimed, "He was not merely a chip of the old block, but the old block itself." The chip did become a block, so to speak, for Pitt went on to become one of England's most famous, rock-ribbed Prime Ministers.

CHOWDER/LASAGNA

Both *chowder* and *lasagna* are well-known dishes in America. A *chowder* is a souplike concoction, usually made with assorted fish or clams, and often served in restaurants on Fridays. *Lasagna,* a popular treat in Italian eateries, is a mixture of wide, flat noodles, meat, cheese, and other ingredients, all cooked together. Certainly these dishes are a delight to eat, but chances are we would not be so delighted if today they were what they were originally. A *chowder* was not a soup. It was, from French *chaudière,* a stew pot. Its ultimate ancestor was the Late Latin *caldaria,* caldron. A *caldron,* of course, is a vat or kettle used for boiling water. A *lasagna,* in Italian, is a cooking pot. Its original forebear makes the dish even less tempting. It was Greek *lasanon,* chamber pot. As time moved on, the names of the vessels were transferred to the contents. The soup became the chowder and the noodles the lasagna. No longer are chowder and lasagna pots; they are the food made in them.

CLOCK

The popular timepieces of today are clocks and watches. Time is told, if not expressed in digits, by noting the position of the hands, one indicating the hour and the other the minute.

The first mechanical clock, invented in Italy in 1335, had no hands. It was, as was true with clocks for many generations, a striking clock—that is, it had bells to sound out the time. The word *clock* comes from the French *cloche,* which means "bell." The root sense of *timepiece,* therefore, is "thing that rings bells."

As everyone knows, timepieces have twelve digits. But a clock once chimed thirteen times, according to a story reported in Brewer from Walcott's *Memorials of Westminster.* A certain John Hatfield, a soldier, who was (believe it if you will) aged 102, served in the army of William III. Hatfield was accused of falling asleep on duty. He asserted, in his defense, that he had heard St. Paul's chime thirteen times and that therefore he could not have been sleeping. According to this fanciful tale, several witnesses confirmed his statement. Perhaps they were all bakers. They had a different idea of what constitutes a dozen.

CLOTHS, NAMES OF

In many instances, the cloth invented by man was named, sometimes with slight alterations, after the town or area where the fabric was first made. *Cretonne,* for example, was produced in Creton, a village in Normandy; *paisley* in the Scottish city of Paisley; *muslin* in Mossul, Mesopotamia, now Iraq. And so with *calico* from Calicut (not Calcutta), India; *shantung,* from the province of Shantung, China; and *jersey,* from the island in the English Channel that bears that name.

Buckram, a coarse cloth made stiff with glue, was first made in Bukhara in Russia. From that country, as well as from adjacent Turkish areas, came *caracul,* sometimes spelled *karakul,* a short, flat, loose, curly fur of lamb or Asian sheep. *Karakul,* literally "black lake," was the name of lakes in that region.

The ancestry of *satin*—a silk, rayon, or nylon cloth having a smooth, glossy side—has not been fully established. Presumably the word *satin* is a refinement of Arabic *zaituni* or *zaytuni,* meaning a fabric from Zaitun, an adaptation of Chinese Tzut'ing, now Chuanchow. *Suede,* a soft leather with a velvety nap, was invented by a Swede who, by holding the fleshy side of leather against a buffing wheel, raised the nap. The name of this leather was popularized by French glove manufacturers who used the phrase *gants de Suède,* "gloves of Sweden." In French *Suède* means "Sweden."

COACH

> The civilized man has built a coach,
> but has lost the use of his feet.
> —Emerson, *Essays,*
> *First Series: Self Reliance*

When a coach rides herd on his players or when a coach, a tutor, drives his students to work harder, or when passengers seat themselves in a coach, linguistically they all have something in common, for the word *coach* in all those senses had the same ancestor. The word was born in a Hungarian town called Kocs. In the fifteenth century King Matthias Corvinus of Hungary ordered the manufacture of a sumptuous carriage to convey his royal highness. Built in Kocs, it was appropriately named *kocsi.* And the era of the *coach,* the anglicized form of *kocsi,* the future favorite means of land transportation, arrived. The word *coach* today has been adapted to a motor bus, a railroad passenger car, and to conveyances charging the lowest fares, all having no relationship to the big four-wheelers called *coaches*. Further afield from that is the use of *coach* to mean "tutor" or "sports trainer." In the former sense the term *coach* evolved in the mid-nineteenth century when the difficulties of a tutor were likened to those who handled the reins of a coach-and-four. Great skill was required and even with that, many carriages were upset. Another thought was that the tutor, like a coach, "carried" the students along to their final examinations. Or just as a coach makes progress as it moves along, so the students progress. Later the term was applied to those directing sports activities because they appeared to guide the athletes in the way a coach-and-four was managed, with great difficulty but with expertise.

COBALT

Cobalt is a hard, brittle metallic element resembling nickel and iron in appearance. In German the name *Kobolt* meant an underground goblin, "a silver stealer," whose habitat was the veins in silver ore.

Scientists in the Middle Ages determined that arsenic found in cobalt-containing ores could cause ulceration of the feet and hands of miners. The unlearned people of that time went a step further. They contended that the gnome *Kobalt* (a variant spelling) was found in *cobalt* and that its proximity to silver ores harmed them. How wrong that folk belief was! Today *cobalt* appears in the Periodic Table of the Elements—atomic number 27—a noninjurious element that happily has proved useful to mankind in many ways.

The five-cent coin, commonly called a *nickel* and made of nickel and copper alloy, also was named after a goblin, the German *Nickel* from *Nicolaus*, similar to the English *Old Nick* for "Devil." The Germans called the copper-colored nickel *Kupfernickel*, meaning "fool's copper," a metal much less valuable than copper. The substitution of the cheap metal for the valuable copper in the ore was attributed to the demonic maliciousness of sprites. Apparently mineralogy is just a stone's throw from German mythology.

COBBLER, STICK TO YOUR LAST

This ancient idiom is readily understood as meaning that one should not presume to interfere in affairs about which he has no experience or of which he is ignorant. The expression is usually applied when one with little knowledge of someone's trade or profession butts in with gratuitous advice.

The story that was said to have given birth to this expression took place in Greece, where a painting by the famous artist Apelles was criticized by a cobbler who found fault with a shoe-latchet. The artist acknowledged and then corrected the fault. Whereupon the cobbler, proud of his success as a critic, found fault with the thigh. At this point the painter, restraining his anger, turned to his critic and said, "Keep to your trade—you understand about shoes, but not about anatomy."

Centuries later the Roman historian Pliny expressed the thought this way: *"Ne supra crepidam sutor indicaret"* (the cobbler should not judge above his last). Which is, in today's simpler language, "Cobbler, stick to your last." Incidentally, the origin of the word *cobbler* is unknown. To *cobble,* to mend, comes from it, but its etymology is, of course, likewise unknown—water can't rise higher than its source.

COBRA

The *cobra* is an extremely poisonous snake found mostly in southern Asia and Africa. In India, as in other Asian countries, jugglers and snake charmers are often seen "charming" cobras by playing a flute. The fact is that cobras, like all snakes, have no ears and therefore hear nothing. They can, however, detect vibrations in the earth, their sounding board. The cobra sways as the flutist plays, not because it hears music, but to get in a position to strike the flute, which the charmer keeps moving to tempt the snake and to keep it dancing.

The original name of the cobra in Hindi was *nag,* but the Portuguese, who arrived in India under Vasco da Gama in 1498, decided to bestow it with a name of their own. They dubbed it *cobra de capello,* which in Portuguese means "hooded snake," because to them the snake's neck and head looked like a hood. *De capello* means "with hood"; *capello* is derived from the Late Latin *cappa*, hood. The *cobra* part is from the Latin *coluber*, which means "snake." Remember that a cobra is extremely venomous. If you encounter one, be not beguiled by its fascinating rhythm, lest you be hoodwinked.

COCK AND BULL STORY

It may sound incredible, but the origin of the metaphor *cock and bull story* cannot be traced precisely to any one source. And even more incredible is the sense of *cock and bull story*, for that is what it means—"incredible"—a stupid, unbelievable tale, a canard, or, as the pun goes, something one *canardly* believe. Although it has been suggested that the expression became proverbial in England after the Reformation, authorities have given that notion little credence. The phrase was supposedly related to a papal bull on which was embossed the seal of St. Peter and the cock. Because such bulls, or mandates, were no longer heeded, any fanciful story was, by transference, called *a cock and bull story*, something entitled to no credit. The more plausible attribution lies in literature, beginning with Aesop's *Fables* (in one a cock was turned into a bull) in which animals were personified—talking, thinking, and behaving like human beings. Since these attributes were impossible, they made real *cock and bull stories*. The French have an equivalent phrase, centuries old, *faire un coq à l'âne,* to make a cock into a donkey. Its sense is "believe this and I'll tell you another." Perhaps English simply borrowed the phrase, metamorphosing the donkey into a bull. The novel *Tristram Shandy*, written by Laurence Sterne (1767), ends pointedly with this "incredible" phrase: "Lord! said my mother, what is all this story about? 'A Cock and Bull,' said Yorick, 'And one of the best of its kind, I ever heard.' " One must conclude that any more theories must be rejected as nothing more than another cock and bull tale.

COLD BLOOD

In zoology *cold blood* refers to such life forms as fish, reptiles, and amphibians, whose blood temperature approximates the environmental temperature. A ten-dollar word that says all this is *poikilothermous.* But whether human beings ever have cold blood, that is, no feeling or emotion, has not been scientifically determined. Through the many centuries the belief has been that the temperature of the blood ruled the temper. Certainly, a person riled, physically overactive, or extremely embarrassed might find his or her face flushed or the neck much warmer than normal. On the other hand, fear can induce a chill, which may suggest a cooling down of the blood. And for those without control of their tempers, the expression still persists—*hot-tempered.* The opposite—remaining tranquil and apparently serene under trying circumstances—passionless, is said to be *cold-blooded,* or, as the French say, *sangfroid.* But all of this may be a myth until these conditions are proved or disproved. What we do know is that body temperature, with its norm of approximately 98.6 degrees, does not deviate to accommodate changes in temper. In any event, we say that a person who's cold as a fish or has reptilian indifference has *cold blood,* particularly when a cruel performance of an unpleasant act is involved. Truman Capote's 1965 novel that described a gruesome murder in detail was appropriately titled *In Cold Blood.*

COLD FEET, TO HAVE

Persons who are regarded as cowards under a certain set of circumstances should not necessarily be criticized. Human endurance can be stretched to a limit, after which it can break. No one can feel the ordeal of a coward. However, throughout history cowards have been roundly condemned and have been tarred with various phrases of denigration. For example, we speak of a coward as having a yellow streak down his back or sneaking away with his tail between his legs. But one idiom that seems justifiably applied to all cowards is *cold feet.* Bear one thing in mind—that anyone afraid is said *to have cold feet,* although there's no scientific proof. But it is generally agreed that fear reduces the circulation to the extremities, causing a loss of normal heat. The loss can be accompanied by the chattering of teeth and shivers and chills, all natural physiological results. This notion of the effect of fear can be traced all the way back to 1605, to Ben Jonson's *Volpone:* "I am not, as your Lombard proverb saith, cold on my feet; or content with my commodities at a cheaper rate than I am accustomed." In any event, the idiom is widely used today as a symbol of cowardice, of a person who backs off from an agreed plan, one who has lost his courage or resolution. (The groom did not show up at the church; at the last minute he got cold feet.)

COLD SHOULDER, TO GIVE ONE THE

A person who's "cold" to another person is being distant, perhaps even disdainful. This attitude, often expressed tritely as *to give someone the cold shoulder,* intimates that a person's acquaintanceship is being rejected. He or she is *persona non grata.*

Although the origin of this expression is obscure, phrase sleuths agree that a human shoulder is not the one being referred to, but a shoulder of mutton or beef. Such a cut of meat, which is inferior to a round roast, is particularly unpalatable when served cold. In olden times, guests who overstayed their visit or became otherwise unwelcome were given a serving of cold shoulder rather than the usual hot meat. It was considered the politest way of telling them to pack up and leave. This practice of conveying a host's disenchantment was customary in medieval France, and although other countries did not adopt it, its figurative sense spread to England and America. Today *to give someone the cold shoulder* is proverbial for "to rebuff or snub."

COLESLAW

If the validity of the term *coldslaw* depended on the number of times it appeared on menus spelled like this, it would be as acceptable as the correct name of this salad—*coleslaw. Cole* is an Old English name for cabbage, and its ultimate ancestor was the Latin *caulis,* stem, stalk, especially a cabbage stalk. From that Latin word has come many names of vegetables: kale, cauli (cauliflower), kohl (kolrabi), and cole (coleslaw). The term *salad* is from Dutch *sla,* which means "salad."

The Dutch made a thinly cut cabbage dish called *koolsla,* literally "cabbage salad." In English, and for no known reason, *kool-sla* became *coleslaw* and eventually *coldslaw.* A punster might have said, "The cabbage got colder with time; it went from *kool* to *cold.*" Coleslaw, it is true, is served cold, and it therefore is a cold sla (slaw) or cold salad. But those who have adopted this erroneous form, unwittingly or otherwise, have, through the process of folk etymology, defeated the purpose of the original name, which described the nature of the dish, simply to make it sound more like what they believe it is and the way it should be spelled. Which leaves some of us as cold as the salad.

COLOGNE

The fragrance surrounding some women comes from the *cologne* they dab on their skin. Cologne, of course, a scented liquid made of alcohol and aromatic oils, is a toilet water, originally called *eau de Cologne.*

Cologne is also the name of a city on the Rhine River. It was built there at the command of Agrippina, mother of Nero and wife of the Roman emperor Claudius. Some authorities believe that she wanted the site honored because it was her birthplace. However, instead of being named after him, the site was named after her, *Colonia Agrippina.* The *Colonia* is Latin for "colony." Later her name was dropped, leaving *Colonia* by itself, which, under French influence, became Cologne, a city whose fragrance has perfumed the world ever since.

COME TO A HEAD, TO

According to the *OED,* the expression *to come to a head* goes back many centuries, long before the discovery of America. A plant that had a peculiar growth pattern was cultivated by farmers who sold their produce on the open market. This plant during its early growth, when its leaves were young and loose, was called *colewort,* our modern coleslaw. When time passed and the plant became hard during the summer months, its name was changed to "cabbage." But at times the cabbage did not harden quickly, and housewives were left without this popular vegetable. Complaining did these shoppers very little good, for they were told that they would have to wait until the plants "came to a head."

Some authorities analogize the expression, alluding to a crisis or the reaching of a culminating point or the maturing of any plan or project, to the ripening or coming to a head of a boil or ulcer that is ready to suppurate, or burst. There's no doubt that if we had to make a choice between cabbage and an ulcer, our pick would be obvious.

COMFORT

How words do change their meanings with time! Take the word *comfort.* It comes from Latin *com-,* together, an intensive prefix, and *fortis,* strong. (Originally these elements combined to make the classical Latin *comfortare* and the Late Latin *confortare,* meaning "to strengthen.") This sense continued for centuries, even to the thirteenth century when the word, both as a noun and a verb, was acquired by the English language. Between the eighteenth and nineteenth centuries, a new meaning of *comfort* evolved, for which there has been no accounting. Its sense became "ease" (verb, "to soothe"; noun, "relief"), its current meaning. The *Oxford English Dictionary* has the following entry: "A state of physical and material well-being, with freedom from pain and trouble, and satisfaction of bodily needs," and cites "Excursion" by Wordsworth (1814): "Their days were spent in peace and comfort."

CONGRESS

> It is two strange serpents entangled in their amorous congresse.
> —Puttenham, *English Posie*

You can't get away from it. Sex, that is. It's everywhere, even in the legislature of the nation. Not exactly. But the word that signifies a formal assembly or a legislature, especially of a republic, is *congress*. That word had a Latin ancestor, *congressus,* which means "a coming together," past participle of *congredi (con,* together, plus *gradi,* to advance, to walk). By 1589, the coming together acquired a more specific meaning, the coming together of a man and woman in sexual intercourse. In *The Historical Bible* by L. Clarke (1737), we read: "They had each of them a Son from that incestuous congress." (Another word with a similar sense, *copulate,* to join together, from the Latin *copula,* link, also acquired a sexual meaning. To *copulate* is to engage in coitus.) Political activity in the colonies centered on a congress, beginning with the Continental Congress in 1774. After the formation of the United States, its legislative branch was named the Congress. But only members of the lower branch, the House of Congress, are known as Congressmen. A member of the Upper House, the Senate, is a Senator, a word that comes from the Latin *senatus,* literally the council of the elders, a derivative of *senex,* old. From *senex* has come *senile,* a word fittingly applied to some Senators.

CONSPICUOUS BY HIS ABSENCE

The absence of a particular person at an important function may be more obvious than the presence of others. When a certain person's presence is expected because the event demands his presence, his absence becomes very noticeable. Tacitus (A.D. 55–117) recorded in his *Annals* that at Junia's funeral, Junia's brother Brutus and her husband Cassius were absent. He wrote: "The images of the most illustrious families . . . were carried before it (the bier of Junia). Those of Brutus and Cassius were not displayed; but for that reason they shone with preeminent luster" (*magis praefulgebant quod non videbantur).* In 1859 Lord John Russell declared before the Electors of the City of London, concerning a provision in Lord Derby's Reform Bill: "Among the defects of the bill, which were numerous, one provision was conspicuous by its presence and another by its absence."

COOK ONE'S GOOSE, TO

A person whose *goose is cooked* is headed for a sad happening, a downfall. He will be done in. The term is well known, but its origin is unknown. Some word detectives attribute its source to an English ballad, recorded in 1851, that took hold in London. The ditty defied papal aggression and expressed contempt at the efforts of Pope Pius IX through a cardinal, Nicholas Wiseman, to reestablish the Catholic hierarchy in England. The doggerel contained these lines: "If they come we'll cook their goose,/The pope and Cardinal Wiseman."

Many years earlier, in fact during medieval times, the story that made the rounds was that the defenders of a besieged town showed their scorn for the attacking force by hanging a goose from a tower. The taunt backfired. The attackers became so inflamed that they put the whole town to the torch, and thus "cooked the goose." According to another story, Mad King Eric of Sweden approached a town with only a few soldiers. The townspeople mocked the poorly manned king by hanging out a goose for him to assault. When the town's defenders realized that King Eric was in earnest, they sent a herald to him to learn what he wanted. With a wry smile the King said: "I've come to cook your goose."

Other word sleuths believe the clue to the source of the phrase *to cook one's goose* can be found in the ancient fable of the goose that laid the golden eggs. In that story the owner-peasants killed the goose to get to its golden eggs, a disastrous move, since the eggs in the goose's body had not yet turned to gold. The couple had ruined the source of the golden eggs or, in the words of a now established proverb, "cooked their goose." Today's kids would say, "They were left with egg on their faces."

COOL AS A CUCUMBER

Although cucumbers are usually served in warm weather because of their coolness, they actually have a temperature below that of the surrounding air. This fruit (and it is a fruit, not a vegetable) therefore lends itself well and easily to the expression *cool as a cucumber.* The simile means self-possessed, unemotional, unruffled, and serene. If involved in an argument, a person said to be as cool as a cucumber would be perfectly composed, and not in the least angry or agitated.

When the expression was first used centuries ago, it signified not coldness of temperature or self-possession, but aloofness. Beaumont and Fletcher in *Cupid's Revenge* (1615) wrote: "Young maids were as cold as cowcumbers." With the passing of years the spelling and meaning of *cucumber* evolved into that of today's. Thomas de Quincey in describing the ancient historian Thucydides used it in its current sense: ". . . is cool as a cucumber on every act of atrocity."

COPPER

Copper is a reddish-brown metallic element used extensively for wiring and water piping. This metal, now commonly found in many countries, was also mined in ancient times. The Egyptians made articles from it. But its source to the Romans was the island of Cyprus, called *Kupros* by the Greeks because from it they imported *copper,* a word meaning "metal from Cyprus." The Latinate term for copper is *cuprum* (from *Cyprian aes,* literally "Cyprian brass"), which is what copper was called during Roman days. This product was so important to the Romans that in 58 B.C. they annexed Cyprus to ensure their having all the copper they wanted. Copper today is still very much in demand, except by a thief who spots one coming at him.

CORPORATION

So many words have an obscure origin that it is a pleasure to find one whose origin is clearly known, one that can be attributed to a specific source. The word being referred to is *corporation,* a coinage of Quintus Septimius Tertullianus. Tertullian, as he was known in the legal profession before turning his talents to religious endeavors (A.D. 190), came up with a word to designate a "body," which he called *corporation-em.* One can easily see within it the Latin *corpus,* body, the physical body of a human being. This *body* since that time has been used in several ways, but primarily, according to a dictionary definition, to mean "a body of persons granted a charter legally recognizing it as a separate entity." For centuries the word lay dormant, but it was revivified during the sixteenth century, when all kinds of corporations sprang up— for adventurers, surgeons, and even ecclesiastic institutions. The corporations were, and still are, considered artificial persons, making its members immune from corporate liabilities and giving the organization the power to continue indefinitely, in perpetual succession.

The less dignified use of *corporation,* one used infrequently, is "one's body." Ciardi points to Bartlett Jere Whiting's *American Proverbs and Proverbial Phrases* (1809): "A fellow who has not so much sense in his whole corporation as your son has in his little finger." A more common but slangy use is a reference to a man's paunch, a potbelly. It is interesting to see how a word that had an ecclesiastic birth could become a keystone of business and financial enterprises and wind up in a man's fat stomach.

COURTESAN

A courtly person is elegant; his behavior is of the quality befitting a court. A *courtier* is "one in attendance at a royal court"; a *courtesan* (from French *courtisane*) is a female courtier. She too is an attendant at a royal court. Both *courtier* and *courtesan* were words of respect. With time, something happened to the word *courtesan.* Through the process of perjoration, the process by which meaning degenerates with time, it came to represent a person of low moral character. (And we have no reason to believe that her male counterpart was any different.) In any event, the courtesan was no longer considered a suitable member of a royal court; she was simply a royal mistress. And with more time the word *courtesan* developed a wider and more derogatory meaning—a woman of pleasure generally, but one catering to an elegant clientele, which, however, need not consist only of courtiers.

A courtesan has never been placed on the low rung of an ordinary *prostitute* (Latin *prostitutus,* to expose publicly), even though their functions are alike. A courtesan is said to have a more discriminating following. Since some dictionaries still list two disparate meanings for *courtesan*—a female courtier and a bed companion for wealthy men—one using that word must be careful that the context makes clear the intended meaning. Certainly, if misused in a royal court, it could cause a royal flush.

CROISSANT

One thing we know about the word *croissant:* It is a French word for "crescent." Another thing we know about the croissant is that it was first made in Vienna in 1689. A croissant, of course, is a flaky roll shaped like a crescent. Beyond that, there is much that has been surmised, but little attested.

It has been said that this puff of pastry was made by a chef to celebrate the Viennese defeat of the Turks. The emblem of the Turks on their flag is a crescent. Whenever the Austrian victors would eat a croissant, they would feel as though they were devouring their vanquished foe. Apocryphal as this may be, it makes a good story. But it leaves one question wide open: Why did the chef select a French instead of a German word to name this roll? Which makes us wonder whether this is a story as flaky as the shell of a croissant.

CRY WOLF

Everyone knows that the nub of the well-known "cry wolf" fable is to give a false alarm. Aesop's story concerns the shepherd boy who, to annoy his fellow shepherds and to have fun at the expense of his neighbors, called "Wolf!" when there was no wolf present. He did this so often that everyone tired of his false calls for help and, no longer believing him, did not respond when a real wolf did, in fact, attack his flock.

In almost every language there is a similar tale. The most startlingly different version comes from China. According to this Oriental fable, the emperor Yu Wang of the Third Dynasty, to amuse his favorite concubine, Pao Tse, rang the alarm bells that warn the people that an enemy is coming. Another version states that the emperor had the bells rung because this concubine was in a state of depression and refused to laugh. In any event, as the story goes, when the concubine saw all the people scurrying about to protect themselves from a nonexistent enemy, she became so amused that she laughed uproariously. But, like the "cry wolf" tale, the ruse did not last long, for the people learned that the ringing of the bells was a hoax, and they no longer responded when the bells were rung. Eventually an enemy did come to the gates of the town, which, since it was unprotected, was easily captured. At long last Yu and Pao found out sadly for whom the bell tolls.

CUCKOLD

> The cuckoo then on every tree
> Mocks married men; for thus sings he,
> > Cuckoo!
> Cuckoo! Cuckoo! O word of fear,
> Unpleasing to a married ear.
> > —Shakespeare, *Love's Labour's Lost*

A husband becomes a *cuckold* if his wife commits adultery. Although the word *cuckold* is infrequently heard nowadays, it was a common term in literary works, particularly in Shakespeare's day. *Cuckold* was derived from *cuckoo* (in Old French *cucu*), a migratory bird that, after eating other birds' eggs, laid its own eggs in the nests of those birds, leaving its young to be reared by the "host." In jest a person may be called a *cuckoo*, meaning "an idiot," but one wonders whether, after all, the bird really was such a fool. It had passed on to others the problem of rearing its young.

Because of the cheating practice of the cuckoo, its name came to be applied to a man whose wife was unfaithful. He was derisively called a *cuckold.* Yet, logically, it is the adulterer who should have been named after the bird. What caused this mix-up has never been explained. Dr. Johnson spoke of it but didn't clarify. He said, "It was usual to alarm a husband at the approach of an adulterer by calling *cuckoo,* which was in time applied, by mistake, to the husband." And so the husband of an unfaithful wife became the *cuckold*; a turnaround that sounds cuckoo.

CUT AND DRIED

> Sets of phrases cut, and dry,
> Evermore thy tongue supply.
> —Swift, "Betty the Grisette"

This cliché has been defined in several ways—routine, arranged beforehand, fixed, all ready and set to use—but they all boil down to the same general sense, something that has gone through a prepared stage. Even hackneyed speech is covered because that which is commonplace has simply been warmed over. However, the questions that have never been answered are to what did the expression apply, and who originated it.

Many products have to be cut and then dried before they can be marketed. A major product that requires cutting and drying is timber. For that reason, most authorities believe the expression originated in lumber camps. But there is not even a guess as to the originator. Other authorities point out that some flowers and tobacco are routinely cut and dried. Still others maintain that physicians during the sixteenth century were known to insist that their herbs be cut and dried and not made from fresh leaves because in their opinion herbs compounded from fresh leaves were not so effective. Coming back to rewarmed literary style, as long ago as the eighteenth century, the Reverend Henry Sacheverell was accused in these words of delivering a stale sermon: "Your sermon was ready

Cut and Dry'd." The expression, as you can see, has really made the rounds.

CUTE

If a boy calls a girl *cute* and she replies, "Don't needle me," it may be that she is an etymologist. The fact is that *cute*, through a process known as aphesis (the loss of an unstressed vowel at the beginning of a word) is simply a clipped form of *acute*, which means "having a sharp point." That meaning evolved from its Latin ancestor *acus*, needle, whence *acutus*, sharp. Nowadays, except for geometry (with its acute angles), *acute* is usually employed figuratively to mean "quick to perceive and respond." A sharp-witted person is said to be acute. Likewise, *cute* is used in the sense of sharp or keen-witted, as in "a cute trick." But with girls, the attractive ones are said to be cute—even though they're all curves and no angles.

CUT NO ICE

The phrase *it cuts no ice with me* goes back to the beginning of the last century. It means, of course, that it (whatever *it* may be) makes no difference to me: what you're doing accomplishes nothing as far as I'm concerned or what you're saying has no influence on me. The phrase may be used of third parties as well. Someone talking to his brother might say that "he cuts no ice" with his neighbors; that is, he makes no impression on them.

It is generally believed that the phrase originated in America, but no one knows for certain who should be given the credit for it. There are surmises, and anyone is free to take a pick. One theory is that the expression reflects the early days of figure skating. Poor skaters were said to "cut no ice." Another, that it comes from the practice of cutting ice during the winter with ice saws and storing it for summer refrigeration. Still another, that it applied to icebreakers that failed to break up ice floes properly. Yet this does not pinpoint the need for or the sense of the expression. A theory that makes some sense, but is unattested, is that employees of an ice-cutting company spent too much time at campfires warming their hands, so the foreman would bawl them out by saying, "That cuts no ice. Get back to work." No matter which theory you pick, if any, remember you'll be, according to another unattested cliché, *skating on thin ice,* arguing from a weak position.

CUT OFF ONE'S NOSE TO SPITE ONE'S FACE, TO

Quite obviously this saying is metaphorical, for no one in his right mind would cut off his nose to spite his face. (An ear, perhaps, as Van Gogh did.) Such a silly move would be as foolish as a farmer, angry at his neighbor, setting fire to his own barn and silo in order to burn his neighbor's growing wheat. The idiom is a reminder not to act out of pique, to avoid perverse revenge, for it will bring only harm to yourself. The origin of this saying has been a matter of speculation, but little has been attested. What is known is that in the early thirteenth century, Peter of Blois recorded it as a proverb. Then there was a lapse of several centuries. In the seventeenth century, Gedéon Tallemant des Réaux, in a history of France, wrote: "Henry IV understood very well that to destroy Paris would be, as they say, to cut off his nose to spite his face." In 1796, Francis Grose noted in his *Classical Dictionary of the Vulgar Tongue:* "He cut off his nose to be revenged to his face. Said of one who, to be revenged of his neighbor, has materially injured himself."

CUT THE MUSTARD, TO

A tale without love is like beef without mustard. . . .
—Anatole France, *La Révolte des Anges*

Mustard, the kind one puts on a hot dog, is a paste made of mustard seeds, wine, and other ingredients. The name *mustard* came not from the seeds, but from the wine. In former times *must* (from the Latin *mustum,* new wine) was mixed with mustard powder to form mustard paste. The literal meaning of *mustard,* therefore, is "seasoned with must."

The idiom *to cut the mustard* does not mean to reduce the size of or the strength of. To the contrary, the idiom means to come up to expectations, to be of good quality. One who has reached a desirable end, accomplishing what he has set out to do, has, according to this slang expression, *cut the mustard*. In Western lingo among cowboys, *mustard* meant "the genuine thing." Then its sense became "the best of anything." O. Henry so used it in *Cabbages and Kings* (1894), calling it "the main attraction," possibly because this condiment gave food zest. He put it this way: "I'm not headlined in the bills, but I'm the mustard in the salad dressing, just the same." On another occasion, in *Hearts of the West* (1907), he wrote, "I looked around and found a proposition that exactly cut the mustard" (a girl, of course). Nowadays a successful person in any field might be said to be one who has really cut the mustard. But be aware that the expression is often used negatively, meaning "not to measure up." If a man has not made a favorable impression on a woman, if he has in the vernacular "struck out," she might remark, "He doesn't cut the mustard with me."

𝒟

DAMON AND PYTHIAS

The essence of friendship—the comradeship that makes two people breathe as one—has been most poignantly depicted by the lives of *Damon and Pythias,* Pythagoreans of Syracuse.

When Pythias was condemned to death by the tyrant Dionysius the Elder, he sought leave to arrange his affairs. To assure Dionysius that Pythias would return, Damon pledged his life as a hostage, an arrangement the despot accepted. Legend has it that Pythias's return was delayed. Damon was being led to the executioner's block when Pythias arrived just in the nick of time. Dionysius was so deeply impressed by this show of deep attachment (especially since he himself, according to Cicero, had no friends) that he immediately pardoned Pythias and implored both men to let him enter into and enjoy their friendship. *Damon and Pythias* has become a classical reference meaning two inseparable friends.

DEAD AS A DOORNAIL

Many suppositions have been advanced to explain the origin of this simile, with its sense of dead, unresponsive, without prospects of success. None of these guesses have convinced all linguists of the logical association of a nail, and particularly a doornail, with death.

Charles Dickens suggested that the phrase would gain in sense if *doornail* were replaced by *coffin nail.* The conventional explanation, that a door knocker struck a plate, sometimes called a *nail,* and that because it was struck so often, all its life must have departed, has not been attested. At one time the ornamental use of nails in doors was common, but word experts see no justifiable comparison between them and death. In any event, the expression is very much alive today, having been in continuous use since 1350 when it appeared in the *Romance of William of Palerne* (as put into present-day English): "When I get relief from my trouble, I'm dead as a doornail"; and in 1362 in William Langland's *Piers Plowman.* In Shakespeare's *King Henry VI,* Jack Cade made this point: "And if I do not leave you all as dead as a door-nail, I pray God I may never eat grass more." And in *King Henry IV,* Sir John Falstaff asked, "What! is the old king dead?" To which Pistol replied, "as nail in door." That's really dead.

DEAD HORSE, TO FLOG/BEAT A

Why would anyone want to *flog a dead horse*? Would it do any good? Of course not. Metaphorically, the phrase refers to an attempt to revive interest in an issue that is entirely hopeless.

According to most authorities, *flogging a dead horse* was a nautical term. The *dead horse* was an advance payment of wages to sailors who signed to ship out, giving them a chance to enjoy a last fling before sailing. But once they boarded the ship, they had to work off the dead horse, which they called *flogging;* hence *to flog a dead horse,* or to pay back by work a prepayment of wages. But its current meaning, which is "nothing can be done to help the situation," is so well entrenched and widespread that it would be as useless to revivify its nautical sense as it would be—well, as it would be to flog a dead horse.

A report from one word sleuth stated that John Bright, an ardent supporter of Earl Russell's 1867 Reform Bill, believed that its passage had no chance for success. He declared that efforts to arouse enthusiasm on its behalf were hopeless; it was like "flogging a dead horse to make it pull a load." It just wouldn't work. Bright's statement was the first known use of this expression in this sense.

DEADLINE

Almost everyone, on occasion, has to meet a *deadline,* a date set when an assignment or task must be completed. Reporters and other kinds of writers constantly have to meet a deadline because, unless their material is presented on time, the entire process of which they're part may be thrown out of kilter.

The American expression *deadline,* as we have come to know it, developed during the Civil War (*deadline* had been previously used in other senses). A Confederate prisoner-of-war camp at Andersonville was notorious for its cruel treatment of prisoners. Hence many prisoner escapes were attempted and some were successful. To deter prisoners from breaking out of their confines, a line was marked out a little distance from the camp's fence, and all prisoners were told that any prisoner crossing the line would be shot on sight. Lossing, in *A History of the Civil War, 1861–1865,* described a *deadline* in these terms: "Seventeen feet from the inner stockade was the dead-line over which no man could pass and live." Today, of course, a deadline, fortunately, does not imply such serious consequences, otherwise there would be few newspaper reporters alive today.

DEBACLE

The San Francisco earthquake was, as everyone knows, a *debacle.* But the chances are that few would believe that that was not what a debacle was originally and that its meaning was unrelated to a catastrophic happening. A *debacle,* when the word entered the English language, was a geologist's term for a sudden breaking up of ice. It referred to the havoc wreaked by a sudden spring thaw, which often caused a violent rush of water, carrying with it debris—stones, boughs, entire uprooted plants. The lineage of *debacle* began with the French *débâcler,* to free, to unbar, which came from *de,* un (the Latin *dis*) and *bacler,* to bar. English acquired the word whole from French with a mere change in pronunciation. With time, *debacle* came to be used of any overwhelming rout or stampede. Then, as further extended, it came to mean any sudden, disastrous catastrophe or any complete, ruinous failure. Today synonyms for *debacle* are *disaster* and *catastrophe.*

DELICATESSEN

Except for the erudite, most people would say that *delicatessen* is a German word meaning "delicate eating," the *essen* part being a German verb meaning "to eat." But that is not so. Beginning with the late nineteenth century, stores called *delicatessen* opened in many American cities. The root sense of "delicate or ready-to-eat food" popularized these stores. The origin of the word can be traced to the German *delikatesses,* in which the French word *delicatesse,* meaning "delicacy," is apparent. *Delicatessen* is a plural form when meaning foods sold at such a store ("Delicatessen *require* little preparation"), but English has also converted it into a singular noun when designating the store itself ("The delicatessen *opens* at 7 A.M.").

The startling thing about this essay lies in the first two sentences; that is, the *essen* in the key word does not come from the common German word meaning to eat and has no etymological association with it.

DELIGHT

The noun *delight* means "great pleasure or joy" or "a thing that gives great pleasure or joy." The original ancestor of *delight* was Latin *delectare,* to please, from which evolved the Old French *deliter* and the Middle English *deliten.* Their noun form was *delit.* During the sixteenth century, a new spelling took hold. A *gh* was inserted in *delit* to ensure a long *i* sound and to bring it into a rhyming pattern with such words as *light, bright, sight,* and *night.* No doubt, to Tin Pan Alley the orthographical change was a delight.

DELTA

Dictionaries offer two basic meanings for the word *delta*. One is a triangular alluvial deposit at the mouth of a river. The other is the fourth letter of the Greek alphabet. The first meaning came directly from the second. The three-cornered tract of land formed at the mouth of the Nile, according to Herodotus, the great Greek historian, resembled the triangular-shaped alphabetic delta, from which comparison came the name for this stretch of land. Many of the largest rivers in the world have clearly defined deltas: the Mississippi, the Danube, the Rhine, the Ganges, the Po.

DERRINGER

Henry Deringer was born in Philadelphia in 1786. After an early training period as an apprentice to a gunsmith, he developed a fiery ambition to manufacture guns. His first venture was the making of squirrel rifles. They worked so well that the demand for them became nationwide.

Deringer was on his way to success. In the 1840s, he invented the gun that immortalized his name—a single-shot, muzzle-loading percussion pistol, small enough to be carried in a vest pocket. The gun was reportedly a favorite of politicians and actresses; in fact, of anyone who might need a weapon in self-defense.

Although Deringer spelled his name with only one *r*, the pistol became a generic term spelled with two *r*'s—*derringer*, a name that was then applied to any similar pocket pistol. As orders for these guns mounted, Deringer found himself unable to fill them all. Whereupon greedy competitors undertook to manufacture similar pistols, representing them as the real thing. Some were signed "J. Deringer" by a firm that employed a man by that name just to use the name. Others signed their pistols simply "Derringer." But despite the competition, Deringer thrived. However, a good weapon can do bad things. It was a derringer that John Wilkes Booth fired at the Ford Theater on Good Friday, 1865.

DESPERADO

Words have entered the English language in various ways. Many have been derived from the classical languages, Latin and Greek; some have evolved from Romance languages, primarily French; others have been borrowed whole, that is, the foreign words were adopted as is. Still others have been coined, made up to fill a need.

The question with the word *desperado,* a desperate criminal, is where does it fit? All etymologists and lexicographers do not agree on how it came about. Some believe it was derived from the past participle of the Old Spanish *desperar,* to despair. Others looked to the Latin *desperatus,* past participle of *desperare,* which also means "to despair, to lose all hope." But many more attribute the word simply to the conversion of the English word *desperate* into a non-Spanish word (but one with a decided Spanish flavor) by appending the suffix -*ado.* This pseudo-Spanish word, and others like it, was an acknowledgment of Spanish world power during the sixteenth century, a power so great as to influence the English language. *Desperado* is now recognized as a standard English word in all dictionaries.

Through the same process, English has accepted the word *bravado,* an alteration of Spanish *bravada,* ultimately *bravo,* brave, and *tornado,* an alteration of Spanish *tornada,* thunderstorm.

DICTATOR

A dictator, according to its dictionary definition, is a ruler with absolute power and supreme jurisdiction over the government of a state. Such a person is, in plain words, a tyrant. Although *dictator* is a cognate of *dictate,* to say, from Latin *dicere,* to say, what a political dictator says is a command. It's final. The world was filled with dictators during World War II, but the names of two of them make interesting stories.

What's in a name? In 1879, a boy was born and named by his shoemaker father and seamstress mother Iosif Vissarionovich Dzhugashvili. Someone might rightly ask, Can a person with such a moniker succeed in this modern world? Possibly not. But the fact is that this particular person became a world power, one who was feared not only in his own country, but also in others. Very few people knew him by that name and fewer could identify it with the one he adopted—a name that became a household word throughout the world. That person's adopted name, which meant "Man of Steel" in his native tongue, was *Joseph Stalin*, General Secretary of the Communist Party of the Soviet Union (1922–1953) and Premier (1941–1953).

One prominent leader of a country who never changed his name but adopted an awesome title was *Benito Mussolini*. The title he adopted, which became a mandatory designation of respect in Italy, was *Il Duce*, Italian for "the Leader." (*Duce* comes from the Latin *dux*, leader.)

The family name *Mussolini* and a thin cotton cloth called *muslin* had a common ancestor. Both names derived directly from the name of a city in Iraq called *Mosul*. Marco Polo, in recounting his travels, wrote: "All those cloths of gold and of silk which we call muslins are of the manufacture of Mosul, and all the great merchants termed Mossulini, who convey spices and drugs in large quantities from one country to another are from this province." In Italian, the word for *muslin* is *mussolina*, which sounds like the Duce's patronym. The fact is that the suffix *ini*, as in Mussolini, simply means "of the tribe or clan of."

Mussolini's first name was not of Italian derivation. It was Mexican in origin. Mussolini's father was a great admirer of Benito Juarez, who became Mexico's president after the assassination of Maximilian in 1867. And so the son was named *Benito*, an Italian variant of *Benedict*, blessed or, more appropriate in this instance, well-spoken, from Latin *bene*, well, and *dicere*, say. Coming events, it is said, cast their shadows before them. Mussolini certainly spoke well. It was, in fact, his fiery oratory that truly made him Il Duce.

DIESEL

But for the Franco-Prussian War of 1870, the *diesel* engine might never have been invented. As it was, the idea of replacing the steam engine with a more efficient one was generated in the mind of the inventor because of a fluke.

Rudolph Diesel during these times was a young boy living in Paris with his parents. Since they were Germans, they fled to England for the sake of safety. So as not to jeopardize the boy or his education, his uncle, who lived in Augsburg, Germany, offered to care for the lad until the war was over. Hence, with a card of identification hanging around his neck, young Rudolph set out on a train for his uncle's home. The trip took eight days, primarily because the engine broke down several times. And of course trains were not expected to run according to schedule during wartime. When Diesel grew to manhood, he remembered this exasperating experience and decided to do something to improve the functioning of these engines.

To this end, Diesel conducted numerous experiments. He succeeded in building an engine that operated without the ignition spark. He clearly was on his way to success when the engine blew up in his face and almost killed him. Undaunted, he began all over again, realizing that his problem was to find a more suitable fuel. He tried many different kinds, from alcohol to peanut oil, until finally he discovered that a semirefined crude oil seemed to be the perfect solution. He was right and the diesel engine was born, a compression ignition engine more economical in the use of fuel than other existing engines.

Diesel's life ended in misfortune. While traveling on the cross–Channel *Diesden* on September 29, 1913, en route to England, he disappeared mysteriously. He had said good night to some colleagues, entered his stateroom, and was never seen again. His bed had not been slept in, and the only clue to his untimely end was his cap lying near the ship's stern. Ten days later the crew of another ship found his corpse floating in the water. The question that has never been resolved is, Was it suicide or murder?

DIET

> Praise is the best diet for us all.
> —Sydney Smith,
> *Lady Holland's Memoirs*

This essay should be as lean as a person should be after a *diet.* This may not be so, however, because the word *diet* has two distinct meanings, one of which is not associated with restricted ingestion. A deliberative assembly of church officials or a parliamentary assembly is a *diet.* The word in that sense was derived from Latin *dies,* day, which in Medieval Latin became *dieta,* meaning a day's journey (or a day's wage), its root sense being that the members of the assembly convened after traveling for a day (or longer). With time, *diet* came to be used not only for a day's journey but also for the assembly, in which sense it had widespread acceptance throughout Europe. In Japan, the *Diet* is still the national legislature or congress.

The word *diet,* meaning a person's usual food and drink or a regimen prescribed by a physician, comes from a Greek word, *diaita,* mode of living. This *diet* came on the English scene in the thirteenth century, at which time it meant food, daily provisions. Chaucer in 1386 wrote: "He wolde been the moore measurable of his diete sittynge at his table." This meaning, food that is restricted in kind or limited in quantity, continues to this day. It is on everyone's lips to govern everyone's stomach.

DOCTOR/PHYSICIAN

> The best doctors in the world are Doctor
> Diet, Doctor Quiet, and Doctor Merryman.
> —Swift, *Polite Conversations*

People may rightly wonder whether the generic terms for those in the healing arts—*doctors, physicians*—are associated with the practice of medicine. Unquestionably today a doctor is generally thought of as a doctor of medicine, a doctor of dentistry, or an optometrist. But originally, when these terms evolved, this was not so. The word *doctor* in Latin means "teacher" (from *docere,* to teach, to lead, from which has come the English *docile,* one who is easily led). A *doctor,* therefore, strictly speaking, is a teacher, an instructor. The ancestor of *physician (fiscien* in Middle English) is traceable to the Latin *physica,* meaning "natural science, physics." In German it became *physike,* knowledge of nature.

Since the words distinguishing a physician from a person involved in physics were confusing, William Whewell, in the nineteenth century, coined the word *physicist* as the name for one engaged in the pursuit of physics. To designate a practitioner of medicine, to the German root *physis,* nature, English added the suffix *ian,* which signifies "one skilled in," as mathematician, musician, politician; hence *physician.* (Incidentally, the initials *M.D.* after a physician's name stand for *medical doctor,* from the Latin *Medicinae Doctor.*)

The word that contains the notion of healing is the English word *medicine.* It comes from the Latin *medicina,* which in turn comes from *medicus,* healer. Perhaps to be finitely accurate, those involved in healing the ailments of others should be called *medici.* Remember the medicine men, the Medicis? They either cured you or killed you. More often the latter.

DOG IN THE MANGER

A person who selfishly, and out of pure meanness, refuses to part with something that he himself does not want, something he has no use for, may be termed a *dog in the manger.* The expression is traceable to an Aesop fable in which a dog stationed himself in a manger near hay placed there for an ox to eat. Every time the ox came up for its rations, the dog would growl and scare the ox away. "Surly creature," said the ox, "you cannot eat the hay and you will let no one else have it." And from that fable, we say that a person who cannot enjoy something, but nevertheless does not let anyone else enjoy it, is a *dog in the manger.* The idiom first appeared in print in 1564. And we still occasionally run into someone who, doggone, fits the description of the idiom.

DOG'S LIFE, TO LEAD A

The dog has been mercilessly vilified in proverbs. In 1542 Erasmus said: "The most parte of folkes calleth it a miserable life, or a dogges life. . . ." To lead a dog's life is considered a bleak, wretched existence. The idiom describes a person harried from morning till night, nagged constantly, and never left in peace. And so it is said *to go to the dogs,* meaning the lowest form of existence, and *to die like a dog,* a miserable end indeed. We speak of a morally base person as *a dirty dog,* one who is *in the doghouse* as far as society is concerned.

But all this has changed, not these derisive sayings about dogs, but man's attitude toward these animals. It all started a long time ago when one interloper had something nice to say about dogs. He said, "Love me, love my dog," which is construed by some people to mean that my dog is so much a part of me that you must love us both, you can't have me alone. But that was not its sense when first written in medieval times by St. Bernard of Clairvaux—*Qui me amat, amat et canem meum.* What was meant was "If you love anyone, you will like all that belongs to him." The breakthrough came in 1876 through the mouth of Senator George C. Vest at Warrensburg, Missouri. He uttered the poignant idiom that signifies the wonderful relationship of man to dog: "A man's best friend is his dog."

DOGS, NAMES OF

The names of dogs have come from various sources. A common source was the place of the dog's origin. The *Pomeranian,* of the silky hair, for example, came from Pomerania; the *Newfoundland,* from the island of Newfoundland; and the flat-nosed *Pekingese,* bred in China, from its then capital city, Peking.

Some dogs were named after an aptitude peculiar to the breed. Two such dogs, the *terrier* and the *dachshund,* were particularly skillful in seeking out and routing badgers from the holes in which they burrowed. Many hunters used these breeds for this purpose. One of them was so suitable for chasing this quarry from its mound of earth that it was called *terrier,* after the Latin *terra,* earth. In

France, where it was first named, the dog was dubbed by French hunters *chien terrier,* meaning "earth dog." (In French *chien* means "dog.") English borrowed the term, dropped *chien,* and applied it to many breeds of dogs, *fox terrier,* for example, used in hunting foxes.

Another badger nemesis was the *dachshund.* This low-slung dog, bred in Germany, displayed such skill in digging out badgers that it was given the name of its prey—*badger.* In German, *dachs* means badger and *hund* is dog or hound. The full name *dachshund* (badger dog) now refers to this lovable, funny-looking pet that, in all probability, has never seen a badger.

DON'T COUNT YOUR CHICKENS BEFORE THEY'RE HATCHED

> To swallow gudgeons ere they're catched
> And count their chickens ere they're hatched.
> This gudgeon is a fish.
> —Samuel Butler, *Hudibras*

Of the many expressions of advice that tell a person what not to do, none is better known, nor makes more sense, than the warning Don't count your chickens before they're hatched. We are constantly being buffeted by many adages of the "Don't" category—"Don't look a gift horse in the mouth," "Don't look back. Someone might be gaining on you," "Don't take wooden nickels," "Don't let the grass grow under your feet," "Don't cry over spilled milk," and "Don't swap horses in midstream." And there are others.

The saying not to count chickens that have not been hatched dates all the way back to Aesop. In this fable a milkmaid while carrying a pail of milk on her head daydreams about all the money she's going to make when she sells the milk for eggs that will hatch and make her so wealthy that she will be able to toss off her many offers for marriage. Unfortunately for her, however, in her exhilarated state she tosses her head and spills the milk. Sadly she learns not to count profits before they are earned. The moral is to make sure a thing is actually yours before you treat it as yours. Erasmus wrote the same moral, but in different words: "Don't

crow till you are out of the wood." Or we might say, in more vernacular speech: "Don't jump the gun."

DON'T LOOK BACK, SOMEONE MIGHT BE GAINING ON YOU

During the early 1900s there was an outstanding black baseball
pitcher named Satchel Paige. He was also a philosopher, for he offered a formula worth following that is hard to beat. It comes in as
fast and straight as one of his speedballs. Here is what he suggested to retain the vigor of youth: "Avoid fried meats which angry
up the blood. If your stomach disputes you, lie down and pacify it
with cool thoughts. Keep the juices jangling around gently as you
move. Go very light on the vices, such as carrying on in society.
The social ramble isn't restful. Avoid running at all times. Don't
look back. Someone might be gaining on you." (Some authorities
believe that these sayings were dreamed up by a newspaper
writer—whose name is unknown—who attributed them to Paige.
Paige did make them his own in effect by repeating them many
times.)

DON'T SWAP HORSES IN MIDSTREAM

The advice *not to swap horses in the middle of a stream* means
that a change in course or policy in the middle of an undertaking
or a change of leaders at the height of a crisis may be disastrous.
Or, in other contexts, it's better to keep what you know you have
than to change for something or someone unknown. This homely
American phrase was made famous by Abraham Lincoln, although
he did not originate it. On June 9, 1864, in replying to congratula-
tions on his renomination, he said (according to W. O. Stoddard's
version): "I have not permitted myself, gentlemen, to conclude that
I am the best man in the country; but I am reminded in this connection of a story of an old Dutch farmer who remarked to a companion that it was not the best to swap horses while crossing the
river." Today we usually say "in the middle of the stream" or
"midstream" rather than "while crossing the river." Of course the
"river" referred to by Lincoln was the War Between the States.

DROP OF A HAT, AT THE

Authorities have no idea who may have originated this cliché or who introduced the practice of *dropping a hat* to signify the beginning of a race or duel. The fact is that a sweeping motion of a hat while held in hand is just as effective as a starting signal for hostilities or some other event. The expression passed into common speech to mean without delay, immediately, at once. A person ready to perform at the drop of a hat is ready to begin at once. And a person told to begin at the drop of a hat had better be ready immediately. When Johnnie's father says he expects Johnnie to get to the store at the drop of a hat, Johnnie had better leave now.

It may be noted that yesteryears' duelists—prominent men such as Alexander Hamilton, Henry Clay, and Andrew Jackson, as well as ruffians from the forests or mining areas—observed one rule before trying to kill their foes. They began the duels only after the starting signal, the drop of a hat.

DRUG ON THE MARKET

A *drug on the market,* according to street parlance, is a narcotic sought by addicts. It does not refer to a therapeutic drug invented for mankind's benefit and for use under controlled conditions. Centuries ago the word *drug* was not confined to pharmaceuticals but also covered ingredients used in dyeing and in chemistry. During the sixteenth and seventeenth centuries ports of call traded in such drugs as tea, chocolate, spices, and sarsaparilla. Clearly, the term covered a variety of unrelated items. With time the idiom came to refer to something for which there is no demand, something in overabundant supply, something unsalable. In simpler terms, if no one wants it, it's a drug on the market.

The origin of this saying is unknown. Holt guesses that the word *drug* came from French *droque,* meaning "rubbish." It sounds like a good guess. At least it seemed so when Robinson Crusoe laughed at the coins found in the wreck on his desolate island. He said: "O Drug! . . . what are they good for?"

DUMB

It is wise to know that the English word *dumb,* unable to speak, mute, slow-witted (a blockhead), has an etymological association with the sense most often attributed to it, "stupid," as in "My neighbor is so dumb he waters his garden in the rain." It is believed that this latter sense came from *Dummkopf,* a German word brought to America by German immigrants and reduced to *dumb* by analogy, with the word *dumb* meaning "devoid of articulate speech." True, one who lacks understanding is likely to remain silent, that is, speechless; hence *dumb.* (The first person credited with the use of this word was James Fenimore Cooper, in 1823.)

The slang term *dumbbell* (not necessarily a *dumb belle*) is, in ordinary conversation, an equivalent of "stupid," the second element, *bell,* serving no purpose, since *dumb* says it all. The origin of this vernacular term can be found in bells that had no clappers, bells used by beginners when learning to chime. Since the bells made no sounds, were inarticulate, so to speak, they came to be called *dumbbells.* And so were the tyros who failed the chiming test.

DUTCH UNCLE

Is an uncle overindulgent or unnecessarily severe? According to the common simile *like a Dutch uncle,* the answer depends on familial circumstances. Ordinarily an uncle is pleased to show his affection and generosity and is usually a welcome guest. But it is thought that when a father dies, the uncle who assumes parental authority becomes unusually severe and strict. The word *uncle* has a similar meaning to the Latin *patrus,* stern and severe guardian or overseer. And since the Dutch were assumed to be particularly strict, the adjective *Dutch* was appended to *uncle* to make a more drastic expression. Joseph C. Neal wrote in *Charcoal Sketches* (1837), "If you keep cutting didoes, I must talk to both of you like a Dutch uncle." In general parlance, *to talk like a Dutch uncle* has come to mean frankness coupled with severity, that the forthcoming advice or tongue-lashing is meant for the listener's own good. And he had better listen or he'll be sure to be in Dutch.

DWELL

If you were to say that your friend dwells in a stunning house, you might be punning on the word *dwell*, taking its ancestry into account. The meaning of *dwell* at its very beginning, according to Shipley, was "to stun." In Old High German, *to stun* came to mean "to delay," from *twellan*, to retard. Certainly a person who has been stunned has had his mobility retarded. And because that which is retarded is said to linger, to abide for a while, *dwell* (through Middle English *dwellen*) came to mean the place where a person lingered, abided in—his abode. The abode, a person's living quarters, is his dwelling place, since from Old English *abidan* ("to wait on") has evolved the meaning "a resting place," "a place to linger," "a habitation."

EAGLE-EYED

A person who is *eagle-eyed* is said to have sharp vision or, to put it in other words, keen and piercing sight, the kind eagles have. The expression is used of human beings in several ways. A fine marksman is regarded as "eagle-eyed" or as possessing "an eagle eye." This quality of having acute vision is a mainstay of supervisors or overseers. Their responsibility is to observe everything and miss nothing. This sharp watch by those with excellent eyesight was enunciated by John Keats in "On First Looking into Chapman's Homer":

> Then felt I like some watcher of the skies
> When a new planet swims into his ken;
> Or like stout Cortez when with eagle eyes
> He stared at the Pacific—and all his men
> Looked at each other with a wild surmise—
> Silent, upon a peak in Darien.

EARMARK

An *earmark,* according to the dictionary, is "a special mark, quality, or feature that gives information about a person or thing." For example, run-down heels are an earmark of a slovenly dresser, just as clear enunciation is an earmark of a polished speaker.

There is also the verb *to earmark,* which literally means "to place an identifying mark on." Its figurative sense, "to reserve or set aside for a specific purpose," is much in common use today.

For example, "One third of the Whites' earnings are *earmarked* for their children's college education."

Originally an earmark, and some people may be unaware of this, was a mark made for owners on the ears of cattle and sheep (usually a notch) as a sign of ownership. The word first appeared in print in 1523 in Fitzherb's *Husbandry:* "Se that they the sheep be well marked, both eare-marke, pitche-marke, and radel-marke."

EARTH

Let's get down to *earth.* The planet Earth (the Old English *eorde*) is the one on which we live. According to Greek mythology, the universe as we now think of it was all mixed up with confused matter surrounded by a whorl of vapor. The Greeks called this matter *chaos* because it was formless and shapeless (in Greek, *chaos* means "abyss," literally "a cleft"). *Chaos* as the word is now used is not too far different. It means a state of utter confusion and disorder.

Out of the word *chaos* came two important mythological figures—the god of the sky, *Ouranos* (a Greek word meaning "sky") and the goddess of the earth, *Gaia* (*gaia* means "earth" in Greek). The name *Ouranos* lives on in the English language, but in its Roman spelling, *Uranus.* Scientists in the eighteenth century gave that name to a newly discovered planet and, later, to a newly discovered metal, but with a slightly altered name, *uranium.* From *gaia,* spelled *gaes* by the Romans (pronounced *JEE-a* in English), comes the combining form *geo* (meaning "earth"), which appears in many English words: *geocentric,* having the earth as center (a theory that all planets, including the sun and the moon, revolve around the earth); *geography,* the Latin *geographia,* description of the earth; *geology,* from the Modern Latin *geologia,* the study of the earth; *geometry,* measurement of the earth. When it came to earthiness, the Greeks had a word for it.

But the Romans, not to be outdone, also named a goddess of earth (the counterpart of Gaia). They called her *Terra,* which stands for "earth" in Latin. This goddess too made a mark in the English language; her name appears in many English words. In fact, because of her we walk on *terra firma,* firm ground; on *territory* belonging to our country; and, when we tire, rest on our *terrace.* And if creatures from outer space could speak English, they would call us *terrestrial,* people bound to the earth. For those who wonder why the word *terra* appears in the name of a sea—the *Mediterranean*—the answer usually given is that the Mediterranean (Latin for "middle land") was in the middle of the land around which ancient Western civilization lived. But many word sleuths think that that etymology is in deep water, despite the literal Latin definition. They are inclined to say that the origin of the sea's name is obscure.

EAT CROW, TO

This metaphorical saying, with its sense of acknowledging an error or humiliatingly eating one's words, would, if done literally, be most distasteful because crows are not good eating. And that is probably how the idiom arose.

In 1888, the *Atlanta Constitution* reported this story. During an armistice in the War of 1812, an American soldier went hunting. He found no game, even though he tramped about for a while. But he did spot and shoot a crow. At that moment a British soldier appeared and informed the American that he had wandered into British territory and that he was a trespasser. But the Britisher quickly added that he admired the American's marksmanship and would enjoy examining so excellent a rifle. The American felt complimented and surrendered the rifle, whereupon the Britisher put it to his shoulder, pointed it at the American, and told him that he would be released only if he took a bite of the crow he had shot. Not having a choice, the American complied. The Britisher then tossed the rifle at his prisoner in disgust, saying that since he had learned his lesson he was free to go but to be sure never to trespass again. The American, now with rifle in hand, covered his former captor and told him that the tables had been turned and that he had better eat the remainder of the crow or face death. With such a dire threat, the amazed Britisher had no choice but to give in. This, a wit once said, is a case of enemies dining together.

The story is a good one. It makes one feel proud that the American soldier was ingenious. But some authorities believe, and rightly so, that without attestation this account should be put into a drawer marked "folk etymology."

ECSTASY

The term *ecstasy* has become a street term to mean "super-delight." It sometimes represents what may be called "mind-boggling euphoria," as witness the many teenage dancers gyrating on a floor to ear-splitting sounds dominated by incessant drum-beats. The dancers may have their eyes closed and their arms flung into the air, up and down, to accompany their bodily movements. They are, they would assure you, in a state of ecstasy, out of this world. And to that extent they have etymology on their side.

The term *ecstasy* was derived from the Greek *ek,* out, and *sta-sis,* a standing, which meant, literally, a condition in which one stands out of one's mind, is beside oneself, or, as the dictionaries put it, "one who has been driven out of his or her senses," possibly because of a religiously inspired fervor. The term may also be properly applied to a person in a trance of rapturous exaltation in-duced by a mystic. But it is not inappropriate nowadays for one, when expressing intense joy or delight, to say, "I am ecstatic at the wonderful performance of my ten-year-old grandson." No longer is the sense of "being out of one's mind" necessarily inherent in all its uses.

END OF ONE'S ROPE, AT THE

Go hang yourselves (critics) ... you shall never want rope enough.
—Rabelais, *Gargantua and Pantagruel*

This idiom has developed from an old expression, *at the end of the tether.* When horses were man's chief form of travel, it was customary, in order to enable a horse to graze, to tie one end of the rope to the bridle and the other to a tree. The horse would then be free to graze, but only as far as the tether would allow. If the horse wanted to eat some grass beyond reach, all the horse could do was strain his neck, since he had come to the end of his rope. And so we say that a person who goes as far as possible has come *to the end of the rope.* This allusion is to the limit of one's resources, strength, patience, money, and so forth. Having exhausted all the options, there is simply no more one can do or tolerate.

A criminal who has come to the end of his rope, if he is being hanged, is dangling from a hangman's noose. But the expression is also used, figuratively, of all kinds of criminals the moment they have been arrested. A bank robber, for example, who has committed a series of bank holdups and is finally apprehended by authorities, may be said to have come to the end of his rope. Perhaps they gave him enough rope to hang himself.

ENOUGH/GALORE

Enough (the Anglo-Saxon *genoh*) may mean "too much" ("You've polished the table enough already"), "barely sufficient" ("We've just enough to pay for the ticket"), or "plenty" ("We've enough to take care of the entire crowd"). But when one switches from *enough* to *galore,* as in, "We have doughnuts galore," the meaning then is that there is more than enough—more than can be eaten.

The term *galore* (from the Gaelic *go leor,* which when allided sounds like *galore*) originally meant merely "enough," and no more. However, in Ireland, where the expression is rooted, it moved up a notch and developed the sense "more than enough," meaning "more than what was bargained for." Later, in Irish sailors' cant, it moved still higher and came to mean "in abundance," that is, far more than enough. In English, *galore* means "well supplied," but it has never risen above an informal level. Note that *galore* (suits galore, opportunities galore) always follows, never precedes, its noun. One can wear Dior suits but never galore suits!

ENTHUSIASM

When Sammy greets the members of his baseball team enthusiastically, you can be sure he's not thinking that he's had a God seizure. He simply has an intense feeling for the team and what it stands for. Any person with zeal for a subject or cause may be said to be *enthusiastic* about it. But at the birth of this word— *enthusiasm*—it meant "inspired by a god," *entheos,* "possessed": *en,* in, plus *theos,* god. The term was applied to those possessed by excessive religious fervor, fanatics. These zealots were said to be under the influence of godly prophecy.

With time this superstitious belief dissipated and then disappeared entirely. No longer does the word describe one experiencing emotional religion. Its use is universally nonreligious, applying to those devoted to a project or cause, as is Sammy with his baseball team.

EPONYM

An *eponym* (Greek *epi,* upon, and *onyma,* name) is a real or mythical person from whom a place, institution, practice, and so forth takes its name. *Caesar* is the eponym for caesarean section; *A. J. Tasman,* a Dutch navigator, for Tasmania; *Mae West* for an inflatable life preserver; *Benedict Arnold* for a traitor; *John Hancock* for a signature.

Its adjective form, *eponymous,* which means "giving one's name," as to a family (Hellen was the eponymous founder of the Hellenic people), is often used to refer to the character of a book that bears the same name as the book's title. For example, *Reynard the Fox* is the eponymous hero of the beast-epic of Hinreck van Alckmer and *Tom Jones* of Henry Fielding's suspenseful romantic novel.

ETHNIC NAMES

Ethnic groups have pet peeves about names that have been thrust upon them. For example, calling a person of Polish ancestry a *Polack* is considered deprecatory. Yet *Polack* in Polish has meant "an inhabitant of Poland." There should be nothing disparaging in such name-calling. Some black people resent the eponym *Negro,* even though Negroid is the proper anthropological term for a distinctive segment of the population. Their new preference is "African-American." And so with the term *dago.* Italians resent that word. Before that term was applied to Italians (and it came to be done so exclusively), it was a designation for Spanish and then Portuguese people because Diego, from which *dago* was corrupted, was a common Spanish name. *Wop,* too, a cutting nickname for Italians, did not originate as a derogatory word. It was not designed to belittle anyone. It started, so the story goes, with Italian immigrants who came to the United States in droves and who had no identifying documents. As these immigrants were processed, the immigration agent would call out to a clerk, "Mark this one as being without papers." And so on and on. Later, to speak quickly and save time, the agent would say, "Here's another wop," meaning another immigrant *without papers.* Here, too, nothing belittling. But there are some respected authorities who contend that *wop* comes from the Italian dialect word *guappo,* meaning "a big, handsome fellow."

EUREKA

Eureka is a joyful, exultant pronouncement of success. The word was immortalized by Archimedes of Syracuse, the famous mathematician. It was he who discovered the principle of measuring the volume of an irregular solid by the displacement of water.

According to the story behind this discovery, King Hiero of Syracuse had commissioned a goldsmith to make a crown of solid gold, which, upon its presentation, was suspected of containing some silver. The king asked his mathematician friend, Archimedes, to test the crown. It is said that while pondering the matter, Archimedes stepped into a bathtub and noticed that the water overflowed. This incident proved to him that a body must displace its own volume in water. If the crown was alloyed with silver, which is lighter than gold, it would displace a greater amount of water because a pound of silver is bulkier than a pound of gold. Excitedly, and triumphantly, he leaped from the tub and, taking no time to dress, ran naked through the streets shouting "Eureka! Eureka!"—which in Greek means "I've found it! I've found it!"

Archimedes's discovery did indeed prove that the goldsmith was a cheat; the era of scientific investigation was born. But it has never been reported whether Archimedes, having exposed his newly discovered principle, was arrested for having absentmindedly exposed himself.

EXCEPTION PROVES THE RULE, THE

Possibly the most absurd proverb, as many people apply it, is *the exception proves the rule*. Distinguished writers through the ages have echoed and re-echoed it, with minor alterations. Cervantes in *Don Quixote* wrote, "There is no rule without an exception." Robert Burton in his *Anatomy of Melancholy* put it this way: "No rule is so general which admits not some exception." And Byron in *Letters and Journals* said, "Exceptions only prove the rule." The chief argument advanced was that the existence of an exception proves that there must be a rule because if there were no rule there could be no exception to it. This, of course, is talking in circles and is sheer nonsense.

Even though this ridiculous proverb is still repeatedly mouthed, it was wrongly construed in the first place because of a mistranslation of the Latin word *probat* in *exceptio probat regulam*. In that aphorism *probat* does not mean "proves" or "confirms." It means "tests." In Latin, *probare* means "to examine, to test, to probe."

All this should be as clear as it was to Sherlock Holmes who, in *The Sign of Four*, remarked to his ever-present Dr. Watson, "I never make exceptions. An exception disproves the rule."

EVEN-STEVEN

> Don't get mad; get even.
> —Attributed to Joseph Patrick Kennedy,
> the father of President John F. Kennedy

When one says, "We'll divide the profits *even-steven*," he means evenly, fifty-fifty. The expression is common, having been with us for generations. But, despite its frequent use, its origin is unknown. The surmise of some authorities (and sense seems to be on their side) is that the term came from Swift's *Journal to Stella:* " 'Now we are even,' quoth Steven, when he gave his wife six blows to one." Steven had a peculiar idea of *even*.

Perhaps the expression took hold for no reason other than its rhythmical, lilting sound, as many other such expressions have evolved and stayed with us: *hocus-pocus, shilly-shally, ding-dong, dilly-dally,* and so on.

FABRICS, NAMES OF

Some of our most popular fabrics were named in odd ways, some erroneously, some facetiously.

The fabric called *tweed,* for example, a woolen cloth with a rough surface used in the making of rather expensive garments— primarily suits, jackets, and outercoats—was mistakenly named *tweed* instead of *tweel* (a Scottish variant of *twill*), supposedly by one James Locke, a London merchant. The alternation may have been influenced by the name of the well-known River Tweed. In any event, but for that error, the horsey set today would look *twilly* instead of *tweedy*. However, some word historians think that this story is nothing more than a fabric of someone's imagination.

Mohair is a cloth made from the silky hair of Angora goats. The name of a cloth used in upholstery, one manufactured from wool and cotton or rayon, is also called *mohair*. The original name of the cloth was *mukhayyar,* which in Arabic stood for "select choice" (from *khayyara,* to choose), since cloth made from angora goats' hair was considered "select." The English spelled it *mocayare,* a reasonably good phoneticism. In an account in *Hakluyt's Voyages* in the sixteenth century appeared this line: "There is also cotton, wooll, . . . chamlets, mocayares." Because the cloth mocayare looked like hair and because its last syllable sounded like it *(mo-cayare),* the English, with time, altered their own alteration further to *mohair*. However, the evolution of this word too has not been authenticated; it may have been fabricated out of whole cloth—presumably not mohair.

FAHRENHEIT/CELSIUS

Thermometers were unknown until the seventeenth century. Galileo invented a thermoscope, but it failed to measure temperature accurately. In 1724 Gabriel Daniel Fahrenheit, a German by birth but a Dutchman by choice, developed the thermometer that bears his name.

Fahrenheit in his earliest thermometers used alcohol, but he later switched to mercury, the only metal that is liquid at room temperature. His first point of reference was the temperature of the human body, which was obtained by placing the thermometer in a healthy person's mouth. This point he arbitrarily set at 98.6 degrees, the accuracy of which has been disputed in a report in the *New York Times* based upon recent research. He calculated the freezing point of water at 32 degrees, because that was what the tube registered when placed in a container of ice and water, and he set the boiling point at 212 degrees. Fahrenheit imagined that the scale would need lengthening to 128 degrees or 132 degrees if the thermometer were to be used for sick people. "Whether these degrees are high enough for the hottest fevers, I have not examined," he wrote. "I do not think, however, that the degrees named will ever be exceeded in any fever." In general usage the word *thermometer* refers to temperature according to the Fahrenheit scale.

The *Celsius* temperature scale was for many years—from 1742 to 1948—called *centigrade,* a term derived from the Latin *centi,* a combining form meaning "hundred," and *gradus,* degree. Anders Celsius, the inventor, was an eighteenth-century Swedish astronomer. His scale ranged from 0 to 100 degrees, from freezing to the boiling point of water.

To convert from Celsius to Fahrenheit, the Celsius reading is doubled, 10 percent subtracted, and 32 added. To convert from Fahrenheit to Celsius, one should subtract 32 from the Fahrenheit reading and then multiply the remainder by five-ninths.

FAIR AND SQUARE

That which is *fair and square* is honest, just, and straightforward. The word *square* today, referring to a person, means "stodgy," dull as dishwater. But when this idiom evolved, *square* meant honest, which makes *fair and square* tautological. It was the ryhming effect of these words that assured the expression's survival, even though *square* is an unnecessary appendage. In 1604 Francis Bacon wrote: "faire and square." Oliver Cromwell, in 1649, when discussing the fate of a Portuguese, said, "There would be no living (for him) unless he ... do that which is fair and square." An honest, cards-on-the-table transaction is said to be a "fair and square" deal, as William Wycherley in *The Gentleman Dancing Master* enunciated in 1673: "You are fair and square in all your dealings." In street language today one is likely to hear "You'll get a fair shake," which has the same meaning. It matters not how it's worded so long as you get it.

FARM

You might not be welcome if you knocked on a farmer's door at an ungodly hour, yet the word *farm* was derived from an Anglo-Saxon word, *feorm,* meaning "hospitality." Its sense also was "food" and "supper."

In medieval times tenants of land were obligated to supply their lord with certain necessaries, primarily food. These necessaries were called *ferme.* When currency came into vogue, the tenants no longer paid in *ferme* but in white money, called *ferme blanche.* The term *ferme* was in effect another word for *rent.* Since the farmers paid *ferme,* or rent, from the money derived from working the land, the land itself came to be called *ferme,* which ultimately evolved into *farm.* And the Middle English *fermour* became the present-day *farmer.*

FATAL

The original ancestor of the word *fatal,* meaning "of or relating to fate," was the Latin *fatum,* what is spoken. The Romans acquired the concept of an ordained future from the Greeks, who believed that whatever was spoken by the oracle was irreversible; it could under no circumstances be changed. That theory has given rise to another concept—*fatalism:* "that events are fixed in advance for all times in such a manner that human beings are powerless to change them." The word *fatal* has suffered from perjoration, the semantic process by which meaning degenerates over time. After all, one's fate, one's prophecy, may prescribe nothing but joy during a healthy life. But nowadays *fatal* is given one meaning—causing death.

One last thought. We speak of a fateful event, one having momentous consequences. The word *fateful* (a combination of *fate* and the suffix *ful*) was a coinage of the eighteenth-century English poet Alexander Pope.

FEATHER IN ONE'S CAP, A

When congratulating a person for having done something exceptionally well, one might say, "Put a feather in your cap" or "That's quite a feather for your cap." The *feather* referred to is a figurative mark of distinction, meaning that something was done to be proud of. Yet some people might be unhappy with the expression if they knew its grisly military background. The custom was to stick a feather in one's cap for every enemy slain—a mark of battlefield prowess. This tradition supposedly began a long time ago with the Lycians. The practice was adopted, in more modern times, by Hungarians, Turks, Abyssinians, and American Indians. It may be that the Hungarians should be credited with having popularized the phrase. A manuscript in the British Museum, referring to Hungary, states that in 1599, "It hath been an ancient custom among them that none should wear a feather but he who had killed a Turk, to whom only it was lawful to shew the number of his slain enemies by the number of feathers in his cap." But some phrase historians argue that a similar custom by hunters, of attaching to their caps a feather from the first bird they had killed, might have given rise to the saying. Others attribute it to the valor of Edward, "The Black Prince," son of Edward III, who, at the age of sixteen, was credited with the victory of English forces over a numerically larger French and allied force at the Battle of Crécy in 1346. He was awarded three white ostrich feathers, the crest of John, King of Bohemia, who was killed in the battle. The crest became a badge of each succeeding Prince of Wales. One might conclude that anyone who can convincingly establish the origin of the phrase would be justified in sticking a feather in his cap.

FEATHER ONE'S NEST, TO

What is meant is clear: to take care of oneself for the future by stocking up on money or other possessions. Or to make any other comfortable provision for oneself. The allusion, of course, is to the practice of birds that build soft nests for their eggs and their future young. The idiom is as old as 1553, at which time it was used in a play, *Republica:* "Now is the time come . . . to feather my nest." In 1590, Robert Greene, a poet, wrote: "She sees thou hast fethred thy nest, and hast crowns in thy purse." The idiom usually registers disapproval except, naturally, where birds are concerned. Which leads one to believe that the expression is strictly for the birds.

FENCE

To *fence* is to defend, to guard. It is also a slang term for a receiver of stolen goods. Many thieves depend on their "fence," for it is the fence that, in one sense of the word, keeps the thieves in business. Viewed from another angle, the receiver, by relieving the thief of his loot, is defending him—is protecting his ill-gotten goods by converting them into money. It is said that formerly the fence would serve as the thieves' defenders against charges brought against them. *Fence* is aphetic for *defence,* which came from the Latin *defendere,* to beat off. The word *fence* was first used in print by Rowlands in 1608: "To fence property, to sell anything that is stolen." It became thieves' cant.

Fend, to keep or ward off, is *defend* without *de;* and *fender,* one who wards off or a guard over a wheel, is *defender,* also without *de.* They both, returning to their Latin ancestor, "beat off," "thrust away," what shouldn't be there.

FILE

The English word *file,* meaning "a collection of papers, a place for keeping papers in order" and "a line, a row of persons, animals, or things, one behind the other," had its original ancestor in the Latin *filum,* thread. Two French cognates evolved to distinguish these different meanings. The first *file* (a set of papers or a container for them) came from *fil,* meaning "thread," because a string or wire was placed through documents to ensure their remaining in order. English borrowed the word and added a final *e* so that the *i* would be pronounced long. The second *file,* from the French *filer,* referred to those who "marched in file." English borrowed this word whole, making no orthographic changes. These *file* words, it might be said, have marched or threaded their way through every phase of American life beginning with the Native Americans, who walked "Indian or single file" to conceal their footprints. Each Indian would step into the footprints of the person ahead, the end man then obliterating the last prints. However, this practice was never verified. Although a good story, it does not seem plausible, for the obliterator to bend and erase all those marks would need a back made of rubber. Let's file this one in a drawer marked "folk etymology."

FINGERS/TOES

> The thumb in chiromancy, we give to Venus,
> The fore-finger to Jove; the midst to Saturn;
> The ring to Sol; the least to Mercury.
> —Ben Jonson, *The Alchemist*

A hand has five fingers. Since everyone knows it, that is not an exciting fact. And neither is there much of a story behind the naming of these digits, but it is interesting to learn what the various fingers were called many years ago and why they were given these names.

The first finger, the inside finger, is the *thumb,* in Old English called *thuma,* meaning "thick" or "swollen." The thumb, of course, is the thick finger. Some anatomists would dispute that statement, for they say that man does not have five fingers. He has four fingers and a thumb. They reason that since a finger has three phalanges and a thumb only two, the thumb is not a finger. (The word *phalange* comes from the Greek *phalanx,* a close battle formation of spearmen carrying overlapping shields, because someone fancied that the small bones in the hands and toes were suggestive of a battle array.)

The second finger, the one after the thumb, is known as the *index finger* because it is used for pointing (*index* is the Latin "informer," "something that indicates," that which points out). In Middle English the index finger was called the *toucher* (spelled *towcher*) because it was so often used to touch things. The third finger, now known as the *middle finger,* was called the *long-man,* for obvious reasons. The next, the fourth finger, now called the *ring finger,* was formerly called the *lecheman* because a leech or doctor used it for testing (*leech* is an archaic word for physician). The fifth finger, the *pinkie,* was called the *little-man,* here again for obvious reasons.

One question still remains to be answered: Who or what was *finger*'s ancestor? Most etymologists surmise that its original forebear was *penkwe,* an Indo-European word meaning "five," from which evolved the form *penkweros,* meaning "one of five." Certainly a finger is one of five. Which makes one wonder, how about the toes? *Toe,* in Anglo-Saxon *ta,* meant "to show." This was its etymological sense all the way up through Middle English. Of course, in ancient barefoot or sandal-wearing times the toes were always "that which shows." This is still true, figuratively, in today's world when a person is made to toe the line. He had better show what the boss is looking for.

FIT AS A FIDDLE

Every book on word origins should include this simile, for that is exactly, in a few words, how we all would like to feel. Dictionaries define the phrase as meaning "in fine shape; feeling good." The phrase, however, is also applied to things nonhuman; for example, we might say, "Our auto is running just fine. It's as fit as a fiddle, in tip-top condition."

A fiddle has been a symbol of fitness for at least three hundred years, but no one knows how this came about. Conjectures are all the experts can offer, one being that people at one time thought the fiddle to be so beautiful an instrument that they would liken a handsome face to it. Interesting, but farfetched. Anyway, the expression appeared as early as 1616. William Haughton, at a time when *fit* meant "appropriate," wrote, in *Englishmen for My Money:* "This is excellent, i' faith; as fit as a fiddle." Currently the expression signifies physical fitness. The sense of "appropriateness" has been discarded, which shows that usage can fiddle with an ancient cliché and come up with a different tune.

FLABBERGAST

Where and how the word *flabbergast* originated remains so obscure that it flabbergasts word sleuths seeking a clue to its genesis. It is one of those words whose survival had best not depend upon a known parentage. Some philologists believe that *flabbergast* is a blend of *flabby* and *aghast.* But others do not go along, since *flabby* (from Latin *flaccidus,* soft or not firm) is unrelated to the word's sense. Those who suggest that the initial element came from *flap,* a slangy expression for "a fight or row" or "loud confusion," may be closer to the truth. No one argues about *aghast* (the Old English intensive prefix *a* and *gaeston,* frighten), for that is how a flabbergasted person feels—shockingly amazed, astonished, practically struck dumb with surprise.

Incidentally, the pursuit to identify the word's forebears began before the American Revolution. It was listed, in 1772, as slang, but it has since been elevated in the literary scale of acceptability. It is now regarded as an informal term, certainly a step upward. But be not flabbergasted if one day it is welcomed into the family of formal English.

FLATTERY WILL GET YOU NOWHERE

Flattery consists of words of praise, but usually those that are untrue or exaggerated. And that is why perceptive people resent flatterers. The word came through French *flatir,* stroke (with the flat of the hand). Even before the days of the Romans, appealing to someone's vanity was recognized as an insidious way of getting into a person's good graces. But the cliché, *flattery will get you nowhere,* is of recent origin; it is a twentieth-century Americanism. Ellery Queen wrote in 1971 in *A Fine and Private Place,* " 'Flattery will get you nowhere, Queen,' the murderer said." The thought, however, as previously pointed out, preceded the Common Era and was given a measure of impetus by Shakespeare in *Richard II,* in which Richard says: "He does me double wrong that wounds me with the flatteries of his tongue."

Flattery has fathered many other clichés. The one that has become the most established is "soft soap," possibly because that kind of soap has an unctuous quality, like the persiflage sliding from the tongue of a flatterer. Sometimes the term is used as a verb, as in Francis M. Whitcher's *The Widow Bedott's Papers* (1840): "Ye don't ketch me a slanderin' folks behind their backs and then sof-soapin' 'em to their faces."

Those who wish to be facetious have taken the expression "flattery will get you nowhere" and twisted it around to say, "Flattery will get you everywhere." And perhaps they're right.

FLOWERS, NAMES OF

The lovely but strong-scented flower the *gardenia* was named after Alexander Garden, a practicing physician in Charleston, South Carolina, who had the heart of a botanist. Garden enjoyed the world of flowers so much that he kept in touch with many eighteenth-century botanists and wrote regularly to Linnaeus, who named this variety of jasmine after him. Hence the *gardenia.* Incidentally, although Garden's granddaughter was named Gardenia, he never saw her, because her father, his son, joined the Revolutionary forces in their struggle against the British. Garden, completely devoted to the Crown, could not accept his son's disloyalty. After the colonists' success, Garden returned to Britain, where he died soon afterwards. It has been said that, appropriately, his grave was covered with gardenias.

Many flowers were named after people, some of whom were

not even associated with the flower. The *fuchsia,* for example, was named after Leonhard Fuchs, a lover of flowers and plants, who became a sixteenth-century botanist, although he was by profession a professor of medicine at the University of Tübingen. Although he collected botanical specimens, his international fame followed the publication of a booklet instructing people on how to protect themselves against the plague. Fuchs was immortalized by the name given this drooping, vivid purplish-red flower by seventeenth-century French botanist Charles Plumier.

Some flowers are named for things they seem to resemble. For example, a *dandelion* owes its name to the French because the jagged edges of its leaf reminded them of a lion's tooth. From the French *dent de lion,* which translates into "lion's tooth," came the sixteenth-century English corruption *dandelion.* The leaf of a *gladiolus* is shaped like a sword (perhaps one wielded by a *gladiator*). From this diminutive form of the Latin *gladius,* sword, came the name of this popular flower—*gladiolus,* literally "small sword."

FLY IN THE OINTMENT, A

It may be hard to believe, but it is true that this saying, *a fly in the ointment,* has been with us since the third century B.C. It was one of many homely bits of advice and warning that emanated from the brilliant mind of a Hebrew sage who penned his works under the name of Koheleth. The phrase became biblical and appears in Ecclesiastes 10:1, the twenty-first book of the Old Testament.

When first written—"Dead flies cause the ointment of the apothecary to send forth a stinking savour, so doth a little folly him that is in reputation for wisdom and honour"—its sense was not that with the fly once removed everything would be restored to a happy state, but that the total good would be destroyed by this one blemish. The passage of time has moderated the effect of the blemish, and its sense is now generally considered to be simply that of a minor imperfection, an obstacle that can be cast aside so that, with the hitch in any plan removed, everything would be properly restored. And so when we say, "There is one fly in the ointment," we mean that one problem must be resolved and that after taking care of this one thing, we can then move along.

FOOL AND HIS MONEY ARE SOON PARTED, A

The sense of this often-repeated saying—a dim-witted person is easily persuaded to buy something or invest his money—is clear. But where and under what circumstances it was first enunciated is far from clear. Authorities are united in saying the source is unknown. One story that seems to have merit, but is unattested, concerns a George Buchanan, tutor to James VI of Scotland. It is said that the tutor and a courtier each claimed that he could compose a coarser, a bawdier verse than the other. And so they made a wager. Buchanan won and, when pocketing his winnings, was heard to mutter, "A fool and his money are soon parted." Somewhat different but yet akin to it is an American adage attributed to Phineas T. Barnum (1810–1891): "There's a sucker born every minute." Who no doubt will soon be foolishly relieved of his money.

FOOL'S PARADISE, A

Children are told of a place of bliss called *paradise*. Some older people dream of it, hoping that they can go there someday. But since at least the year 1462, people have been aware that the notion of paradise may be illusory and one based on ignorance. In that year William Paston wrote in his *Passion Letters:* "I wold not be in a folis paradyce." The expression took hold, and it was used by many of our great literateurs, including Shakespeare and George Bernard Shaw, who in *Misalliance* (1910) wrote: "Beguiling tedious hours with romances and fairy tales and fools' paradises." Today a person who knows he's being "sold a bill of goods" because he's thought to be gullible may rightfully say, "I'm not interested in a fool's paradise."

FORTY WINKS

The term *forty* has many biblical connotations and has, to an extent, been treated as sacrosanct. For example, "Moses was on the mount forty days and forty nights"; "Elijah was fed by ravens for forty days"; "the rain of the flood fell forty days"; and "forty days passed before Noah opened the window of the ark." And there were legal restrictions based on *forty*. A *quarantine* (from Italian *quaranta*, forty) was the period a ship suspected of carrying infectious disease was compelled to lie in port. A widow entitled to a dower was permitted to remain in her deceased husband's house for forty days. But what has all this to do with *forty winks*, and why forty?

A *wink* has been an informal term for "a short nap," "a doze," since William Langland wrote *Piers Plowman* (1377): "Thenne Wakede I of my wink." But the story that has been bruited about for centuries, one that has set *forty winks* deeply in a cement block, was an apocryphal account concerning the required reading of the thirty-nine Articles of Faith that the clergy had to accept during the reign of Elizabeth I. The reading was tedious and, as might be imagined, soporific. And that gave a writer for *Punch* the idea to pen an article (1872) that concluded: "If a man, after reading through the thirty-nine Articles, were to take forty winks . . ." The writer was probably offering sound advice. Nevertheless, as a matter of record, the term first appeared in print in 1828 in Pierce Egan's *Tom and Jerry:* ". . . (an) uncommonly big gentleman, told out, taking forty winks." But it took *Punch* to put punch into this expressive term.

FREEMAN/SLAVE

> It is better to be a mortal freeman than an immortal slave.
> —R. G. Ingersoll, *Voltaire*

A *freeman* is a person who may make his own decisions subject to no external controls. The word *free* has evolved through several languages having somewhat similar forms. But chiefly it was a legacy from the Franks, a Germanic tribe which in the sixth century conquered Gaul and gave its name to France, with its meaning of "free" or "open." The members of this tribe—the Franks—considered themselves honest, forthright, and given to sincere expression.

English derivatives from the tribal name are *frank, franchise (enfranchise)*—in French, *affranchir* means "to set free"—and the term *franking privilege,* which means free mailing privileges on one's signature.

The condition antipodal to freedom is slavery. During the Middle Ages Germanic tribes, after conquering much of central Europe, took their captives and sold them to the Romans, Franks, and Spanish Moslems. The racial name in Latin for a captive was *sclavus.* From it came the English word to designate one forced into bondage—*slave.* But there was an in-between step. The Slavs of Eastern Europe were enslaved people so oppressed and so cruelly treated that their name, modified to *slave,* slipped into English.

Despite this semantic genealogy of *Slav,* it remained a name that those tyrannized people were proud of, for in their language Slav meant "glory."

FROM PILLAR TO POST

This old, well-known expression is one whose origin has never been convincingly established. Word history mavens have come up with several possibilities, but on none can all agree.

One belief advanced is that the phrase came from early riding academies, where posts were set on the perimeter of the ring around which riders would maneuver. The pillar was in the center. Because of this riding regimen, the phrase originally was called *from post to pillar,* which is in reverse form. Another theory is that the expression was born on a tennis court to represent the banging of the balls.

But a more likely belief is laid at the doorstep of the cruel Pilgrims, who punished minor offenders by putting them in a *pillory,* a yoke around the neck that kept the culprits standing on tiptoe, while the populace was encouraged to pelt them with stones and mud. More serious offenders were punished at the public whipping post. And so a person who went from the pillory (later corrupted to *pillar*) to the whipping post was said to be going from bad to worse. The idiom, figuratively, is used to mean repetitive drifting from one thing or place to another monotonously and without definite purpose.

The term *pillar* by itself is used of an important person, perhaps a self-important person. It is a sarcastic reference to one who thinks he's influential. The phrase *pillar of the church* is not uncommon but, according to Eric Partridge, was common in its pejorative sense and highly objectionable.

FROM THE SUBLIME TO THE RIDICULOUS

From great to small, success to failure, noble to ignoble. One can more poetically phrase the meaning "from one extreme to another" by saying *from the ridiculous to the sublime. Sublime* (the Latin *sub,* under, up to, plus *limen,* the lintel, the upper edge of a door and originally coming up to below the lintel) means "noble," "lofty," "majestic." *Ridiculous* (Latin *ridere,* to laugh) means "absurd," "laughable."

Some philologists at one time credited this expression to Napoleon because in a letter to the Abbé du Pratt he wrote about his return from Russia (1812) and, referring to the retreat from Moscow, said, *"Du sublime au ridicule il n'y a qu'un pas,"* which, translated, reads: "From the sublime to the ridiculous is but a step." However, most of today's researchers of word and phrase histories have joined the ranks of those who place its origin in Tom Paine's *Age of Reason* (1793): "The sublime and ridiculous are often so nearly related that it is difficult to class them separately, and one step above the ridiculous makes the sublime again."

FURY

> Heaven has no rage like love to hatred turned
> Nor hell a fury like a woman scorned.
> —Congreve, *The Mourning Bride*

Fury is extreme anger. But originally it represented a more serious state. It was (from a Latin word, *furia*) a rage, a madness. This came about because in Roman mythology three female avenging spirits, called *furia* (Alecto, Tisiphone, and Megaera, who had snakes for hair), instilled madness in those whose misdeeds had not been avenged. Nowadays the word *fury* does not have such a strong connotation. A furious person is not thought of as being mad, only very angry. Even the fury of a woman scorned is not madness, although she is, in popular parlance, quite mad.

FUNNY BONE

A bump on the elbow can be painful, certainly not a laughable matter. But what is funny is the name given to this area—the enlarged end of the bone where the ulnar nerve is exposed to the elbow. It's called the *funny bone*. The name is fitting, however, not because an amusing sensation arises there, but because of a pun— the bone that descends from the shoulder to the elbow is the *humerus*. Americans, according to Mencken, can't see the humor in it; many of them call it the *crazy bone*. Why? No one knows. Although according to the *Dictionary of American Regional English*, more Americans call it the *funny bone* than the *crazy bone*.

GADGET

All of us occasionally have lapses of memory, especially when it comes to remembering names. If we want, say, the calipers, and we can't think of the name, we're likely to say, as we point, "Pass me that *thingamajig* or that *whatsis* or that *doodad* or that *gadget.*" The first three combinations of letters that pass for words, of course, are not words and are not listed in dictionaries. The last, however, *gadget* (a word first recorded in 1886, but in common usage long before), is an accepted word for a handy mechanical device. Its admittance into the English language, however, may have been based on tenuous grounds, a whimsical conjecture by some wordsmiths that *gadget* had two etymological bases: one, a French word, *gachette,* a catch or staple or a small hook; the other, a Scottish term, *gadge,* gauge. Most authorities dispute these sources. They say the origin of *gadget* is unknown.

What is known is that *gadget* was a term commonly used by seamen when they forgot the name of a small tool or mechanical device. The seamen's lingo ultimately reached land and spread into towns and villages. Nowadays almost everyone—seamen and landlubbers—accepts the word *gadget* as the equivalent of "that thing," and it has become as ordinary a term as its origin is obscure.

GAFF

To stand the gaff, meaning to bear with equanimity stress, pain, or punishment, is an expression that almost everyone understands.

But whether the word *gaff* by itself is fully understood is another matter. The fact is that *gaff,* between standard English and slang, has many meanings.

A *gaff* (from the Old French *gaffe*) is a light fishing spear, a metal hook fastened to a pole used to boat large fish. A *gaff* is also the name of a metal spur attached to the leg of a gamecock. Other meanings are a hoax or trick, used of a gaming device so set that no one can win (the device is said to be *gaffed*). In slang, *gaff* is the equivalent of harsh statements or treatment, or, in *to blow off the gaff,* "to blab, to disclose secrets." So which *gaff,* one might ask, is involved when one *stands the gaff*? Word historians opt for pain or stress, like the kind inflicted on a gamecock when struck by spurs during a cockfight. The cock that quits, we must conclude, couldn't stand the gaff.

Gaffe, the immediate ancestor of *gaff,* has been accepted whole into the English language. It has a completely unrelated meaning, "a clumsy social error," or *"faux pas,"* French for "a false step."

GAME

> Play up, play up, and play the game.
> —Sir H. Newbolt, *Vitai Lampada*

The adjective *game* may be used to describe a person who has endurance, is lively and spirited, or is plucky and courageous. Informally speaking, such a person is ready and willing. Which makes one wonder why a *game leg* should hinder a person from playing in a game. The answer seems to be—although the imprint of authorities does not appear on this one—that *game* in *game leg* came from *gam* (rhymes with *dam),* a form of Welsh and Irish dialect meaning "crooked or bent." Which is no reason not to look at your girlfriend's *gams.*

The noun *game,* from Middle English *gamen,* means "sport or amusement," a sense that has not changed as its present-day spelling evolved with its final *n* clipped, except that *game* is now usually applied to a contest.

GANGPLANK

> The best laid schemes o' mice an' men
> Gang aft a-gley,
> An' lea'e us naught but grief an' pain,
> For promis'd joy!
> —Robert Burns, *To a Mouse*

The first line of this verse is well known, but not the second. *Gang aft a-gley* in Scottish means "often go wrong."

In today's usage, the word *gang* refers to a group of people, a group of hoodlums, a group of laborers, or a set of tools. The *gang* in the verse of course means none of these things: it means "go," as will be seen shortly.

First let us consider the word *gangplank*. Is a gangplank a plank over which a gang or a group of people walk? It is that in a sense, but the *gang* in *gangplank* has none of the usual meanings attributed to *gang* in the preceding paragraph. Beginning with Old English and through Middle English, the sense of *gang* was "going," and was applied to "the act of walking," specifically along a passage, since in Anglo-Saxon the walking was along a path or course. Hence the term *gangplank,* a passage between a ship and a landing place on which passengers and crew enter or leave the ship. They are doing what Middle English claimed: each one is "going."

GAS

Many coinages have enriched the English language. Alexander Pope coined *bathos;* Horace Walpole coined *serendipity;* Samuel Foote invented *panjanadrum.* But possibly the commonest word ever artificially created is *gas*—the magic flame that works for man.

Gas was first noticed by a shepherd who thought his sheep acted oddly when they grazed on a certain mountainside. Upon investigation, the shepherd found something emanating from around the rocks which made him light-headed. The ancient Greeks didn't take this matter lightly, however. After meditating about it, they decided that what was escaping from the ground was the breath of

Apollo. And so they erected a temple at that place—Delphi—
where the oracle came to sit and answer questions brought by the
people. Of course, what the shepherd found escaping from the
ground was natural gas, a form of gas used by many peoples. More
than three thousand years ago, the Chinese learned that this substance would burn; later their knowledge spread to Europe.

The first manufactured gas was a discovery in 1609 in Brussels
by Jan Baptista van Helmont, who was studying the vapors produced from burned charcoal. His accidental finding was serendipitous, for he was an alchemist looking to make gold. To name this
matter, he coined the word *gas* (one of the few invented words to
enter the English language). That coinage, so to speak, was made
out of thin air. Helmont wrote: "I have called that spirit *gas,* as being not far removed from the Chaos of the ancients." Note the
word *spirit.* Helmont was an occultist, and he sometimes referred
to his find as "ghost" or "wild spirit." In referring to Chaos,
Helmont used the name in Greek classics for the substance of the
universe as it was composed before the Creation gave solid form to
some of it.

GENEROUS TO A FAULT

For those who wonder how generosity can be a fault, bear in
mind that *fault* here means "excessive." Any excess is on the verge
of becoming a defect. Hence liberality carried to an extreme may
indicate a psychological weakness, an effort to rebut an inferior position. But of course when it comes to ourselves, we do not hesitate
to be "generous to a fault."

GET ONE'S GOAT, TO

Although some city dwellers have never seen a live goat, they
might nevertheless say, if they lose their temper, "That gets my
goat" or "That gets my nanny." Both expressions have the same
meaning (a nanny goat is a she-goat). But this is not to say that
their rural cousins do not express themselves in like terms. In fact,

the notion of *getting one's goat* can be traced far from urban areas—to horse country.

It was the practice some years ago to provide a high-strung racehorse with a companion, a docile animal, one that would stay close whenever the horse was in its stall. A stablemate tended to quiet the thoroughbred so that it didn't become restive. Since thoroughbred horses, especially stallions, become competitive when near each other, and since a mare might excite them, a goat was used instead. The continued presence of the goat as a companion put the horse at ease. Then the bright but nefarious idea arose that if someone would get the goat, that is, steal it before a major race, the horse might become nervous and lose its composure and, in all likelihood, the race, too. Sure enough, once a thief got a horse's goat, the horse became upset and irritable, which is exactly how a person feels when someone unfelicitously gets his goat.

The expression first appeared in print in Christy Mathewson's *Pitching in a Pinch* (1912): "Then Lobert . . . stopped at third with a mocking smile which would have gotten the late Job's goat."

GET THE SACK, TO

> I wonder what red Fogg 'ud say, if he knew it.
> I should get the sack, I s'pose—eh?
> —Charles Dickens, *The Pickwick Papers*

To get the sack (or *to be sacked*) is to be dismissed from employment or, as is more commonly said, to be fired. This phrase may have originated in France in the seventeenth century *("On lui a donné son sac")*, but it became current in England a century later. Many explanations of this expression have been advanced, but none thoroughly established. One belief is that the Turkish sultan, when he lost interest in one of his harem, would have her put into a sack and then tossed into the Bosphorus. Another is that the custom of Turkish lovers generally was to dispose of their unwanted women in the same fashion. Workmen, especially in textile mills, provided their own tools, which they brought to work in a sack. Being told to get the sack, therefore, was a disguised notice of dismissal—"get your tools and go." It was also thought that, tools apart, an employer, to rid himself of an unsatisfactory work-man, would simply hand him an empty sack. Everyone knew what that meant. In Spanish, the verb *sacar* means "to dismiss," which is also a possible source. In football, a quarterback who is caught in his tracks before he can move is said to be dumped or *sacked*. No matter. If you get it, you're a sad sack.

GIBBERISH

A person who talks *gibberish* speaks meaninglessly. What he utters is senseless chatter. It is unintelligible speech belonging to no known language. Although the meaning of *to talk gibberish* is clear, its origin is unknown.

An Arabian alchemist named Geber who lived in the eleventh century wrote with words that made no sense; they constituted his own peculiar jargon. He used this unintelligible language in order to baffle the ecclesiastics. Had his writing been clear and under-standable, he would have subjected himself to a severe penalty, possibly death for dealing with the devil.

Dr. Samuel Johnson credited the origin of the word *gibberish* to the man who wrote in those terms, Geber. But most authorities do not go along with Dr. Johnson. They contend that the word is imitative, like *jabber, gabble,* and *giggle*.

GIDDY

A *giddy* person is, according to the dictionary definition, light-headed, perhaps reeling about, as one might say: *dizzy*. In a less severe state such a person may be more kindly described as frivolous, lighthearted, or even *flighty*.

Like many another English word that is in common usage, the story behind it is far afield from its original meaning. The progen-itor of *giddy* was Old English *gidig,* which meant "insane" but sig-nified one "possessed by a god," certainly a form of madness. With time, the sense of *giddy* went through a process of melioration and acquired the meaning of "foolish" or "stupid." In the fourteenth century, in another semantic change, the term came to mean "dizzy." Some three hundred years later there was another decided movement in the meaning of *giddy*. It then came into its modern sense of "causing dizziness" and its more accustomed sense of "exuberantly silly." Although such a person may be regarded as "wacky," that is not the same as insanity.

GIFT OF GAB

Is *the gift of gab* a social grace or an undesirable trait? The answer depends on what you consider it to mean. If you regard it as "fluency of speech," it is something we all would admire, but if you think it means "a tendency to boast" or "prattle"—much talk about nothing, loquacity—we would frown on it. The word *gab* *(gob)* is an old Gaelic and Scottish word meaning "mouth." In 1695, Samuel Covil in his *Whiggs' Supplication* said: "There was a man called Job . . . He had a good gift of the Gob." With time, *gob* had a phonetic change to *gab,* as in William Godwin's *Caleb Williams* (1794): "He knew well enough that he had the gift of the gab." Its sense "to boast" comes from a distant ancestor, the French *gaber,* to boast. It certainly seems that the English *gabble,* to talk incessantly and inanely, may be onomatopoeic of *gab* and a derivative. Should any of this raise questions, perhaps a gabfest may straighten it out.

GILD THE LILY, TO

This cliché is so well known that it needs no introduction. And probably everyone thinks he or she knows its meaning, "to add excessive or superfluous ornaments or decoration to something already beautiful." But what some might not know is that this is not an accurate quotation of Shakespeare but a misquotation. The story behind the expression is that King John, having illegally seized the throne after his brother's death in 1199, now thinks that a second coronation might reinforce his weak position and strengthen the waning affection of his people. Lord Salisbury thinks otherwise, that a second coronation is a "wasteful and ridiculous excess." He says:

> Therefore to be possess'd with double pomp,
> To guard a title that was rich before,
> To gild refined gold, to paint the lily,
> To throw a perfume on the violet,
> To smooth the ice, or add another hue
> Unto the rainbow, or with taper-light
> To seek the beauteous eye of heaven to garnish,
> Is wasteful, and ridiculous excess.

Quite clearly the words *gild* and *paint* have changed positions in the minds of most people, which leaves both phrases less fitting.

GIN

Some people drink *gin;* others clean cotton with it.

The cotton *gin,* a mechanical invention of Eli Whitney's, separates the seed from the fiber. Its name came from the second syllable of *engine,* in Old French and Middle English spelled *engin,* but ultimately from the Latin *ingenium,* natural disposition, talent; whence *ingenuity.*

The spiritous liquor known as *gin* originally was spelled *geneva.* It all started with *juniper,* dubbed *juniperus* at its Latin birth. The *geneva* from which the product gin is manufactured is a corruption of the French word for the juniper berry, *genièvre,* called *genever* by the Dutch. The English soldiers who fought in the Lowlands also called it *genever* but pronounced it *geneva.* With time, *geneva* was shortened to *gin.*

Incidentally, two myths that should be exploded are that there is gin in ginger, a pungent rootstock used as a flavoring or spice, sometimes medicinally, and that Eli Whitney once told his drunken neighbor, "Keep your cotton-pickin' hands off my gin."

GIVE ONE'S EYETEETH FOR, TO

What this hyperbolic expression means is that a person will go to great lengths to satisfy a strong desire or to obtain something that he or she yearns for. Surrendering the upper canines would destroy a person's ability to bite and chew well. So a person who says, "I'd give my eyeteeth for that (or her)" is theoretically prepared to give up something of great value, and eyeteeth have the deepest roots and are hardest to pull. The probabilities are, however, that although the term has been used since the mid-nineteenth century, no one has actually given up eyeteeth for that purpose. The expression is most likely made only for its dramatic effect. W. S. Maugham in his *Cakes and Ale* (1930) wrote, "He'd give his eyeteeth to have written a book half as good."

Other clichés echo the same thought, a willingness to give up a part of one's body to obtain what is desired. (Remember Van Gogh and his slashed-off ear?) Occasionally one hears, "I would give my pinkie (the little finger) for that," but more often, "I'd give my right arm for that." None of these hyperboles are spoken seriously of course or are to be taken seriously. It is unlikely that anyone would sacrifice his right arm for a whim or even an unusually strong desire. Robert G. Dean used the term in *Layoff* (1942): "He'd cut off his right arm for her, as the saying goes." But he didn't. These lavish thoughts can trigger ridiculous statements. Take Ciardi's example: "I'd give both arms for a chance to pitch for the Yankees." If so, how would he do it?

GIVE SOMEONE SOMETHING TO BOOT, TO

To give someone the boot has a meaning entirely different from *to give something to someone to boot.* The first means to direct your boot, as with a swift kick, so as to punish or to rid yourself of someone. The second means "besides or in addition." A person hired to wash the exterior of a car who also cleans the interior—*to boot*—has performed an additional service—free of charge. Any trade in which something is given besides the object bargained for is said to be given to boot. The idea behind this generosity is to make the recipient feel good, perhaps that he has profited from the transaction, which was what *boot* (Anglo-Saxon *bot*) meant originally, "profit or advantage."

But the "besides or in addition" may not always be what a person was looking for. For example, "Andy lost his wife, his money, and his car to boot." Perhaps that was what his father-in-law gave him, too.

GLAD

> Shall I seem crest-fallen in my father's sight?
> —Shakespeare, *Richard II*

To be *crestfallen* is to be dispirited, dejected. In times past, however, *crestfallen* referred only to a rooster that, having lost a fight, drew back, his crest adroop. He was truly crestfallen. The opposite emotion to depression is gladness. The word *glad,* from the Old High German *glat,* smooth, became in Old English *glad.* It did not connote happiness, but brightness. *Glad* meant "shining, bright," and its cognate meant "smooth," "polished," as exemplified by an anonymous sixteenth-century poet when he wrote: "leves new, Som very rede, and Som a glad light greene." But because bright and shiny things bring pleasure, the sense of *glad* evolved into its present meaning: "pleased, feeling or displaying joy," a sense that Dr. Johnson entered into his *Dictionary.*

In 1915, Mrs. Eleanor Hodgman Porter wrote a book called *Pollyanna, the Glad Girl.* The gist of the story hinged on the life of an orphan who regularly played a game of finding something to be glad about. The word *Pollyanna* (from two Hebrew words meaning "bitter grace") has become a generic term for "a person who always sees the bright side of things," "one who is constantly cheerful and optimistic," or, we might say, "one who wears rose-colored glasses." Cynics, nevertheless, deprecate pollyannaism by saying it is foolishness to cover up the sordid reality of this world. They may be right, but there's no doubt that cynics are not "glad" about gladness.

GLAMOUR/GRAMMAR

> Grammar, which knows how to control even kings.
> —Molière, *Les Femmes Savantes*

Most students would agree that *grammar* is anything but *glamorous,* yet there is a relationship between those words. From the days of antiquity through the Middle Ages and until the days of the Enlightenment, reading and writing were kept arcane. The ordinary people, and that was the vast bulk, were awed—and suspicious—of scholars and the grammar that was a part of their learning. *Grammar,* from the Latin *grammatica,* became associated in their minds with occult learning or black magic, since it too was a learned art. From that Latin word, with its sense of "pertaining to letters or literature," as well as other unrelated senses later dropped, emerged through Old French the English word *grammar.* In Scotland during the sixteenth century, *grammar,* through orthographical changes, became *glamer* and then *glamour* (these were Scottish mispronunciations of *grammar),* but it still retained the sense of black magic. Sir Walter Scott was responsible for bringing the corruption of *glamour* from *grammar* into common usage. *Glamour* developed a magic of its own, the alluring charm that excites a person's imagination. In the United States, Madison Avenue commercialized it. Undoubtedly, today, if you have glamour, you can get along without grammar.

GO AGAINST THE GRAIN, TO

Anyone who has tried to saw a piece of lumber has learned the literal application of this term. The grains of lumber run in parallel lines. Following the grains with the saw makes the cutting easy. Cutting the lumber obliquely or at right angles to the grains will make the job difficult. Carpenters plane a board with the grain rather than against it. And so it is with life. One learns, with time, that it is easier to go along with expectations and instructions and to follow established rules than *to go against the grain.* Otherwise, to borrow another cliché, it is like swimming upstream.

As true as all this might be, Ciardi says that it is common error to take "grain" to be the organic set of wood texture in "to go against the grain." He points out that the base word is French *gré,* "natural capacity for pleasure, agreeable." Hence the key phrase means "against nature."

GOBS

Sailors have many nicknames, but among the most popular is one that is an etymological mystery—*gobs*. The word sounds of the Orient, and indeed some authorities believe that it was Commodore Matthew Perry who imported the word to the United States from Japan after opening its ports to world commerce. The Office of Naval Intelligence supported a similar thought, but only in part, declaring, in 1928, "Undoubtedly it was brought back from the Asiatic Station and is derived from the Japanese word meaning a fighting farmer."

According to another theory, the French *garde de l'eau,* water guard, was picked up by Americans but pronounced *gobbyloo,* which was later shortened to *gob.* H. L. Mencken in *The American Language* has this to say: "*Gob* has been traced variously to *gobble,* an allusion to the somewhat earnest methods of feeding prevailing among sailors, and to *gob,* an archaic dialect word signifying expectoration. The English coast-guardsmen, who are said to be free spitters, are often called *gobbies.*" A punster might conclude that these various beliefs and theories have spawned gobs of unverifiable ideas.

GO HAYWIRE, TO

To go haywire is to act uncontrollably, to be all snarled up, to be crazily unpredictable. At the least the term applies to one who is confused, if not mentally unbalanced. Although many present-day Americans have never seen haywire, the term, since the beginning of the twentieth century, is still alive and much in use.

Haywire is a pliable wire that comes in coils and is used by farmers to bind bales of hay. Because the ends of these wires protrude, they can easily lacerate the farmers' hands. In fact, to open a bale of hay with a hatchet and avoid being struck by the whirling wire required skill and mental alertness—and a good measure of luck. Further, the farmers often saved the wire to bind other things—implements of all sorts that abound in a farmyard. It became the means for repairing things and also served as a makeshift tool. But haywire rusts quickly and is unsightly. Nevertheless, with all the work to be done on a farm, temporary repairs tend to become permanent, and after a while the tangled haywire makes for a disorderly place that looks as confused as a person who is said "to go haywire."

GONORRHEA/SYPHILIS

From the goddess of love, the Roman Venus, have come two words associated with acts of love. One, *venery,* which means "the pursuit of sexual pleasure," describes the practice of a Lothario or lecher. The other, *venereal,* a more common word, means "relating to sexual pleasures" but is best known in connection with diseases transmitted through sexual intercourse ("a contagious inflammation affecting the genital organs"), which, until the discovery of penicillin, was a scourge of much of the male population.

The most prevalent form of venereal disease is *gonorrhea* (from the Greek *gonorrhora,* compounded of *gonos,* that which begets, a seed, plus *rhoia,* a flowing). This medical term was coined by an Italian physician in 1530, but it first appeared in print in 1547 in Boorde's *Breviary of Healthe:* "The 166 Chaptairs doth shew of a Gomary passion." *Gomary* was an early name for *gonorrhea.*

Syphilis, a virulent infectious venereal disease, was first mentioned in a Latin poem titled *Syphilis, sive Morbus Gallicus* ("Syphilis, or the French Disease"), written in 1530 by Girolamo Fracastoro, a Veronese physician and poet who is said to have been the first known victim of the disease. The poem's hero, a shepherd named *Syphilus* (an altered form of the name of the disease), was also so afflicted, but as a punishment for having blasphemed the Greek god Apollo.

> He first wore buboes dreadful to the sight,
> First felt pains and sleepless past the night;
> From him the malady received its name.

The word *syphilis* may have come from the Greek *suphilos,* "lover of pigs."

GO SCOT-FREE, TO

When one has been excused from paying for something or has escaped punishment for a crime or other harm one has committed, we say, "He's gotten off *scot-free*." The expression is not related to anyone named Scott or to Scotland. It was derived from the Anglo-Saxon *sceot*, reckoning or contribution, especially payment for entertainment. In later usage it referred to a customary tax paid by subjects according to their ability. But the tax frauds of yester-year were not concerned with ability any more than today's tax dodgers are. Those who wriggled out of paying their just taxes were said to have gotten off scot-free. In its current parlance, *scot* is used simply as an intensifier meaning "absolutely." A defendant at a criminal trial who has been exonerated is said to leave the courtroom scot (absolutely) free.

GO THROUGH FIRE AND WATER, TO

A person who says he'll *go through fire and water* for a friend means he is willing to undergo any hardship for him. It's a prover-bial but flamboyant way of saying, "If I can do anything for you, let me know." Interestingly enough, there was a time when people did go through fire and water for others—literally. And the phrase has continued, but metaphorically, until this day. Under English law, during the Middle Ages, ordeals determined questions of crim-inality. If an accused whose hand was thrust into boiling water showed no ill effects or if he walked barefoot on red-hot iron and showed no wounds, he was judged innocent; otherwise, he was guilty. An accused person had the privilege, however, of hiring a deputy—a surrogate—to undergo the ordeals for him. Sometimes a friend volunteered. These proxies truly went through fire and water for another. And so today expressing a willingness to go through fire and water, a relic of English trial by ordeal, signifies man's highest test of friendship, even though the language, of course, is figurative.

GRASS WIDOW

If someone were asked what a woman separated from her husband may be called, a correct answer would be *grass widow,* even though the term is no longer popular. If instead of "separated from her husband" the question was worded "divorced from her husband," again a correct answer would be *grass widow.* If a mistress is abandoned or a woman becomes the mother of a child without the benefit of matrimony, there too the term *grass widow* may be applied. All of this means that one cannot know precisely the status of a woman called *grass widow* without further explanation. Perhaps for this very reason the term is seldom used anymore.

Some word sleuths believe that the expression *grass widow,* a term used at least since the sixteenth century, emerged into modern English from the French phrase *veuve de grâce* (widow by grace), a woman divorced or separated from her husband by the dispensation and grace of the church, and not by death. During early times Catholic divorces and separations were granted only by the authority of the Roman Church. It is believed, however, that *grass widow* originally referred to an unwed mother. A parallel expression in German is *Strohwitwe (Stroh* means "straw," which, like grass, alludes to the bed on which the child was begotten). According to this thinking, only legitimate children are conceived in regular beds.

GREEKS BEARING GIFTS, BEWARE OF

> I fear the Greeks, even when they bring gifts.
> —Virgil, *Aeneid*

The classics are indebted to Homer's *Iliad* not only for the history of the Trojan War, a conflict most of us had to learn as students of the classics, but also for some of the most expressive proverbs that are used to this very day.

The Greeks had laid siege to Troy for ten years. To gain entrance to the city, they employed a strategy unknown up to that time. They declared themselves war-weary and presented the Trojans with a peace offering in the form of a large wooden horse. The

Trojans drew the horse into their city, unfortunately unaware that it was hollow and filled with Greek soldiers. That night the hidden warriors emerged, slew the guards, and opened the city gates for the Greek troops. The capture of Troy followed. Laocoön, a priest of Poseidon, had tried to dissuade his countrymen from taking in the wooden horse, and so he kept repeating the warning. But the Trojans ignored him—and they were indeed "taken in" by the duplicity of the Greeks. The rest of the tale is told: "The topless towers of Ilium" burned to the ground, but the *Iliad* survived to become the most famous epic poem in all literature.

The term *Trojan horse* (it actually was a Greek horse) has come to symbolize treacherous infiltration, a so-called fifth column. It refers to "a person, thing, or factor intended to undermine or subvert from within." Hence this warning: Do not trust enemies who pretend to be friends. (But how can you know?)

GREEN-EYED MONSTER, THE

A distinctive metaphor for jealousy is *the green-eyed monster.* The expression comes from Shakespeare's all-time classic of jealousy, *Othello,* in which Iago says:

> O! beware, my lord of jealousy;
> It is the green-ey'd monster which doth mock
> The meat it feeds on.

The monster is thought to be a feline, a cat or tiger, since many of those animals have green eyes. The reference to "mock" is to the way these cats play with a trapped animal before eating it. And so it is thought that a jealous person mocks his victim, first loving and then hating before taking advantage of it. At one time it was believed that a greenish complexion indicated jealousy. Not so, but the notion persists. It is still not uncommon to hear it said that someone is "green with envy."

GREENHORN

During the wave of nineteenth-century and early twentieth-century immigrants to the United States, a common name for an immigrant was *greenhorn,* an allusion since the fifteenth century to the green horns of young horned animals. During the seventeenth century, the term was applied to humans, particularly immigrants, who, like immature, inexperienced animals, had much to learn to adapt to their new environments. Eventually *greenhorn* came to mean anyone inexperienced in business or politics. It did not refer just to aliens. In short, any novice was known as a greenhorn. Today the term is seldom used.

GRIN AND BEAR IT

This expression has been in use since the eighteenth century. Its sense is that if you have to put up with something unpleasant, if resistance is hopeless, you may as well put on a pleasant face. A frown will not cause adversity to disappear, whereas a grin helps make the best of the situation, and that will make you feel better, too. The wording of this proverb has changed. It used to be "Grin and abide" and was so documented as late as 1802, as witness the earlier Erasmus Darwin's *Zoonomia* (1794): "We have a proverb where no help could be had in pain, 'to grin and abide.' " The movement to today's language had already begun but hadn't as yet captured the whole field. That its inception was as early as 1775 appears in William Hickey's *Memoirs:* "I recommend you to grin and bear it" (a term common to sailors after a long spell of bad weather). The nautical sense is no longer exclusive. We all should grin when we have no choice but to bear it. A wiseacre might say, "If we have no choice, we'll bear it better with gin than with grin."

GROG

> Gossips in grief and grograms clad.
> —Praed, *The Troubadour*

Although *grog* is no longer so popular a beverage as it used to be, it was at one time the chief drink of British sailors. In fact, *grog* was issued daily to both crew and officers and became a name for rum. But to get to the story behind the word. In the eighteenth century, a tough British admiral, Edward Vernon, decided that reforms should be made in his command, especially those that would encourage sobriety. To that end, he ordered that the daily portion of rum be diluted with water so that his sailors would not be incapacitated after drinking the spirits, which was usually the case. The sailors dubbed the beverage *grog* after the Admiral's nickname, which was "Old Grog," a moniker given him because he was often seen wearing a grogram coat. (Incidentally, the word *grogram,* a coarse fabric, came from the French *grosgrain—gros,* coarse, plus *grain,* grain.) The name *grog* eventually reached land and came to be used as the general name for rum.

From *grog* evolved an adjective, *groggy.* A person who has imbibed too much grog, or any other intoxicant, is unsteady on his feet, shaky, and somewhat disoriented. He is said to be *groggy.* And so is a prizefighter who appears wobbly. He's said to be punch-drunk, but not because he has drunk too much punch or grog. And note that anyone, even a person as sober as a judge, if he is dazed or giddy, feels groggy.

GUARANTEE/WARRANTY

A *guaranty* (or *guarantee*) and a *warranty* have different legal significances, even though some dictionaries list them as synonyms. A *guaranty* is "an agreement by which one person assumes the responsibility of assuring payment or fulfillment of another's debts or obligations." A *warranty* has several meanings, but it comes into comparison with *guaranty* when meaning "an assurance by the seller of property that the goods or property is as represented or will be as promised." Despite that difference, *guaranty* and *warranty* ancestrally are the same word. Both stem from the French *werento,* from *weren,* to protect. These words were borrowed into French from Old High German, but the initial *w,* as was done in other cases, was changed to *gu,* as in *guarantee. Warranty,* according to Klein, was the Middle English *warrantie,* corresponding to the Old French *guarantie.* The *y* ending represents the French *ie.* The replacement of the initial *g* with *w* gives *warranty* a Germanic sound.

GUMBO LIMBO

Gumbo limbo is a compound word derived from the African Bantu. *Gumbo* came from *nagombo,* meaning "anything pertaining to slaves," and *limbo* from *ulimbo,* meaning "birdlime." However, the origin of this word is listed in dictionaries as unknown. *Gumbo limbo* is the name of a tall, tropical American tree that marks the perimeter of the Tropical Zone. Its name, through the centuries, has gone through a litany of change, beginning with *goma elemi,* meaning "gum from the *elemi,"* but no one knows where *elemi* originated. The tree yields sweet, aromatic resin used in the making of varnishes. In Florida, the tree was mostly used as a birdlime. The sap of the tree, after being boiled, became sticky. Indians spread this gummy substance on the limbs of trees where prized songbirds perched. When the feet of the birds became stuck, the birds were caught. The gumbo limbo is humorously called the "tourist tree" because both are always red and peeling.

HABERDASHERY

Remember Harry S. Truman,
a fine haberdasher and a great President.

Haberdasheries today are more commonly known as men's stores. The chief difference between a true haberdashery originally and a men's store is that the haberdashery specialized in men's furnishings—ties, shirts, hats, and so forth but not in suits. The proprietor of a haberdashery is called a *haberdasher.* That word has no analogous English element. Authorities have conjectured about the word's origin in an effort to unravel the mystery of its ancestry. Two theories have emerged. One is that the source of *haberdasher* can be found in an Icelandic word, *hapurtash,* meaning "sacks of oats." The other is that its source lies in the Norman French word *haberdasher,* which had come from the Old French *hapertas,* cloth or a width of cloth. But no one knows how Old French acquired the word. A *haberdasher* (or *hapertasser* or *haberdasser*) was a dealer in that cloth. The word *hapertas* came into prominence when its width was a matter settled by the Magna Carta, which indicates how important the width of cloth was in those days. Of the two theories, certainly the second seems more plausible. However, neither one, without more evidence, will be adopted by word historians. Chaucer used the word *haberdasher* in his Prologue to *The Canterbury Tales.* It was the first literary use of the word. But since he did not explain what the word meant, it has remained a mystery. No one could know what a *haberdasher* did. All he said was:

An haberdasher and a Carpenter,
A Webbe, a Dyer, and a Tapsier,
Were with us eke, cloth'd in one livery,
Of a solemn and great fraternity.

The *Tales* contain no further reference to *haberdasher.*

HAIRSBREADTH

A *hairsbreadth* escape from a serious accident can make one's hair stand on end. If the narrowness of such an escape measured merely a *hairsbreadth,* it would be, according to the measurement established by the Jews, only a forty-eighth part of an inch. And that is too close for comfort. On that point, we can be sure, no one would care to split hairs. The word *hairsbreadth* was first printed in 1584. R. Scot in *Discovery of Witchcraft* wrote: "Limits . . . beyond the which they cannot pass one haires breadth."

HALF A LOAF IS BETTER THAN NONE

This homely saying is one that should be easily accepted, for it is sensible to get a part of something than nothing at all. And quite clearly it is better to try to be content with what you've received, even if it is not all you want. Additionally, remember you weren't shut out, deprived of everything. In fact, you got half, which is a substantial portion. Back in 1546, John Heywood wrote in his *Proverbs:*

Throw no gift at the giver's head;
Better is half a loaf than no bread.

Daniel Rogers in 1642 was quite severe in expressing his opinion. He said: "He is a foole who counts not halfe a loafe better than no bread, or despiseth the moonshine because the sun is down." A more modern version was given by G. K. Chesterton in *What's Wrong with the World:* "Compromise used to mean that half a loaf was better than no bread. Among modern statesmen it really seems to mean that half a loaf is better than a whole loaf."

HANDKERCHIEF

What, one may ask, can be said about a *handkerchief,* a small square of cloth used especially for wiping the nose or mouth? Not much in terms of its utility, but much in terms of its incongruous etymology. In the fourteenth century the word from which *handkerchief* evolved was a square cloth used to cover the head, from the Norman French *couvre,* cover, and *chief,* head, possibly a misspelling of the Old French *chef.* Of course, this cloth could serve many purposes, and by the sixteenth century it became the usual cloth for wiping the nose, and the mouth, too, where no napkin was available after a meal. At that time the *kerchief* also became a fashionable accessory of clothing, something to be carried in the hand with an air of casualness.

And so the full word *handkerchief* was born. But the bastardization of this now-common word did not stop there. As the specialization of *handkerchief* evolved primarily as a nose wiper, the word *pocket* was added because that was where the handkerchief was normally kept. This whole thing becomes particularly confusing because we're saying that a *handkerchief* is a covering worn on the head, held in the hand, and put in the pocket. But hold it! Women usually carry a handkerchief not in a pocket, but in a handbag. And fashionable men, although carrying the handkerchief in a pocket, use it not to wipe the nose but as a colorful addition to their attire. So much for etymology.

HANDS DOWN

Everyone seems to know what "Hands up!" means—the order given by captors to prisoners just taken—but not necessarily what *hands down* means. Fewer may know where this latter phrase came from. But it's no mystery. The full expression is "to win hands down," and therein lies a clue. Anyone who has watched a horse race must have noticed the way jockeys urge their mounts onward, especially as they're approaching the victory ribbon. Their hands are up and then down as they whip the horses, and then up again, and so forth. The fortunate jockey who is far ahead of the field, relaxed and winning easily, has no need to whip his horse and therefore no need to raise his hands. He may ride *hands down.* This racetrack term is now used in many unrelated competitive activities, all to the same effect. A basketball team far ahead of its opponent or a candidate in an election who is garnering a heavy vote may be said to be winning "hands down," as is true of anyone who finishes way ahead of the field and therefore triumphs easily.

HANDWRITING ON THE WALL, THE

Cassandra, the prophetess of doom, might have said, "I see the handwriting on the wall," except that she was a figure in Greek mythology, whereas the statement is a paraphrase from the Bible. But since it is a foreboding of some future calamity, a prediction of disaster, it could conceivably have been uttered by her.

During a feast given by the Babylonian king Belshazzar for his wives and concubines at which the guests drank from goblets that had been plundered from the Temple at Jerusalem, cryptic words appeared on the wall, *"Mene, mene, tekel, upharsin."* No one could decipher them. Daniel was summoned and his translation (which appears in Daniel 5:25–31) was "This is the interpretation of the matter . . . God has numbered the days of your kingdom and brought it to an end. . . . You have been weighed in the balances and found wanting. . . . Your kingdom is divided and given to the Medes and Persians." (The phrase means "numbered, weighed, and divided.") It is said that on that very night Belshazzar died, and his kingdom was eventually conquered by the Persians.

Although "the handwriting on the wall" is a term for a warning of doom, nowadays it more often refers merely to a warning of danger, which, if heeded, may enable one to avoid serious consequences. In America's urban centers, the handwriting on the wall is called *graffiti.*

HARD AS NAILS

One might ask, Is it desirable to be as *hard as nails*? The question is best answered if the simile is divided into its physical and figurative senses. *To be as hard as nails* physically is to be tough, to be able to withstand physical rough treatment. Athletes, especially football players and boxers, train to that end. But otherwise the phrase describes a person who is brusque, stern, unsympathetic, bigoted, rigid, and therefore unyielding and uncompromising. This definition probably applies to fundamentalists and our distant puritanical cousins. In either of these senses—the physical (athletes) or the figurative (fundamentalists)—these people can accept blows in the one and ignore social sensitivities in the other in the way nails can withstand the pounding of a hammer. The expression was a favorite of George Bernard Shaw. Charles Dickens employed it in *Oliver Twist*. To Fagin's question as to whether the gang of thieves had been hard at work this morning, the Dodger replied, "Hard," to which Charley Bates added, "As nails."

HARP ON ONE STRING, TO

> This word revenge he still harpt upon.
> —Sir T. Herbert, *Trav*

To harp on something is to dwell on a subject incessantly, refusing to give it up. The result is that the bored listener probably thinks the speaker is a crank. But why the word *harp*? A harp, of course, is a large stringed instrument played by plucking the strings. Today's harps have many strings and foot pedals so that they are truly musical instruments. But that was not so in medieval times. Harps then had fewer strings and no pedals. Unless the harpist was a master, his performance was bound to sound monotonous. It would seem, in fact, to be a repetition of sounds, as repetitious as a person who cannot let go of a subject but keeps cranking away at it. And so the idiom *to harp on something,* as wearisome as the sounds of a harp.

A sister expression, *to harp on the same string,* is also associated with the playing of a harp—but the plucking of only one string. If a harpist plucked one string over and over again, listeners would soon be bored. And so a person is tiresome who repeats the same story over and over again or constantly returns to the same argument. He is, it might be said, harping on the same string.

HAVE YOUR CAKE AND EAT IT TOO, YOU CAN'T

Quite clearly, if you spend a thing, you cannot have it too. This ancient platitude was first propounded by the dramatist Titus Plantus in his *Trinummus* over two thousand years ago. From it has evolved the modern version: *You can't have your cake and eat it too,* meaning you can't spend your money and still keep it. But how modern this homily is and when it originated cannot be answered because no one knows. The first time this saying appeared in print was said to have been in 1546 in John Heywood's *Proverbs:* "Would ye both eat your cake and have your cake?" Since the *Proverbs* was a compilation of well-known sayings, it certainly must have previously circulated for many decades, possibly centuries. An English poet, George Herbert, who died in 1633, in a poem entitled "The Temple: Sacred Poems and Private Ejaculations," wrote:

> Enact good cheer?
> Lay out the joy, yet hope to save it?
> Wouldst thou both eat thy cake, and have it?

During early times, cake was usually pieces of baked bread rather than cake as we know it today.

HEAR NO EVIL

It might very well be that a person who hears no evil will think no evil. Regardless, the best and easiest way of going through life is to think the best of everything. As one sage said, echoing the Latin *male audire,* it is better to be fooled occasionally than to be suspicious constantly. This adage is not the equivalent of a form of pollyanaism, foolish optimism. It is, instead, a way of maintaining a state of serenity, tranquility. The complete *hear no evil* proverb has been in place since the seventeenth century, carved over the front door of the Sacred Temple in Nikko, Japan. It is a legend atop the Three Wise Monkeys that reads: "Hear no evil, see no evil, speak no evil." Excellent advice for everyone.

HEAD OVER HEELS, TO BE

It's been traditional for schoolkids to complain about their onerous school chores and, to show contempt, even to strike back at those in charge. Perhaps the reason is that teaching is not always a process of education according to its literal meaning (*teach* is Anglo-Saxon *tacan,* show; *educate* is Latin *e,* out, and *duco,* lead). More often *to teach,* rather than to show, is to inculcate (Latin *in,* in, and *calcare,* to trample, literally "to tread in" by grinding with the heel). The knowledge inculcated has, so to speak, been ground in. Those who resent the grinding of a heel sometimes rebel against authority by figuratively using their own heels. They become *recalcitrant*; they kick back (Latin *re,* back, and *calcitro,* kick with the heel). The Romans applied the term to horses. Nowadays it is used not only of balking animals but of any obstinate or refractory person.

Possibly the silliest phrase involving heels is *head over heels,* as in "She's head over heels in love with Tom." Of course, what is meant is "completely and uncontrollably." But since having one's head over the heels is normal, whereas the implication is entirely opposite—that the person is so wildly in love as to be acting abnormally—it would be more in keeping with the intended sense to say "heels over head." That might graphically suggest how one bitten by the love bug feels—utterly and helplessly unbalanced, upside down. Perhaps the whole thing is a mistranslation of Catullus, who wrote: *per caputque pedesque,* over head and heels.

HIDEBOUND

Hidebound is a word, as might be imagined, that relates to cattle. The term first appeared in print, according to the *Oxford En-*

glish Dictionary, in 1559 in Cooper's thesaurus, *Coriago:* "The sicknesse of cattall when they are clounge, that their skynnes dooe cleve fast to their bodies, hyde bound." In former times, before the advent of veterinary science, farmers were unable to protect and care for their cattle adequately. It was common to find that cattle during the winter months had become diseased and, if they survived at all, that the layer of fat between hide and flesh had been consumed. Without that fatty tissue, with the hide clinging to the flesh, the cattle could move, but stiffly; and when they died, their hide could not be removed. To flay cattle having no layer of fat separating skin and bone is almost impossible.

Today *hidebound,* as a metaphorical term, refers to a person so narrowminded, inelastic, or stubborn that he is incapable of altering his opinions. One may consider a likeness of his rigidity of mind to the lack of mobility of emaciated cattle. A pseudophilosopher might twist the words around and say that an archconservative is so bound to rigidity that he can't hide it.

HIDE ONE'S LIGHT UNDER A BUSHEL, TO

This ancient idiom appears in the Bible: "Neither do men light a candle, and put it under a bushel, but on a candlestick." Its sense expresses extreme modesty possessed by few men, if any. It would be difficult, if not impossible, to make progress in this world if no one knew of your merits, talents, or accomplishments. Which does not mean that, oppositely, one should boast about unique or enriched attributes. What is not readily understood is the meaning of *bushel* in this saying. It refers to a container that holds a bushel, four pecks, not to the unit of weight.

HIGH AND DRY

A job unfinished and never to be completed, a person forgotten or ignored, and certainly one who has been abandoned, are said to be left *high and dry.* This metaphor had a nautical genesis. A ship that had gone aground or was placed in dry dock was high and dry. With time, however, the idiom has come to be employed figuratively, and today its origin is no longer remembered. It may be noted that another saying—*hard and fast*—has the same sense. A ship out of water for any reason is said to be hard and fast. That the ship could not move under those circumstances gave rise to a figurative sense that is common today: rigid, fixed. A person who lacks flexibility is as rigid as a ship that has been grounded. Then the term came to be applied to "rules" that must be rigidly kept. This is its chief use today. J. W. Henley in 1867 said in the House of Commons: "The House has deliberately, after long consideration, determined to have no 'hard and fast line.' "

HIGH ON THE HOG, TO EAT/LIVE

To live high on the hog or, as it is sometimes put, *to eat high on the hog* is to live sumptuously, with no thought of the cost. Certainly one who lives or eats so well is affluent. The expression is centuries old. From the days of the Norman Conquest, when royalty ate loin chops and roast, they ate high on the hog (the part above the belly), where the best cuts of pork are. The low parts— sow belly, pig's feet, hog jowls, and so on—were left to the underlings to dine on. And so when we say that someone is living or eating high on the hog, we mean he is prosperous and his lifestyle shows it.

HIT THE NAIL ON THE HEAD, TO

The sense of this idiom is obvious. To hit something on the head is to guess right or to reach the right conclusion. In terms of words, its sense is an accurate and clear understanding of the idea posed, which in the vernacular means to hit the bull's eye. The saying was known in the days of Caesar, but, although it meant in effect "to hit the nail on the head," its actual sense and wording, quite naturally, were different. The Romans said, *"Acu rem tangere,"* meaning "to touch a matter on the point." The expression has had a long, varied, and ubiquitous life. According to Brewer, the French say, *"Vous avez frappé au but"* ("You have hit the mark"), and the Italians say, *"Avete dato in brocca"* ("You have hit the pitcher"). The English version first appeared in print in 1508 in John Stanbridge's *Vulgaria:* "Thou hyttest the nayle on the head." Which nails down this essay.

HITTING BELOW THE BELT

This essay, to borrow the subject expression, is to a certain extent like *hitting below the belt* because it doesn't have a story behind it. But the cliché historically was interesting, and so it has been included.

Boxing until the nineteenth century was prohibited by law. Bouts of fisticuffs were frequently staged, but they were done on the sly, in out-of-the-way places. The boxers fought with bare hands and took advantage of their opponents as best as they could. This meant that they were free to strike wherever possible, even in parts of the body that could cause permanent injury. The eighth Marquis of Queensberry decided to draw up a code of fair play. Together with John G. Chamber, he prepared a set of rules that, among other things, outlawed hitting below the line of the belt (in the groin area). Such a low blow would be a disqualifying foul. Although not welcomed and even resisted, the rules thus formulated gradually gained acceptance, and the prohibition against low blows stands to this very day. In fact, the rule is widely used figuratively in all walks of life; that is, one who takes unfair advantage or speaks unfairly could be said to be hitting below the belt.

HOGWASH

If one tells you that you are speaking *bushwah, nonsense,* or mere *hogwash,* he has mixed slang with colloquial English. *Bushwah* or *booshwa(h)* or *boushwa(h)* is a slang term that since 1920 has been used to mean "bunk" or "blah." *Nonsense* is clearly an English word in good standing. And so is *hogwash.* Although *hogwash* sounds like slang, it's not. In fact, it has been good English since the mid-fifteenth century. The *Oxford English Dictionary* has this entry, dated 1440: "They in the kechyn, for iape, pouryd on here hefd hoggyswasch." What was said is clear except for *iape,* which means "jest": "They in the kitchen, for jest, poured hogwash on her head." What a sense of humor! *Hoggyswasch,* now spelled *hogwash,* is pig slops, swill of a brewery or a kitchen given to hogs. In later centuries *hogwash* colloquially came to mean "nonsense" or "bushwah," which returns us to the first sentence. But be not misled. In no way is *hogwash* related to the washing of hogs.

HOLD AT BAY, TO

The expression *to hold at bay,* which first appeared in print in 1344, is commonly associated with hunting dogs, the image being of dogs barking or baying at treed prey until the arrival of the hunters. Such a scene was painted by the renowned English painter Edwin Henry Landseer, *The Stag at Bay.* A translation in 1530 of French usage by John Palsgreve was "Yonder stagge is almost yelden; I here the hounds hold hym at baye." And so we say that to hold something at a standstill or to keep a difficult situation from getting worse is to hold it at bay.

But phrase sleuths dispute the correctness of that usage, pointing out that the idiom was derived from the French *tenir à bay,* which means "to hold in a state of suspense or inaction." It is synonymous with "to hold in abeyance" (from the Old French *bayer,* through the Late Latin *badare,* to gape) or, literally, "to hold agape" or "to hold with mouth open." The word *gap* can be seen in the middle of *agape.* The opening implied by *gap* has come to designate allotted space, as between two columns or the median strip on a highway. The recesses thus suggested have given us such words as *horse bay* (a stall) and *sick bay* (a ship's hospital). Of course, a possible connection is that the treed animal might have been so surprised that its mouth was agape.

HOMAGE

Homage, as the word is used today, is flattering attention or even reverential regard. A person to whom homage is paid is usually given a publicly expressed tribute. Occasionally *homage* is used of an idea, as in "With the exception of peace, no social ideal receives more *homage* than education."

In the Middle Ages, however, homage was a ritual in which a tenant made a public avowal that he would be the "man" of his future lord (the word *homage* stems from the Latin word for "man," *homo*). According to *Black's Law Dictionary,* homage was the most honorable service of reverence that a tenant could perform for his lord. The oath was administered in the following ceremony: The tenant, ungirthed (without weapons) and with bare head, knelt before the lord; the latter sat, and the tenant, who extended his own hands and joined them between the hands of the lord, said: "I become your man from this day forward, of life and limb and earthly honor, and to you I will be faithful and loyal, and bear your faith, for the tenements that I claim to hold of you, saving the faith that I owe unto our sovereign lord the king, so help me God." Having concluded, the tenant then received a kiss from the lord. Like a marital vow, homage was sealed with a kiss.

HOMOSEXUAL

Homosexuality is a word that raises not only social problems but linguistic ones as well. Socially it is in conflict with heterosexuality, sexual commingling of the different sexes (in Greek *heteros* means "different"). Homosexuality, on the other hand, involves sexual relations with members of the same sex. And therein lies the crux of the matter that irked some philologists. The word *homosexual* consists of two prime elements, each coming from a different classical source. One is Greek *homo-,* which means "the same" (note that *homo-* in Latin means "man"), and the other is Latin *sexus,* which means "sex." Such bastardized terms are irritants to language purists. *Studies in the Psychology of Sex,* a tome by Havelock Ellis, published in 1897, contained the first instance of the word *homosexual* in print. Ellis disliked the word so much that he said, *"Homosexual* is a hybrid word, and I claim no responsibility for it."

Members of the homosexual community have also created a linguistic furor by taking for themselves the word *gay,* meaning "a homosexual." No longer do some people feel free to use the word *gay* in its traditional sense of "merry" or "happy." And although homosexuals have a right to call themselves gay, it becomes chancy for others to express happiness by saying that they're happy and gay.

HORS D'OEUVRES

It is American custom for persons attending an affair to be offered *hors d'oeuvres.* Obviously, that term is French, but it has been adopted by the English language and appears in American dictionaries. In fact, the term is irreplaceable; there is no English synonym. The term *canapé* is offered as a synonym by some dictionaries, but that word, also borrowed from the French, describes, accurately speaking, a spread on a cracker or a piece of bread that is considered a thing apart from an hors d'oeuvre by knowledgeable chefs. Hors d'oeuvres are appetizers, other than canapés, served before a regular meal to whet the appetite. The expression *hors d'oeuvres* literally means "outside the main work" (*hors,* outside, plus *de,* of, plus *oeuvres,* work). Its origin, however, is completely unrelated to a savory appetizer. It was an architectural term used to refer to a structure, an outbuilding, apart from the main design, and was, therefore, "outside the work" of the original project. The culinary borrowing of the term was logical, however, because hors d'oeuvres are edibles served outside or in advance of the main meal. All this means that hors d'oeuvres may architecturally please the eye or gastronomically please the palate.

HORSE LATITUDES

Seamen who manned sailing ships called the region in the North Atlantic between latitudes 30 and 35 the *horse latitudes.* The area has unsettled wind conditions. Sometimes the winds were baffling; sometimes ships were so becalmed that not even the slightest breeze blew. The region received its name, according to one theory, from the fact that when it was necessary to lighten a horse-transporting ship to take advantage of any breeze that might be stirring, the horses aboard would be jettisoned. A related theory differs only in the reason for casting the horses overboard. It was to save on water or, according to still another theory, because of lack of food. Yet another notion is that the name came from the Spanish phrase *golfo de las yegas,* which translates into the "Mares' Sea." It may be pointed out for the benefit of non-horsemen that mares have a reputation for being unruly. And apparently the Spanish had a feeling that the winds in this region could be compared with the fickleness and boisterous nature of mares.

HORSE OF A DIFFERENT COLOR, A

This term is used to mean "something entirely different from what is being considered" or "a situation that is altogether unlike the one being discussed." Its origin is uncertain, but there is every reason to believe that it is old, certainly that it antedated Shakespeare, who had Maria respond to Malvolio: "My purpose is, indeed, a horse of that color," the first literary record of that expression. It has been suggested that Shakespeare's terminology change was a punning change. The usual sayings are *that's a horse of a different color* or *of another color.* A conjecture, but one rejected by most philologists, is that the source of the expression can be found in the archaeological mystery of the White Horse of Berkshire, a crude, large figure of a galloping horse that changes from green to white when the locals clear the surrounding landscape of grass and weeds. Another suggestion that has been advanced is that during the period of tournaments on horseback in which knights competed, the contestants were distinguished by the color of the horses they rode. It is easy to imagine that a maiden watching the festivities and then seeing a distant rider unseated may have, after peering through lenses, remarked, with a sigh of relief, "My lover is safe. That was a horse of a different color."

HORSELAUGH

> Laugh and be well.
> —Matthew Green, *The Spleen*

Although you have never seen a horse smile, you have probably heard a *horselaugh*. That is, not a *horse laugh* (two words) but a *horselaugh* (one word), a loud, coarse, raucous, vulgar laugh. The term *horselaugh* is centuries old. It was used by Pope in 1710, but it first appeared in the writings of Richard Steele in 1713: "The Horse-Laugh is a distinguishing characteristick of the rural hoyden." Whether the term is likened to the loud neigh of a horse or whether *horse* is simply a corruption of *coarse* has not been established. Each side has its proponents. True it is that the neigh of a lusty horse sounds somewhat like a human laugh, but the semantic development of *horse* in the sense of "coarse" has been wide. Consider *horseradish, horseplay,* and *horse-faced.* William Makepeace Thackeray once wrote: "And the old gentleman gave his knowing grin and coarse laugh." One must conclude that an etymologist who thinks horse sense will settle this matter will get naught for his troubles but a horselaugh.

HORSE'S MOUTH, STRAIGHT FROM THE

One can understand that his grandfather takes *catnaps* (because he frequently dozes, as cats do) and that his grandmother goes to *hen parties* (because her friends gather together and cluck like a bunch of chickens). But what is not easy to understand is how anyone can get tips *from a horse's mouth.*

The fact is that horses are not so knowledgeable nor generous to give tips—or else no one would ever bet on a loser. Yet the expression has been with us over the years, having started from a longstanding practice of examining a horse's mouth to see whether the animal is healthy. It was then decided that a horse's age could be told by studying its teeth (that's why we say, "Don't look a gift horse in the mouth"). From this practice came the notion that from a horse's mouth comes the truth of its age. It was not a long step to generalize when asked whether what was said was true that it surely had to be, for it came *straight from the horse's mouth.* Figuratively the phrase, of course, means "the truth"; "the straight dope"; "from the best authority."

HOUSEWIFE

What a difference the times make. No one would dare call a *hausfrau* a *hussy.* A *hussy,* as everyone knows, is a prostitute, a trollop, a hustler. But before the sixteenth century that is what a housewife was called, "a hussy," a contraction of *huswif* (in Medieval English *hous,* house, and *wif,* woman, wife), sequentially *huswif, huswife, housewife.* Today a bustling housewife may hustle, but she's not a hussy or a hustler in the street sense of the word. Incidentally, that same Anglo-Saxon *hus,* house, is still found in the word *husband,* which means "the master of the house." Times certainly have changed.

HUMBUG

Humbug sounds like slang, but it is a respectable English word, so listed in all dictionaries, and it means "hoax or fraud" or "nonsense." The last, *nonsense,* is particularly applicable because *humbug* sounds as though it suggests "nonsense." Yet its meaning when it entered the language from underworld cant in 1750 was unknown, and how it originated cannot be established because the facts of its origin appear to have been lost. One belief is that during the war between the German states so many unreliable reports were distributed that it became commonplace to say, when another report was touted, "You must've gotten that from Hamburg." With little time and less effort *Hamburg* was slurred and *humbug* emerged. Another is that it came from the Irish *uim bog,* soft copper (sounds like *humbug*), a debased coin that James II had minted in Dublin and used widely in England. But it had almost no value; hence a thing real in appearance but worthless in merit. Or it may refer to a bug whose humming frightens people, a real humbug. There is almost no limit to the fanciful etymologies advanced by some sources. Charles Dickens set this word in cement through Scrooge's "Bah, humbug!"

Although *humbug* as a verb is no longer commonly used, it became a popular expression toward the end of the nineteenth century, thanks to Phineas T. Barnum. In England he delivered a lecture on the subject of *humbuggery,* entitled "The Science of Monkey Making, and the Philosophy of Humbug." Barnum once said, "The American people like to be humbugged," which was the same thought expressed by Horace Greeley, but in more picturesque language: "The public is one immense ass."

HUNCH

A *hunch* is an intuitive feeling or guess. It is an idea based on no facts or experience. Almost everyone at least once in his or her lifetime has had a hunch that has led to the making of a decision, a method of reaching a decision particularly true of gamblers. Deformed persons who have a "hunch" or "hump" in the spine, a malformation known medically as *kyphosis,* were thought for many centuries to possess psychic powers. Their curved back was a sign of demonic affiliation, a league with the devil, which endowed them with foresight, the ability to predict the future. And so today a flash of insight is said to be a *hunch.* Coming back to that word's etymology, we must add that as to its paternity, no one has even a hunch.

HUSKY

The word *husky,* in the minds of most people, is immediately identified as a kind of sled dog, a strong and rugged man, or a hoarse throat. Can you imagine a word having such disparate meanings? The sled dog was a breed developed in Siberia. When Europeans found in the Arctic a breed of dog that lived in snow, ate fish, was powerful enough to pull a sled, and yelped like a wolf, they likened it to its Siberian cousin. North Canadian Indians called this dog *uskimi,* which meant "Eskimo." The explorers thought they were hearing "huskemaus," but they called the dogs

Eski, a shortening of *Eskimo.* Eventually they corrupted the contraction *Eski* by fronting it with an *h,* and from it *Husky* emerged—and stayed.

The informal term *husky,* meaning "big and burly," refers to the strength of a Husky likened to a stocky and muscular man. Harriet Beecher Stowe used the term in a story published in 1869. (A football player may feel flattered if described as "husky," but does he know he's being compared to a sled dog?) A husky throat, on the other hand, is a dry one that has lost the timbre of its voice, possibly from dust after *husking* corn.

Coming back to *Eskimo,* that name may have come from the Micmac *eskameege,* meaning "eaters of raw fish," but the supposition is unattested. The Eskimos of North America, as distinguished from those living in Asian lands, call themselves *Inuit,* which means "people."

I

⊰⊱

ICICLE

The word *icicle* goes way back to Old English, when it was spelled *gicel* and meant "a point of ice." With time *gicel* experienced trifling alterations in spelling, first to *ikel* and then to *ickle*. Old English *ice,* from a Sanskrit root, was *is,* to glide, as on a smooth surface. When the Old English forms were combined, *is gicel,* they were standardized, leaving *icicle* alone to glide into modern speech.

IMP

This word is both a noun and a verb. Almost all people who have occasion to use the word use only its noun form, which means either a mischievous child or a small demon, an evil spirit. Its most common use refers to a misbehaving child, as in this excerpt from Jonathan Swift's *Gulliver's Travels* (1726): "I once caught a young male of three years old . . . but the little imp fell a squalling, and scratching, and biting."

During the period of Old English, *imp* was spelled *impa* and referred to a young shoot of a plant. And an imp still is "a graft," from Greek *emphytos,* "engrafted," "implanted." But this sense of a young shoot gave rise to the now-archaic meaning "offspring," as in *The Faerie Queen* (1590) by Edmund Spenser: "Fayre ympe of Phoebus and his aged bryde." A century later the meaning "a small devil" caught on, and it too is still with us. In "A Long Story," Thomas Gray (1753) wrote as follows:

> ... thereabouts there lurk's
> A wicked Imp they call a Poet,
> Who prowl'd the country far and near
> Betwitch'd the children of the peasants,
> Dried up the cows, and lam'd the deer,
> And suck'd the eggs, and kill'd the pheasants.

The verb *imp* went through stages of meaning, but they all were related to its present sense "to graft (new feathers) onto the wing or tail of a falcon to repair damage or increase flying capacity."

IN A (PRETTY) PICKLE, TO BE

The sense of this phrase is that one is in a state of disorder, in trouble, in a bad way, or at least in an embarrassing situation. The phrase was said to have come originally from the Dutch—*in de pekel zitten*—meaning "to sit in brine," certainly an uncomfortable position to be in, *pekel* or *pickle* not being the edible that comes with today's corned beef sandwich, but the brine itself. The expression was used in 1585 by John Foxe, who said: "In this pickle lyeth man by nature, that is, all wee that be Adams children." Shakespeare in *The Tempest* borrowed the phrase when he had Alonso say to his fellow conspirator, "How cam'st thou in this pickle?"

Ciardi's theory is that the phrase may not mean merely "in a mess," but "done in, dead." During wars on foreign soil it was customary to bury the hearts of leaders where they fell in battle and to ship home for internment the remains in a barrel of brine. He pointed out further that Nelson died aboard his ship, which was considered a part of England, and so his whole body came home— but preserved in rum, as befitting an admiral.

INDIAN

It's hard to believe that people are saddled with a name over which they have no control (not only individuals but also racial groups), and that the name continues for centuries and will perhaps continue forever. The name that comes to mind is *Indian*.

As everyone knows, Columbus sailed forth in the fifteenth century expecting to reach India. He landed on islands in the Caribbean Sea and naturally thought that he had reached his goal. What he saw in the area, the West Indies (Columbus thought he was on the western side of India), were high-cheeked, red-skinned inhabitants. Naturally enough, they were called by the Europeans after the land that had presumably been discovered—Indians. That is why today we have two kinds of Indians—Indians who live in India and Indians who live in the United States, who are not really Indians at all.

INDIAN GIVER

The term today is used derogatorily, of someone who has changed his or her mind after making a gift and now wants it back, a most ungracious move. Hence an *Indian giver* is a person frowned on. And yet it was a normal custom, according to the *Handbook of American Indians* (1907), prepared and published by the Smithsonian Institution, for an Indian, having given someone a gift, to expect in return an equivalent. If no exchange was made or if dissatisfied with the exchange, the gift giver had the privilege of demanding the return of his gift. It was the gift giver's right by custom.

INFLAMMABLE

The English word meaning "capable of being ignited" or "susceptible of combustion" is *inflammable*. The repetitious definition is given in the hope of avoiding a possible disaster that a misinterpretation of that word might cause. Apparently many people have not been sure what *inflammable* means. Even wordsmiths have disagreed on whether the word was confusing on petroleum trucks and whether the word should be replaced by another that would plainly signify that something is combustible. The traditional English word has been *inflammable,* from the Latin *inflammre,* to set on fire. This Latin verb consists of the prefix *in,* in, and the noun *flamma,* flame. The concern was that since the prefix *in* also means "not" (for example, *indestructible* means "not destructible"), some people might construe the *in* in *inflammable* to mean "not," a semantic error with potential dire consequences.

To eliminate any possible misunderstanding, the word *flammable* has replaced *inflammable,* the thinking being that *flammable* is a more unmistakable warning. It is now generally recommended, and most transporters of combustible material go along, that the terms *flammable* and *nonflammable* be used instead of *inflammable* and *noninflammable.* Perhaps pictures painted on these trucks would make the vehicles even safer.

INOCULATE

For generations people have been *inoculated* against certain diseases. It has been a standard practice, for example, to immunize schoolchildren against smallpox. This is done by injecting a small amount of the virus responsible for the disease. And yet the origin of *inoculate* is unrelated to medical science; it is a horticultural term. And it refers to a procedure involving no injection and one that will produce no immunity. In fact, *to inoculate* had a quite different effect. In the first place, it referred to the insertion of a bud in a plant, an "implanting," in order to propagate it.

The Roman poet Virgil may have been the first to record this horticultural phenomenon. In his *Georgics* (36–29 B.C.) he speaks of the grafting of an *oculus* from one plant to another to cause propagation. Thus Latin *inoculare,* "to put a little eye in," from *in,* into, plus *oculus,* eye. The botanists of that day spoke of this grafting procedure as *inoculatio,* which was anglicized as *inoculten.*

After medical scientists concluded that the injection of a virus can immunize against a normal attack of some dread diseases, English researchers latched onto the words *inoculate* and *inoculation* and accepted them as their own. And so they have remained.

However, our evolving language did not relegate the use of those words to scientists only. The terms can be used as common figurative expressions, as witness this excerpt from H. L. Mencken's *Prejudices* (1923): "The theory . . . is that a taste for music is an elevating passion, and if the great masses of the plain people could be inoculated with it they would cease to herd into the moving-picture theaters."

INTERNECINE

> Th' Aegyptians worshipp'd Dogs and for
> Their Faith made internecine war.
> —Samuel Butler, *Hudibras*

People, in most instances, have to live with their mistakes, a price we have to pay for negligence or ignorance. And so does the English language. Take the word *internecine,* for example. We use it today as the dictionaries define it—"mutually destructive." It may pertain to a struggle within a group or organization, the usual bickering one might expect. But this was not what *internecine* meant, and its present prevalent use came about through a lexicographical error. When the word *internecine* originated in Latin it meant "to kill without exception," "to massacre." If there was no bloodshed, it was not internecine. The word consists of *necare,* to kill, and *inter,* an intensive form meaning "down to the last person," a completed action, which in this case meant "to the death." The crux of the problem is the prefix *inter,* which often is used to mean "between," but not here. In *internecine,* as was previously stated, *inter* is acting to make *neco,* kill, more emphatic.

The great Samuel Johnson in his dictionary of 1755 defined *internecine* as "mutually destructive," assuming that *inter* meant "between." His definition, "endeavoring mutual destruction," has remained and is the sense in which we use it today. There can, of course, be internecine wars, those that result in serious bloodshed to both sides, but that usage receives little play. In its widespread general use, *internecine* is not marked by bloodshed but rather by squabbles within a group.

IN THE SAME BOAT, TO BE

Persons in similar positions, taking the same risks, engaged in the same business, or pursuing the same cause may be said *to be in the same boat.* The allusion—to be at sea in the same boat and therefore to be undergoing the same risks—is evident. It is said that this figure of speech was first used by Clement, Bishop of Rome (A.D. 91 to 100), in an effort to resolve matters of dissension in the Church of Corinth. The expression has come a long way. In 1584, Thomas Hudson wrote in his poem "Judith": "Haue ye pain? So likewise pain haue we;/For in one boat we both imbarked be." And so through the years. In 1862 the idiom was expanded by the inclusion of the word *all—we're all in the same boat*—as evidenced by Artemus Ward's *The Draft in Dinsville:* "We are all in the same boat." But of course the *all* is unnecessary, for if we're in the same boat, we're all in it.

INVEIGLE

To *inveigle* is to allure or to seduce by beguiling. A salesman might inveigle a customer into buying four hats, although initially only one was wanted. The sense of *inveigle* is enticement, deception, figuratively leading someone blindfolded. The French forebear of *inveigle* was *aveugler,* to blind, and that, in turn, came from the Latin *ab,* from, and *oculus,* eye, which together means "eyeless."

Some etymologists believe that when *inveigle* was borrowed into English from the French, the initial *a* in *aveugler* was misconstrued as a prefix (meaning "not") attached to a base verb *(veugler).* In accordance with an English trend, the *a* was replaced by the more common prefix *in,* from which emerged today's *inveigle.* But for this blunder, one would now be *aveigled* into seeing the *Late Late Show* rather than *inveigled.*

ISLAND

> No man is an island, entire of himself . . ."
> —John Donne, *Devotions upon Emergent Occasions*

> Every man is an island . . ."
> —L.S., *People's Liberty*

It would seem that the words *isle* and *island* are etymologically related, especially since phonetically and orthographically they are similar. One might imagine that *isle* is an abbreviation or a poetic shortening of *island.* But none of this is so. The ancestry of the word *isle* is traceable to the Latin *insula,* island, a word of uncertain origin. An idea advanced by one authority was that the *sula* part of *insula* was related to the word *salum,* the open sea, the thought being that an island was a piece of land in the sea, surrounded by *sal,* the Latin salt (water). Most etymologists, however, remain unconvinced. In Old French *isle* was spelled this way but with time the *s,* because it is silent, was dropped and the word became *île.* During the fifteenth century the French restored the *s* to make the word conform etymologically to Latin *insula.*

Island can be traced back to the Old English *igland.* Divided into syllables, we find *land,* which means "land," and *ig,* meaning "island." The *s* in *island* replaced the *g* under French influence in the sixteenth century and *island* with its present meaning emerged.

ITALIAN VOICES

> Music hath charms to soothe the savage breast.
> —Congreve, *The Mourning Bride*

The English language is indebted to Italian for the names that designate the range of voices of singers. Those names, with few exceptions, have been absorbed into English with no or little alteration in spelling or meaning.

The lowest range of a male's singing voice is called *bass. Bass* is the same word as *base,* which means "bottom," and which was altered to *bass* in imitation of the Italian *basso,* a word derived from the Late Latin *bassus,* low. (A bass voice with the lowest range, such as the one used in "Ol' Man River," is called a *basso profundo*.) The name of the male voice in the next highest range, the *baritone*, the voice between the tenor and the bass, comes from the Italian *baritono*, whose Greek ancestor was *barytonos, barry*, heavy, and *tonos*, tone. The highest natural adult male voice is the *tenor*. It arrived in Middle English from the Old French *tenour*, which in turn had come from the Late Latin *tenor*, meaning "uninterrupted course" (a holding on of the melody). Its sire was the French *tenir* (Latin *tenere*), to hold. A tenor still holds the audience spellbound, that is, because he usually is, in opera, the dominant male character. But note that Don Giovanni is a bass and the Flying Dutchman is a baritone, and each one thrills the audience.

The next voice range is the female voice called *alto*, from the Latin *altus*, high. Strangely, the *alto* is not the highest but the lowest female singing voice. This incongruity came about because *alto* formerly was applied to the highest male singing voice. The term generally used today for the lowest female voice, rather than *alto*, is *contralto*, a compound of Italian *contra*, opposite to, and *alto*, high. The highest singing female voice is the *soprano*. The term *sopra* (Latin *supra*), above, suggests its singing position. *Soprano* is said to be a variant of Italian *sovrano*, meaning "highest" and also "supreme or sovereign," from the Late Latin *superanus*, chief.

One last thought. If you enjoy the singing and rise and shout "Bravo! Bravo!" remember that in Italian *bravo* means not only "excellent" but also "desperado," a man, according to Johns, who murders for hire. Be careful. The singer might think you're trying to get your money back.

ITCHING PALM, TO HAVE AN

It is a pleasure for those who pursue the origin of words and expressions to come across one whose source has been clearly established. The expression being referred to, which was probably well known before its literary record, is *itching palm*. An avaricious person or one looking for a bribe is said to have an itching palm. This idiom-metaphor was penned first by William Shakespeare. In *Julius Caesar*, Cassius complained to Brutus about his criticism of Cassius's friend for taking a bribe. Brutus replied: "Let me tell you, Cassius, you yourself/Are much condemned to have an itching palm." If only this were not figurative, how easy it would be to identify all the felonious politicians as they scratched their palms.

A sister expression—*grease the palm or fist*—which developed many years later first appeared in print in 1807. It, too, means that money so placed is bound to have an effect on that extremity. It won't cause it to itch but, like a piece of lubricated machinery that runs smoothly, it will get you what you want quickly and easily. What corruptible power money has! Today the term most often used is *payola*.

Grease my fist with a tester or two, and ye shall find it in your pennyworth.

—Quirles, *The Virgin Widow*

J

JANUARY

The name of the first month of the year, as everyone knows, is *January*. The month was named by the Romans after Janus, their god of gates and doors, because he had two faces, one looking backward and the other forward (the English word *janitor* comes from the same Latin root, *janua,* and means "doorkeeper"). All of this is fitting because Janus knew the past and foresaw the future—an attribute that can be symbolically represented by a door or gate, for every door looks two ways.

The Romans must have had some doubts about Janus's trustworthiness, however. His temple in the Roman Forum had two doors, which were closed during peace but open during war. During wartime the open doors meant to the Romans that the god had gone out to assist their warriors. During peacetime, the doors were closed to make certain that this god, the safeguard of the city, would not escape. Clearly the Romans took no chances with Janus; when at peace they would slam the doors shut in both his faces.

JEEPERS CREEPERS

The expletive or mild oath *by jiminy,* sometimes given as *jiminy crickets,* has received etymological buffeting. During Roman times *Gemini,* meaning "twins," and referring to Castor and Pollux, was sworn to as today a person might swear on his honor. With the passage of time *Gemini* was corrupted to *jiminy* and then became a slang term for Jesus. *Crickets* followed as a stand-in for Christ. Hence *by Jiminy* came to mean "by Jesus" and *jiminy crickets* the full "Jesus Christ." Illogical as all this might seem, even less believable but nonetheless supported by some authorities is *jeepers creepers* for "Jesus Christ." Which shows how far some people might go when they wish to swear without being offensive.

JEOPARDY

A person *in jeopardy* believes he's in trouble, that he's vulnerable and exposed to some possible injury or loss. He is, it might be said, at risk. The danger he senses is far from the exhilaration a participant in a game might feel. Yet the word *jeopardy,* from the Late Latin *jocus partitus,* meant simply "a divided game" because the players divided the wager. When the word was acquired by the French, it became *jeu parti* and referred to a game in which the chances of losing and winning were exactly balanced. But since the outcome was uncertain, the implication arose that the stakes were in peril, that one must be concerned about the possibility of loss, which is a worrisome state to be in. From this sense of danger, *jeopardy* became equated with hazard or risk of loss or of something harmful. The balanced sense of *jeu parti* was not merely jeopardized but gone.

JINGO

The meaning and origin of the word *jingo* and the phrase *by jingo* have never been satisfactorily established. Diverse opinions abound, but no proof. One theory is that *by jingo* is related to the word *jingo,* a blatant patriot. Another is that it is simply a euphemism for "by Jesus" or even a corruption of "by Jainko," the supreme god of the Basques (Edward I used these Basque mercenary troops in his wars against the Welsh). *Jingo* was a term frequently used by seventeenth-century conjurers, but they never revealed its meaning. It remains an arcane formula in their jargon.

What is known is that *jingo* became a common word during the Russo-Turkish War in 1877–78. England was seeking to become embroiled in it, and as sentiment in favor of intervention mounted, the refrain of a music-hall song, which included the phrase *by jingo,* became so popular that it was on almost everyone's lips. The song, addressing the threat of war with Russia, was written by G. H. Hunt.

We don't want to fight,
Yet by jingo! if we do
We've got the ships, we've got the men
And got the money, too.

Jingoism, meaning a bellicose foreign policy, has become an established word ever since it was cradled in a jingle. A synonym, nurtured in France, is *chauvinism.* It is defined as "extreme nationalism or exaggerated patriotism."

JOT/TITTLE

Till heaven and earth pass away, one jot or one tittle shall in no wise pass away from the law, till all things are accomplished.

Matthew 5:18

In the sense used, *jot* means "iota" and "tittle," any point that indicates pronunciation (like a dot over an *i*). Today one who declares that there will be no change in what he or she has said or written—not a jot or tittle may be altered—speaks adamantly, that what was said or written will stand subject to no correction.

The verb *jot* means "to write down briefly and hastily," "to record essential details," as in "The student jotted down the last-minute instructions." *Jot* also is a noun meaning "a little bit" or "a very small amount." William Tyndale first mentioned it in English in 1526 when he wrote, "One iott or one tytle of the law shall not scape."

In the Hebrew alphabet the smallest letter was its tenth letter, *yodh.* Its equivalent in Greek was *iota,* the smallest letter in its alphabet. Like *jot, iota* has taken on a meaning reflecting its alphabetic smallness in the sense of "a very little, the lesser quantity possible." Horatio in *Hamlet* said, "No more, ha?—Not a jot more, my lord," and Sir Andrew in *Twelfth Night,* "No, faith, I'll not stay a jot longer." Nothing could be smaller in quantity or shorter in time.

JOE MILLER

Poor Joe Miller. A stale joke is now called "a Joe Miller"—and no one would relish having his name become an eponym for a stale joke. At one time, however, the joke book best known and used by comedians was *Joe Miller's Jest-Book,* subtitled *The Wit's Vade Mecum.* It was the complete resource for jokes both in Great Britain and the United States.

Joe Miller himself was an outstanding comedian in eighteenth-century England. But he did not write the book that bears his name. And so his memory is being unfairly tarnished when the name *Joe Miller* is associated with a stale jest taken from this old book. In fact, Joe never saw the book. It was compiled in 1739, a year after his death, by a great admirer, a man named John Mottley.

Indeed, it is possible that all this has immortalized the great comic's name, for labeling a worn-out joke a Joe Miller may itself never wear out. Come to think of it, Joe couldn't have written that book. Joe was unschooled. He could neither read nor write.

JUMBO

The entry *jumbo* appears in dictionaries as meaning "larger than average." And so we speak of jumbo shrimps, jumbo sundaes, and jumbo airplanes. Where the word came from, however, is, according to the *Oxford English Dictionary,* uncertain. It may have been the second element in *Mumbo Jumbo,* a name applied to a West African divinity or bogy. The West African Mandingo *māmágyombō,* meaning a shaman, one who dispels the troubled spirits of the ancestors, has been adopted into English and given a number of meanings, including meaningless incantation, meaningless object of worship, and gibberish. As the name of a particular elephant, *Jumbo* was popularized during the latter half of the nineteenth century. The elephant, an unusually large one, weighing six tons and reaching ten feet nine inches, was a favorite of children at the London Zoological Garden. But in 1882, Phineas T. Barnum of circus fame purchased this stupendous animal and its name *Jumbo.* The name was so well known that it became, in the minds of children and circus promoters, a generic term for "elephant." Coming back to the origin of the name, according to some authorities the elephant was dubbed *Jumbo* by the natives who captured it. In Swahili the word *jumbo* means "chief."

KAPUT

Kaput is a German word meaning "finished, defeated, ruined." But that definition is not entirely accurate, considering its ancestor, the French *capot*. Although *capot* signified defeat, it was a loss in a game of cards only. The term *faire capot,* to make capot, meant to have taken not a single trick. In this sense, of "having lost it all," the Germans picked it up, modified its pronunciation, and gave *kaput* (they spelled it *kaputt*) the meaning of "finished," "useless," or "destroyed." It is now often used to mean someone or something that is done for—"washed up."

It may be said that a card player who has made no tricks is kaput, all washed up. But the commoner expression is *schneider,* a Yiddish term that literally means "tailor." Why a tailor should be associated with "no score" has never been determined. Tailors in fact score daily—before cutting a piece of cloth.

KEEP A STIFF UPPER LIP, TO

The English language abounds in many "keep" idioms. For example, there is *keep your eyes peeled,* meaning "be watchful, alert" (or *keep an eye on,* which has a related sense); *to keep at arm's length,* meaning "to prevent another from becoming too familiar"; *to keep your head above water,* that is, "to remain financially sound, to avoid disaster." And then there is *keep your shirt on,* don't get angry, stay calm; *keep the ball rolling,* take measures to sustain an activity, which may be only a conversation (and *keep the pot boiling,* with the same sense except "at a brisk pace"). Also *keep your chin up,* meaning "not to lose courage"; and *keep your nose clean,* meaning "stay out of trouble, avoid any suspicion of wrongdoing."

And then there is *to keep a stiff upper lip,* meaning "to remain stoical, to appear resolute, showing no emotion in adversity." The controversy this idiom generates rests in the belief that the lower lip, not the upper, is the one that trembles when tears well up in a person's eyes. If the belief is true, then this saying pays mere "lip service" to an idiom that's more than a century old.

KETTLE OF FISH, A FINE

As the whole company go to the water-side today to eat a kettle of fish, there will be no risk of interruption.

—Sir Walter Scott, *St. Ronan's Well*

A *fine* (*nice* or *pretty*) *kettle of fish* is truly not considered fine, nice, or pretty. In fact, the expression implies disgust at the way things have turned out. This ironic saying for "a sorry state of affairs, a messy predicament" has been with us for centuries. It was first recorded in *Joseph Andrews,* written by Henry Fielding in 1742.

According to the understanding of some authorities, the phrase is attributable to an eighteenth-century custom of gentlemen who, residing near the River Tweed, entertained neighbors and friends by holding picnics along the riverbank. These outings were called *fêtes champêtres,* meaning "kettles of fish." The guests were served broiled salmon that had been thrown into kettles. But sometimes the meals did not come off as planned. Some salmon would escape by jumping out of the kettles. Some were overcooked, some undercooked, and some improperly seasoned. And occasionally a kettle would be upset. All in all the picnics were messy, and saying "a fine kettle of fish" was a reminder of an unpleasant experience. However, some phrase sleuths are unconvinced that these early fish fries were responsible for the homely phrase. To them it sounds fishy. And who can pick a bone with them?

KICK THE BUCKET, TO

Despondency may make you kick the beam and the bucket at once.
—Thomas Hood, *Hood's Own*

Many substitutes for *to die*, both euphemistic and facetious, are used in America as well as in Britain. Perhaps the most popular one is *to kick the bucket*. Although the origin of this phrase is uncertain, two theories have been advanced, one resulting from a common practice in England, especially in Norfolk, and the other a reference to a form of execution or suicide indigenous to no particular country.

In Norfolk the word *bucket* had replaced the word *beam* (the Old French *buquet*, French *trebuchet*, balance). A bucket was a frame from which slaughtered pigs were hung from their hind legs. Presumably before the pigs died they thrashed helplessly and no doubt kicked the *bucket* (the *beam*); hence the association with dying. The theory that seems to be most plausible is that *bucket* refers to a "pail," its more usual meaning. A person wishing to commit suicide could accomplish his purpose by tying a rope around his neck and the other end to a beam. Then, standing on a bucket, all he need do, to address the future, is kick it. An interesting pertinent passage in *Henry IV, Part II*, is "Swifter than hee that giblets on the Brewer's Bucket."

KIT AND CABOODLE

Kit and caboodle means "the whole lot, group, or bunch," and is usually expressed as *the whole kit and caboodle*. Its competing, unassailably American idiom, which has the same meaning, is *lock, stock, and barrel*. The meaning and origin of the two elements—*kit* and *caboodle*—are a subject of dispute among word historians. Some say that *kit* came from the Middle Dutch *kitte*, a wooden tub or tankard. Others surmise that *kit* is an abbreviated form of the Latin *cithara*, a three-stringed lute (a small fiddle was a *kit*). Still others think that *kit* was an old army term referring to the sack in which soldiers carried their gear and personal belongings. And since *kit and caboodle* is often used to refer to a collection of people, at least one authority believes that *kit* is a corruption of *kith*.

Today a *kit* is a container—a tool kit, a survival kit—in which equipment is stowed. *Boodle* probably came from the Dutch *boedel,* meaning "household property."

Some phrase mavens had preferred *kit and bilin* (probably for "boiling"), but *boodle* was the more plausible choice, and it took hold. With time, *boodle* became mysteriously prefixed by *ca-* so that the expression *kit and caboodle* became a corruption of *kit and boodle.* All this is so mixed up that one might say, "Why not forget the whole thing," which is what *kit and caboodle* has come to mean, "the whole thing."

KNOCKED INTO A COCKED HAT, TO BE

To be knocked into a cocked hat is understood to mean "to completely destroy," "to defeat," or "to ruin." Yet the expression and its current explanation seem incongruous. Ruination and a cocked hat have nothing in common.

The origin of this phrase is as uncertain as the tricorn hat is obsolete. One theory is that its original reference was to the striking of something so sharply as to cause it to go limp, and thus to be transportable under the arm, like an old-fashioned hat of the eighteenth century. Another idea is that the foppish French courtiers sported a three-cornered hat with a turned-up brim, which made them look cocky and was therefore called a cocked hat. Generals in the American Revolution also customarily wore a cocked hat. The common saying was that if a general could make something go wrong, it was bound to happen; it would in effect be knocked into a (his) cocked hat. But most authorities, if forced to vote, would favor a derivation only remotely associated with headgear. They would say that the reference originated in a game of tenpins in which the initial ball left three pins standing in a triangle, the headpin and two corner pins. The pins, figuratively speaking, were knocked into a cocked (a three-cornered) hat, indeed a disastrous situation to be in, for it is almost impossible to knock them all down with one ball.

KNOCK ON WOOD

When someone proudly says he has reached his goal or that something lucky has come his way and then adds (and does) "Knock on wood," he is warding off punishment for his boast. At least that is his superstitious belief. Just as prevalent is the superstitious belief that tapping on wood will avert bad luck or misfortune. How this common practice came about is unknown. But it goes back a long way.

Many theories have been advanced to account for the belief in the protective power of wood. One theory attributes it to the child's game of "tag" in which a child who touched wood, usually a tree, is free from capture. Another is that rapping on a tree called up the friendly, and helpful, spirits in the tree, since a notion existed that spirits dwelled in trees. (Remember the druids—Greek *drus,* oak tree. The druids worshipped trees.) And so the practice developed, when ill luck or danger seemed imminent, to rap on a tree. Or, if no tree was available, to touch the wooden statue of a deity. Then there is the Christian version, that knocking on wood is associated with touching the wooden cross on which it is said that Jesus was impaled. According to Jewish legend, the doors of synagogues during the Middle Ages were made of wood and, to gain admission, congregants would have to knock on a wooden door. The thought here is that a person, by knocking on wood, was, once inside, safe from the turbulence and cruelty of the outside world.

In a story circulated during World War II, Winston Churchill, when Lord of the Admiralty, was recounting to the House of Commons the successes of the fleet, at which point a member of the House exclaimed, "Touch on wood!" Churchill replied, "I sympathize with that feeling. I rarely like to be any considerable distance from a piece of wood." He then touched his wooden dispatch box.

KNOW THE ROPES, TO

A person who is so well informed about the details of a task as to be thoroughly familiar with what is to be done is said, in the vernacular, *to know the ropes.* One might imagine that the origin of this idiom is fully established as having come from a maritime background. And in the opinion of many word detectives the term is attributable to the days of sailing ships with their seasoned sailors who knew the rigging and, as the saying goes, "knew the ropes." This notion is given further support by Richard Henry Dana, who, in his *Two Years Before the Mast* (1840), wrote: "The captain, who ... 'knew the ropes' took the steering oar." But everyone is not convinced. Ciardi said, "The use of *ropes* for *lines,* to the best of my knowledge, is unprecedented. Have I missed some earlier maritime form *to know the lines?*" Others believe the expression arose on a racetrack, where *ropes* referred to *reins.* Then the expression was applied to anyone who handled reins well, whether or not on a racetrack. He was said to know the ropes, and eventually it was said of a person thoroughly familiar with any situation or procedure.

LAVALIERE/GORGEOUS

A *lavaliere* is a pendant ornament that dangles from a chain around the neck. This style of necklace was popularized by a mistress of King Louis XIV who frequently wore an oversized pendant. Her name, one might guess, was La Vallière: Louise de La Vallière; hence as anglicized, *lavaliere.*

Another kind of neckpiece, but one that is not always an adornment, came by its name from an entirely different source. This one was anatomical—a neck or throat. In Late Latin the word for *throat* was *gurga* (which possibly sired *gargle*). From this background emanated an Old French word for neckpiece—*gorgias,* which, phoneticized, sounds like the English adjective meaning "dazzlingly beautiful" and which, to fit the pattern of English, was suffixed *-ous: gorgeous.* Hence every woman, etymologically speaking, can rightfully boast of at least one gorgeous part of her anatomy—her neck.

LAY AN EGG, TO

This cliché in today's vernacular means "to fail utterly," "to flop," "to bomb out," or "to make an embarrassing mistake." An egg is ovoid, but it is round enough to resemble a zero. Hence the expression *to lay an egg* came to be a term in sports, used of the team with no score. In cricket, where the term *to lay an egg* originated, "no score" was called a *duck's egg;* in baseball, a *goose egg;* and in tennis, *love,* a corruption of French *l'oeuf,* which means "an egg." With time, *to lay an egg* also became an expres-

sion in the field of entertainment. A theatrical performer whose audience reaction was zero is said to have laid an egg. Today one has
laid an egg if his business fails or if disappointed in a romance. It's
amazing how many eggs can be laid without a chicken.

LAY ON, MACDUFF

This cliché, meaning "to attack fiercely and violently, to do
your damnedest," is usually employed in a different sense, one
completely unrelated to the original quotation. The idiom is the last
utterance of Macbeth before he is slain by Macduff. But usage has
twisted the first word from "Lay" to "Lead," and the resultant
phrase, "Lead on, Macduff," is now commonly used to mean
"Let's begin."

The fatal wounding of Macbeth by Macduff occurs in a fight at
the end of the play.

> I will not yield,
> To kiss the ground before young Malcolm's feet,
> And to be baited with the rabble's curse.
> Though Birnam wood be come to Dunsinane,
> And thou oppos'd being of no woman born,
> Yet I will try the last: before my body
> I throw my warlike shield: lay on, Macduff;
> And damn'd be him that first cries "Hold, enough!"

LEAD-PIPE CINCH

What is a *lead-pipe cinch*? Its sense is clear, "an absolutely certain thing" ("It's a lead-pipe cinch that we'll win") or "an easy
thing to do" ("Seeing the graph makes the assembling of this gadget a lead-pipe cinch"). O. Henry in a short story titled "The
Sphinx Apple" (1907) said: "An engagement ain't always a lead-
pipe cinch." But no idiom has challenged the imagination of folk
etymologists more than this one. Efforts to establish its origin have
proved fruitless. Its source is unknown.

The word *cinch,* from Spanish *cincha,* belt, is easy to understand. A cinch under a horse's belly, if properly fastened, assured the rider that his saddle would stay in place, that it would not become unbuckled; hence a sure thing. But what does *lead pipe* mean? And why was it added? Historians can offer only conjectures. One, that a lead pipe was sometimes used as a blackjack and that a person struck with one would be sure to go plunk. Another, that *lead pipe* became a plumber's expression because such flexible pipes could serve where a rigid pipe could not. Holt says that the expression *lead-pipe cinch* makes no sense, but it is euphemistic and conclusive. One must assume that coming up with a more convincing explanation of the idiom's origin will be no lead-pipe cinch.

LEAVE IN THE LURCH, TO

A person abandoned or deserted in a difficult or embarrassing position, and no one offering a helping hand, has been, it might be said, *left in the lurch.* But that meaning was inapplicable some 400 years ago. Then, *lurch* (from the French *lourche*) was a popular dicing game in which the loser acquired a "lurch," which meant that he was vulnerable to his opponent. To have a lurch or to be left in it was untenable; the player's position became indefensible—akin to a king in check in chess, to a skunk in cribbage, and to a schneider in gin rummy. But with time the sense of *lurch* changed to any kind of abandonment or difficult position. Gabriel Harvey in his *Letter-Book* (1576) used it that way: "Lest he fail in his reckoning . . . and so leave himself in the lurch"; and Richard Tarton in *Jests* (1611) wrote: "He leave him in the lurch and shift for my selfe." In any case, it is not a good position to be left in.

LEAVE NO STONE UNTURNED, TO

A common bit of counsel—*leave no stone unturned*—was first voiced, according to Euripides, by the oracle at Delphi to the Theban general Polycrates when, in 477 B.C., he sought advice on locating a treasure supposedly buried under the tent of the defeated Persian general Mardonius, one that, despite a thorough search, could not be found. Polycrates took the oracle's advice, returned to the site of the tent, and sure enough, under a stone, discovered the treasure. As used today, the proverbial saying means that one should not spare trouble, time, expense, or effort, and so on, to fulfill a purpose or to accomplish an aim. In other words, be thorough in a quest.

Ogden Nash turned the cliché around and came up with an amusing one: "When I throw rocks at seabirds, I leave no tern unstoned."

LED BY THE NOSE, TO BE

Many expressions in popular speech have to do with man's most conspicuous feature, his nose. For example, *look down one's nose,* which means "regard disapprovingly" or "treat disdainfully"; *to nose around,* to investigate or look about secretly; *to pay through the nose,* to pay too much; *to poke (stick) one's nose into,* to meddle in someone else's affairs; *to keep one's nose to the grindstone,* to stay hard at work; and *to follow one's nose,* to go straight ahead. Also *to turn up the nose,* meaning "to act contemptuously"; *on the nose,* which means "exactly"; and *under one's very nose,* in full view or in plain sight.

Of them all, and there are others, the one that is most degrading is *to be led by the nose,* which means submissive obedience, as characterizes a person who has no will to resist but meekly allows himself to be guided by a stronger character. He is utterly dominated. The metaphoric reference is to the way horses, asses, bulls, and so forth are led by the nose either by bit and bridle or by a ring through the nostrils. As early as 1583 Golding wrote: "Men ... suffer themselves to bee led by the noses like brute beasts." Shakespeare had Iago say, when referring to Othello: "The Moor is of a free and open nature/That thinks man honest that but seem to be so,/And will as tenderly be led by th' nose/As asses are." The expression has biblical sanction. Isaiah said: "Beause thy rage against me ... is come up into mine ears, therefore will I put my hook in thy nose ... and ... I will turn thee back."

LET HER RIP

It is not unusual to hear an airline passenger mutter, as the airline is picking up speed to begin its lift-off, "Let her rip!" What he means is, "Let her go!" It is also not unusual for a man who has just had his motor repaired and who then asks the mechanic whether the car is safe to drive to hear, "Let her rip!" The mechanic is saying in vernacular language, "Everything is all right. Go."

How and where this expression originated is anyone's guess. No evidence has been uncovered to justify an authoritative opinion. Conjectures are all we're left with, and even they enjoy no consensus. Was the sense of this saying that a train or ship was to rip along as well as it could—full steam ahead—or is *rip* a humorous takeoff on R.I.P., tombstone initials for *requiescat in pace,* may he rest in peace? *The Daily Morning Herald* of St. Louis printed this excerpt in 1853: "We've got 'em on the hip. Letter Rip! Letter Rip!" Perhaps someday someone will rip off the shroud of mystery that cloaks its origin.

LET SLEEPING DOGS LIE

The sense of this ancient saying is self-evident: leave well enough alone, don't stir up potential trouble by seeking to make changes. Although the expression lends itself best to figurative uses, if a live dog is involved, it probably is a watchdog that should be avoided. Geoffrey Chaucer expressed this proverb first in *Troilus and Criseyde* (1374):

> It is nought good a sleeping hound to wake,
> Not yeve a wight a cause to devyne.

This quotation continued for about four hundred years. John Heywood made no basic change in *A Dialogue Conteyning Prouerbes and Epigrammes:* "It is ill wakyng of a sleapyng dogge." But by the time Charles Dickens wrote *David Copperfield* (1850), the proverb had assumed the usage presently with us: *let sleeping dogs lie.*

LEWD

A reference to a *lewd* person during the days of Old English would not be to one who was licentious, but to one who was unlettered. From Old English *laewede, lewd* referred to laymen as distinguished from *clergy.* Literacy was an accomplishment only of churchmen. The people in general, being unlettered, were said to be lewd. Puttenham in 1589 wrote of making "the poore men rich, the lewd well learned, the coward courageous." And since the upper classes frowned on the unlettered, even though they themselves in the most part were uneducated, they called the lower classes *lewd,* that is, "illiterate." From that meaning, *lewd* traveled down a pejorative hill, degenerating as it moved along. From "unlettered" the sense of *lewd* became "ignorant," then "ill-mannered," "vulgar," then "wicked," ending up with its current meaning, "lascivious." *Lascivious,* of course, means "marked by a lust," an attribute that is not solely in the domain of the unlettered.

LIBERAL

The basic meaning of *liberal,* ignoring political and moral concepts, is "generous." A liberal person tends to give freely. Yet when used of an academic discipline, subjects that have cultural value *(liberal arts)* rather than practical value, there is not even a modicum of generosity inherent in that course of study. The root sense of *liberal* comes from the Latin *liber,* which means "free," a term used to distinguish a *freeman* from one born a *slave.* Since a freeman came from a high class of society, he was thought of as being gentlemanly. When a course of studies was prepared at schools of higher education for the freeman, it was called *liberal arts,* meaning "studies befitting a freeman" (the Latin *liberalis,* the ancestor of *liberal,* had as one meaning "studies a freeman should be versed in").

In years past the liberal arts program consisted of two segments: the *trivium* (grammar, logic, rhetoric) and the *quadrivium* (arithmetic, geometry, music, astronomy). No longer are many of these studies considered as important as the pursuit of athletics.

LICK AND A PROMISE, A

A homely remark, when someone had promised to do a job promptly and well but the work turned out to be a disappointment, is, "All I got was *a lick and a promise.*" This saying is particularly appropriate when a washing or cleanup job is done quickly but superficially. For then it most nearly approximates the source of the expression—the way a cat gives a quick lick to its dirty face (not much of a wash), even though it may wash more later. The idiom is over a hundred years old. W. White in 1860 wrote: "We only give the cheap ones a lick and a promise."

LICK INTO SHAPE, TO

> I had not time to lick it into form, as a bear doth her young ones.
> —Robert Burton, *Anatomy of Melancholy*

Pliny the Elder, who died in A.D. 79, said: "Bears when first born are shapeless masses of white flesh a little larger than mice, their claws alone being prominent. The mother then licks them gradually into proper shape." For many, many centuries the belief was as Pliny put it. In 1578, Seigneur Du Bartas in *Divine Weeks and Works* said in verse:

> Not unlike the bear which bringeth forth
> In the end of thirty days a shapeless birth;
> But after licking, it in shape she draws,
> And by degrees she fashions out the paws,
> The head, and neck, and finally doth bring
> To a perfect beast that first deformed thing.

And so we have the idiom *to lick into shape,* meaning "to make presentable" or "to get one's studies in order" or "to bring up children properly," and so on. But lest our ancestors be unfairly criticized for their false belief, it should be borne in mind that bear cubs are exceedingly small and are nursed for several months. Mothers did lick their cubs, but we now know it was only ablutionary.

LIMELIGHT

To the boys in the back room. They do not sit in the limelight. But they are the men who do the work.

—Baron Beaverbrook, *Broadcast*

It should first be agreed that the *lime* in *limelight* does not refer to a citron fruit, but instead refers to calcium oxide, which has a brilliant luminosity when incandescent. In 1825, a British army captain named Thomas Drummond, after having heard lectures on the luminosity of lime when heated, decided that this lighting system would be most useful between distant survey stations. He was able to produce a steady beam that carried for many miles, and the practicability of this method of lighting became clear.

In those days no satisfactory means to light the stage of a theater had been found. The *limelight* beam became the solution to that problem. Equipped with a lens, the limelight emitted a powerful light that could be concentrated on the area of the stage where the main action was to take place. This meant that the leading actor, being under a bright light, would be distinctly visible, often to the exclusion of the other actors. Because the leading player was made so conspicuous, he was said to be *in the limelight*. The name given this light originally was the "Drummond light." But that name was dropped, as was the use of limelight when more modern lighting methods were invented. What did remain from all this brilliance, and pass into common speech, was the phrase *to be in the limelight*—a pithy way of saying that someone is in the full glare of public attention or notoriety or, to borrow a theatrical term, "on center stage."

LIMERICK

A *limerick* is a humorous verse of five lines of which the first, second, and fifth rhyme with one another and the third and fourth with each other. Most of the verses were bawdy improvisations by men at drinking parties. After each verse, all the men would join in and chant, "Will you come up, come up? Will you come up to Limerick?" Although limericks became popular in the eighteenth century, they are supposed to have been a form of Roman entertainment. Who regenerated interest in this kind of verse is unknown. Edward Lear, an English writer in the mid-nineteenth century, popularized this verse form, although he did not use the name *limerick*. According to the *Oxford English Dictionary*, "a nonsense verse such as was written by Lear is wrongfully so-called—who applied the name to the indecent nonsense verse first, it is hard to say." The verses were dubbed *Limerick* because of the refrain, but why Limerick, a county and city in Ireland? And why should anyone want to come up to Limerick?

Although most verses were meant for male ears only, some were fit for mixed company. An example:

> There was a young lady from Lynn
> Who was so exceedingly thin
> That when she essayed
> To drink lemonade
> She slid down the straw and fell in.

LION'S SHARE, THE

This expression, now used to mean "the greater part of something," harks all the way back to Aesop. According to the fable, a lion went on a hunt accompanied by other beasts of the forest. As the animals were readying to divide the spoils, the lion announced that since he was the king of beasts, he was entitled to one quarter of the take in right of his prerogative, another quarter because of his superior courage, a third quarter to feed his dam and cubs, and "as for the fourth, let who will, dispute it with me." And so *the lion's share* came to mean all or almost all—"almost all" because in one version of the fable, the fox became the "who will, dispute" and snatched some of the meat. In today's usage *the lion's share* refers to "the best or largest," not to "all."

LITERARY TERMS

Many of us fail to realize that we often grace ordinary activities with literary terms. When first written, these expressions sparkled, garnered attention, and provoked thought. But today, because of frequent usage, the sayings, even though from the pen of distinguished writers, have become stale. They are now called clichés. For example, *light fantastic* as a synonym for dancing.

> Sport, that wrinkled Care derides,
> And Laughter, holding both his sides.
> Come, and trip it, as you go,
> On the light fantastic toe.
> —John Milton, *L'Allegro*

or take your pick, for

It's just six of one and half a dozen of the other.
> —Frederick Marryat, *The Pirate*

or let me go by myself, since

He travels fastest who travels alone.
> —Rudyard Kipling, *The Winners*

or be sensibly careful because

The better part of valor is discretion.
> —Shakespeare, *Henry IV, Part I*

LITTLE BIRD TOLD ME, A

> He guides me and the bird. In His good time!
> —Robert Browning, *Sordello*

Probably one of the oldest idioms still extant is *a little bird told me*. It means, of course, that I have information from a secret source. The idiom may have originated in the Koran (Mohammed received instructions from a pigeon who whispered in his ear). Or its origin may have been the Bible. In Ecclesiastes appears the following: "Curse not the king, no not in thy thought and curse not the rich in thy bedchamber; for a bird of the air shall carry the voice, and that which hath wings shall tell the matter." We find in Shakespeare's *Henry IV, Part II* "I heard a bird so sing," and in Jonathan Swift's *Letter to Stella,* in 1711, "I heard a little bird say so." The *Oxford English Dictionary* advanced the thought that the basic idea was in the swift and noiseless flight of a bird. From another source, in 1837, came the suggestion that the key phrase may have originated from a Dutch expression, *Er lij t'el baerd,* which phonetically sounds like "A little bird," but means "I should betray another." Most authorities spoof this surmise; they say, "It's for the birds."

LOBSTER NEWBURG

A supper club delicacy, and a favorite dish in many seafood restaurants, is *Lobster Newburg* (or *Newburgh*). It is cooked lobster meat, heated in a sauce of heavy cream, egg yolk, and sherry. Who dreamed up this dish has never been satisfactorily established. Dictionaries do not mention the name of its chef.

The story that has made the rounds is that in the nineteenth century a West Indian ship captain (some say a shipping magnate) named Ben (or Charles) Wenberg recommended a concoction to the chef of the famous Delmonico Hotel. The creation turned out to be a gastronomic delight, and in time it became a popular main course. But that is getting ahead of the story. The chef was so pleased with this delicacy that he named it *Lobster Wenberg,* after the man who supplied the recipe. But shortly thereafter, the chef and Wenberg had a terrible row. The chef accused Wenberg of conduct unbecoming a gentleman and told him never to return. Not satisfied with that edict alone, the chef penalized Wenberg further. He transposed the first three letters of the dish so that *Wenberg* became *Newburg,* and perhaps also to honor a favorite city on the Hudson. In any event, that's the name he gave it, and that name has remained until this day.

LOCK HORNS, TO

> Blessed are the horny hands of toil!
> —James Russell Lowell,
> *A Glance Behind the Curtain*

It is easy to imagine, and interesting to know, that the expression *to lock horns* alludes to a battle between two buck moose, probably over (what else) a cow. Moose are tall animals with very large antlers, some weighing over sixty pounds. Although the males are usually not aggressive, when the mating season begins and they become horny, they'll use their horns to shunt off a competitor from a mate. If a battle does develop between two males, their antlers can easily become interlocked. If the bucks cannot free themselves, they will starve to death. Which suggests how serious locking horns, even metaphorically, can be, a fact that people who engage in violent argument should remember. In any event, when it appears that disputants are unlikely to resolve their argument, although smooth of head, they are, from an allusion to fighting bucks, said *to lock horns*.

LOCK, STOCK, AND BARREL

Lock, stock, and *barrel* refer to the three component parts of an old-fashioned firearm. The expression in general usage follows along the same path; its sense is "an entirety," "the whole thing." If someone offers to buy a merchant's inventory *lock, stock, and barrel,* he means he will take the whole lot, all of it—the whole shooting match.

In Great Britain, the idiom often followed the writing of John Gibson Lockhart in his biography of Sir Walter Scott (1617): "Like the highlandman's gun, she wants stock, lock, and barrel, to put her in repair." *Stock* and *lock* eventually were transposed to make the idiom more euphonious—*lock, stock, and barrel*—and has remained so rather than the way it was originally written.

LOGGERHEADS

> Solid men of Boston, go to bed at sundown;
> Never lose your way like the loggerheads of London.
> —Anonymous, *Billy Pitt and the Farmer*

It is idiomatic when persons are disputing with each other to say they're *at loggerheads*. A dispute meriting this description is usually not an ordinary one, but one in which the disputants are in hot argument, contending seriously about their differences of opinion.

Through the centuries *loggerheads* had two basic meanings, neither of which related to a quarrel or disagreement. One was "blockhead," an equivalent of dunce. It was stated that loggers were blocks attached to the legs of grazing horses to prevent them from straying. The idea developed that these blocks were dumb things, and so the word *loggerhead* came to mean a thick-headed or stupid person, a blockhead. The other referred to long-handled ladles with which soldiers poured melted tar from the top of a wall onto the heads of a besieging enemy or with which sailors hurled pitch and tar onto an attacking vessel. In addition, it might be noted that large-headed animals were called *loggerheads*. One of these was the *loggerhead turtle*, a snapping turtle. Perhaps therein lies the clue to the allusion of squabbling sharply. Such turtles snapping at one another might seem to be at loggerheads.

LOOSE ENDS, TO BE AT

To be at loose ends is to be uncertain of what to do next or to have nothing planned. Or such a person may be unemployed. Eric Partridge may have been the first to suggest that the expression is derived "from a horse whose tether has broken or slipped." Evans points out that Heywood in his *Proverbs* (1546) says: "Some loose or od ende will come man, some one daie," a version that suggests some other origin.

The phrase *loose ends* usually refers to the final stages of a pending contract or the handling of final details of any transaction.

And if they are concluded, tied up neatly, then one, to use a sister cliché, has *tied up the loose ends.*

LOVE ME, LOVE MY DOG

It has long been proverbial to say, "Love me, love my dog." The idiom, which first appeared in English in 1867 in Heywood's *Proverbs,* is taken to mean either that if you want me, you'll have to take me with all my faults or that if you love me, you'll like all that is mine. The gist of the expression was written as long ago as the twelfth century, but in Latin. St. Bernard, an abbot of Clairvaux, wrote: *"Qui me amat, amat et canem meum"* ("Who loves me, also loves my dog"). That St. Bernard, however, despite his name and its reference to a dog, is not the St. Bernard de Mentheon who lived a hundred years earlier and founded the famous hospice, and after whom the St. Bernard dog was named.

M

MACABRE

Think positive; avoid the *macabre*. Fine, except the advice ignores the realities of life. *Macabre* means "gruesome," "ghastly," that which is suggestive of death. During the bubonic plague of the Middle Ages, carts filled with corpses traveling to graveyards were commonplace. Those still living were so sure that soon they would be carted away too that they spent the expected short life left to them in revelry. Dances with the theme of death, with a dancing skeleton leading men to their graves, became the diversion of the times. Jean de Fèvre composed an early one with verses, *Danse macabrée.*

All this does not give us the paternity of *macabre,* and that is because no one knows. One thought is that the word came from a painter named Macaber or Macabré, but this is unverified. Another is that it came from the Late Latin *Chorea Maccabaeorum,* "dance of the Maccabees," people who so much believed in the worship of one God only that they refused, although threatened by Antiochus IV with death, to worship the many Greek gods. Judas Maccabeus and his many followers bravely endured insufferable torture, all finally succumbing, but they never wavered, and their beliefs remain the foundation of the Judeo-Christian religion.

MAD AS A HATTER

The odd thing about the *attar,* a large, venomous, multicolored reptile, is that it always looks angry, infuriated. This strange characteristic came to be applied to people who seemed angry or mad at someone. They were said to be *mad as an attar,* which more often sounded like *mad as a hatter,* a combination of words that is now proverbial. Today the *attar* is called an *adder* and a furious person *a mad hatter.* What is even stranger about all this is that no one really knows whether this story has any basis in fact or whether it is the raving of a person gone mad from an adder's bite, which is supposed to cause insanity. Or is it that hatters become mad from the mercuric nitrate used in the making of felt hats? This chemical, a poison that can cause all kinds of emotional and mental problems, is believed responsible for the jerky, involuntary movement of hatters, and possibly, in some cases, outright insanity. Conjectures have followed conjectures. One is that Australian miners were called *hatters.* Since they often worked alone, they were said to be eccentric, if not mad; hence *mad as a hatter.* The only thing on which everyone can agree is that Lewis Carroll in 1865 popularized the phrase with his Mad Hatter in *Alice's Adventures in Wonderland.*

But note an earlier use in 1837 by Thomas Haliburton in *The Clockmaker:* "Sister Sal . . . walked out of the room, as mad as a hatter."

MAD AS A MARCH HARE

This peculiar expression dates back at least to the time of Chaucer, who, in 1386 in his "Friar's Tale," said: "Mad were as an Hare." March is the breeding season for hares, and, quite naturally, during that time they seem frolicsome if not wild, but possibly romantic to other hares. When in marshes, according to the eminent Dutch theologian Erasmus, they are even wilder. He said: "March hare is marsh hare. Hares are wilder in marshes than elsewhere because of their greater flatness and the absence of hedges and cover." The question one might ask is whether this is a hairy tale. Lewis Carroll in *Alice's Adventures in Wonderland,* through his character the March Hare, has helped make *mad as a March hare* proverbial:

The March Hare will be much more interesting, and perhaps, as this is May, it won't be raving mad—at least not so mad as it was in March.

Whereas *mad as a March hare* implies lunacy, a sister expression, *mad as a hen,* refers to an angry person. There isn't even a clue as to the origin of this simile, but P. G. Wodehouse in 1942 used it in his *Money in the Bank.* Today the common expression is "mad as a *wet* hen."

MAKE A MOUNTAIN OUT OF A MOLEHILL

He changes a fly into an elephant.
—John Ray, *English Proverbs*

Many languages have many ways of saying that a problem should not be magnified, especially that a small matter should not be enlarged out of all proportion. The Romans said: *"Arcem ex cloaca facere"* ("to make a difficulty from trifles," literally, "to make a citadel out of a sewer"). In English this sense—to give great importance to something that is really insignificant—is popularly expressed by the phrase *to make a mountain out of a molehill.* Although the expression is of proverbial age, it is believed that the English love for alliteration has given us this saying. In other countries, particularly France and Germany, the images conveying this thought are entirely different—"to make an elephant out of a fly," an idea, and a combination of words, first concocted by the Greek essayist Lucian in his "Praise for a Fly." In French it became *"Faire d'une mouche un éléphant."* It may be that the English version first appeared in print in Thomas Bacon's *Catechism* (1560), "They make of a fly an elephant, and of a molehill a mountain," even though generally Foxe's *Book of Martyrs* (1573) is credited with having first recorded the phrase "makeying mountaines of Molehills." The proverb became solidified by Gabriel Harvey in his *Letter-Book* (1573): "To make huge mountains of small molehills," which, of course, is the very opposite of making a mouse from a mountain, as appears in Horace's *Ars Poetica:* "The mountain labors, and a ridiculous mouse is born." Roper, in his *Life of More* (1557), wrote: "Thus was the great mountayne turned scant to a little mole hill." But Foxe, in *A & M* (1570)—"To much amplifying things yt be but small, makying mountaines of Molehills"—made the allusion used today.

MAKE HEAD OR TAIL, UNABLE TO

This idiom, which dates back to the seventeenth century, clearly indicates that a person sees something unclearly. What is seen is so obscure or what is being considered is so obfuscating that one is *unable to make head or tail out of it.* The allusion, of course, is to something that has a head and a tail, and that something is probably either an animal or a coin—the animal being indistinct and the coin worn clean on both sides. Margery Mason in her *The Tickler Tickled* (1679) wrote: "Their Tale . . . had neither Head nor Taile." Cicero remarked, *"Nec caput nec pedes,"* neither head nor feet, which translates into complete confusion. In any event, if you can't make head or tail of something you're looking at or a problem you're considering, you don't understand it.

MAKE NO BONES ABOUT IT, TO

The phrase *to make no bones about (it* or *a matter)* was first used by Nicholas Udall, an early sixteenth-century writer, in *Apothegms from Erasmus,* a story of Abraham and Isaac. Abraham was commanded to sacrifice his son. Udall wrote, "He made no manier (manner of) bones . . . but went in hand to offer up his only son, Isaac." Hence its present sense of "to show no hesitation." However, the genesis of the expression, in the belief of some phrase hunters, lay in the eating of soup. If a person eating soup encountered no bones in it, he would find no difficulty in eating it unhesitatingly. The expression has entered general usage to signify what has to be done without flinching, straightforwardly, or, if speaking, fully and frankly. In either case the person is *making no bones about it* ("Arthur dislikes his mother-in-law, and he *makes no bones about it*). Another theory that has some, but little, support relates bones to dice. Anyone visiting a casino will see some crapshooters follow a ritual before flinging the bones. To encourage Lady Luck, they might breathe on them, toss them in the air, or even tickle them. Those players who avoid such shenanigans, merely shaking the dice in their cupped hands before flinging them, are said "to make no bones about it." They're getting directly to the point to try to make their point.

MAKE ONE'S HAIR STAND ON END, TO

Sudden fright or an unnerving experience can cause one's hair to stand on end. Certainly this phenomenon is noticeable with cats and dogs. When frightened, the fur of a cat or the mane of a dog becomes rigid. And this too is so with human beings. According to Brewer, citing a Dr. Andrews of Beresford Chapel, the hair of criminals about to be executed rose gradually and so remained for a while. Hence the idiom *to make the hair stand on end* has come to indicate that something was exceedingly frightening or terrifying.

This notion goes all the way back to biblical times. The following appears in Job 4:14–15: "Fear came upon me, and trembling, which made all my bones to shake. Then a spirit passed before my face; the hair of my flesh stood up."

Its opposite idiom was created by Jane Austen: "He never turned a hair." The sense there is that the hair on a calm, cool horse remains smooth, but it roughs up when the horse is disturbed. Then its hair, but not literally, "stands on end." The expression *he never turned a hair* is applied to people to mean that they are completely composed and are not visibly perturbed. A quipster might add that these people have had no hair-raising experiences.

MAKE THE GRADE, TO

In some government bureaus during World War II, a passing grade of 80 was required from applicants in all examinations. A high grade indeed. If someone failed the course and said that he didn't make the grade, he would be understood idiomatically but not historically; that is to say, the idiom *to make the grade* applied to railroad talk and had no relationship to examinations. The grade in this expression is an incline that a puffing train must overcome. The steam train before the Civil War had great pulling power but lost much of it when navigating a slope or incline. Trainmen would nervously hold their breaths until the train reached the top of a difficult pull, and then, relieved, would say, "We made the grade." The expression today is used in all fields of activity; it need not apply solely to the upward pulling of a train. A person who reaches the highest point he's seeking or finally reaches his goal might rightly say, "I've made the grade." Even if he's on the level.

MARGARINE

Margarine is a happy invention. The product, although now widely accepted, went through several stages on its way to the grocer's shelf, primarily changes in spelling and pronunciation. The full name for this butter substitute is *oleomargarine* (*oleo* is a combining form meaning "oil"). The word *margarin* (margarin is a mixture of vegetable fats and oils) was coined by the French chemist Marie-Eugene Chevreul in the nineteenth century. He selected that word because one of the product's chief substances was *margaric acid* (in French, *acide margarique*) and because the product's crystals had a pearl-like color. (English *margaric* and French *margarique* come from the Greek *margaron,* meaning "pearl.") The inventor of *margarine* was Hippolyte Mege-Mouries, a French chemist, the winner of a contest to develop a satisfactory substitute for butter. The contest was arranged by Napoleon III, who sought a butter replacement during the Franco-Prussian War of 1870. The initial color of margarine is white. It is artificially colored yellow to imitate the natural color of butter.

To follow its parent's pronunciation and spelling, *margarine* should be pronounced *MAR-guh-rihn* and spelled with a final *e*. These pronunciations and orthographic changes have had no bearing on the product's general acceptance, especially by those who say it's better than the real thing.

MASHER

Masher is an uncommon word in today's parlance, but it is still heard in reruns of old movies and is seen in books whose plots are set in earlier eras. The word first appeared in print, according to the *Oxford English Dictionary,* in 1882. Mashers were chorus girls who flirted with men in the audience, enticing them to meet at the stage door—to become stage-door Johnnies. The slang term was derived from the gypsy *masher-ava,* which, appropriately, means "to allure with the eyes." With time the application of the word changed its sex; it came to describe a male flirt. No matter how you look at it (or no matter who winks first), the twain shall meet. But note that some dictionaries on slang regard a *masher* as a man whose attentions are forced on an unwilling woman. He's more than a winker.

MAYDAY/MAY POLE

If you need help quickly and you use the radio voice code *Mayday,* it would not be expedient for you to inquire where the expression, the equivalent of *SOS,* comes from, since it's not etymology that's going to solve your problem. But at some point after you've gotten help, and you feel thankful, you may be interested in knowing that *Mayday* is pidgin French—an anglicized version of the French phrase *(venez) m'aidez* (pronounced with a long *a,* as in *hay*) and means "(come) and help me."

The *May pole* and *Mayday* are not related terms, even though some of the merrymakers around a May pole, in early times, may have been inclined to yell "Mayday." Despite what may appear today to be an innocuous festivity—students dancing, singing, and romping about the pole to welcome the spring—such frolicking was not always so well regarded. Before going into the sordid history of the May pole, bear in mind that in ancient times the dance was a rite to ensure fertility. The pole was considered a phallic symbol. In London, which had a May pole in the Strand, the Puritans one day rampaged and tore it down to stop what appeared to them to be a bacchanalian frenzy of those romping around it. This excessive puritanical bigotry was surpassed only by the staid Pilgrims in Boston who, revolting at the merriment of Indians and others gathered around a pole erected by Thomas Morton, proceeded not only to tear the pole down but also to burn Morton's property. Which makes one wonder how the May pole could have received such prominence, to the delight of the girls at such a chaste and decorous college as Vassar.

MEDUSA

> Beauty is that Medusa's head
> Which men go armed to seek and sever:
> It is most deadly when most dead,
> And dead will stare and sting forever.
> —Archibald MacLeish, *The Happy Marriage*

Medusa, the ugliest woman in the annals of Greek mythology, was so hideous that a person seeing her would be immediately revolted. Instead of hair on her head, she had writhing, hissing snakes, and these serpents had wings, brazen claws, and enormous teeth. Athena made her into a gorgon, which meant that anyone who looked at her was turned to stone. Perseus was ordered to secure her head. So as not to become petrified, he watched her through the reflective surface of his highly polished shield. Despite his awkward position, he was able to cut off her head with a single stroke of his sword. He later presented this trophy to Athena, who placed it in the center of her breastplate. The Loggia dei Lanzi in Florence, Italy, houses Cellini's famous statue of Perseus proudly holding aloft the severed head of Medusa. Today an ugly woman may be called a Medusa, but prudently not to her face.

MESS

> I confess that you three fools lack'd me fool to make up the mess.
> —Shakespeare, *Love's Labour's Lost*

A *mess* is a dirty or untidy mass, or a state of disorder, or a difficulty, said of one who bungles something—"He's made a mess of it." The original meaning of *mess,* however, bore no relationship to any of those senses. It referred to a portion of food on a table, like a mess of pottage (for which Esau sold his birthright). Its Latin ancestor was *mittere,* to send, but its sense in Rome was "to set in place," from which came the Late Latin *missus,* a course at dinner, but literally "a thing put as on a table." (In Old French *mes*—now spelled *mets*—meant food or a serving of food.) With time, the sense of *mess* changed. It came to refer to small parties, normally of four persons, who were seated together and who helped themselves from the same dishes. These groups were called *messes*.

A hostess would be discomfited if she were one short to make a mess. R. C. Trench in his *Dictionary of Obsolete English* cites a sermon, "There lacks a fourth . . . to make up the mess." (Even today hostesses sometimes have need for a fourth, in bridge.) With more time, the sense of *mess* was further extended to include any number and came to be applied especially to soldiers and sailors *(messmates)* who dine together. Perhaps the sense of untidiness for *mess* developed from the litter left at the dining table in the mess hall.

MILK OF HUMAN KINDNESS, THE

No act of kindness, no matter how small, is ever wasted.
—Aesop, "The Lion and the Mouse"

A person whose natural sympathy, affection, compassion, and understanding seem limitless may be said to be *full of the milk of human kindness*. That expression is now a cliché, but it was an unsurpassed gem when it first appeared in *Macbeth*.

Lady Macbeth, it may be recalled, was concerned that her husband lacked the ruthlessness to find his way to the crown by committing murder. His nature was much too gentle, his concern for humankind much too great to carry out the schemes she envisioned. She said, "Yet do I fear thy nature;/It is too full o' the milk of human kindness/To catch the nearest way. Thou wouldst be great,/Art not without ambition, but without/Thy illness should attend it."

The story concerning this now hackneyed expression that has gotten around is that an aged bishop visited a guru in Bombay. The guru talked incessantly but always with deep piety and insufferable sanctimoniousness. When the bishop rejoined his party, the guide asked: "What did you think of this charismatic character?" "Well," replied the bishop, "I've often heard of the milk of human kindness, but I never dreamed I would meet the cow."

MIND YOUR P'S AND Q'S

A person who *minds his p's and q's* is on good behavior, watchful of what he says or does. He is being careful and precise. Hannah Cowbley wrote, in 1779, in *Who's the Dupe?*: "You must mind your *p*'s and *q*'s with him, I can tell you." Although the meaning of this homely expression is clear, its origin is not. The various sources attributed to it range from the classroom to the barroom.

The letters *p* and *q* are identical except that their vertical lines, called descenders by printers, are reversed. It was therefore conjectured that teachers counseled their pupils to *mind their p's and q's*; that is, to be alert to the distinctive formation of those letters. (But why not "to mind their *b*'s and *d*'s"?) Another theory is that wives of sailors were concerned with the soil on the collar of their husband's pea jackets from their queues or pigtails. Being told to *mind your p's and q's* in this instance meant to keep the pigtail away from the collar or, to put it differently, to keep the pea jacket free of the queue.

The most likely story is that the practice of bartenders was to keep tabs on how much a customer drank by chalking up on a blackboard a number one under a *p* (for pint) or a *q* (for quart) every time a tankard was ordered. Those who went away drunk quite obviously failed to mind their p's and q's.

MONEY BURNS A HOLE IN HIS POCKET

There are all kinds of money. There is *butter and egg money, found money, pin money, ready money,* and *blood money*. But no matter what kind it is, in the hands of certain persons, it will not remain long because it will *burn a hole in his pocket*. The allusion is to a person who cannot keep his money, that is, cannot restrain himself from spending it as quickly as possible. Of course, the idiom is metaphorical, not literal, because if the money had burned a hole in his pocket, the money would be burned, and he would have no money to spend. But this idiom has spawned siblings: *to spend money like water, to let money run through your fingers,* and *to spend money like a drunken sailor*. Regardless of the cliché used, the sense is the same: prodigal recklessness.

MONKEY WRENCH

A *monkey wrench* is so called, it has been said, because it resembles the animal after which it is named. Perhaps, but certainly not everyone agrees. As all mechanics know, a monkey wrench is a hand tool with adjustable jaws for turning nuts of varying sizes, and its movement does resemble that of a monkey's jaw. Conjecturing that the device was given its name because of this resemblance, however, has not garnered the votes of many authorities. For a long period, since about 1856, it was believed that this implement derived its name from a man credited with its invention, Charles Moncke, a London blacksmith. According to this legend, the inventor's name was pronounced *monkey* because the true name of the inventor was not generally known. The *Boston Transcript* rebutted this English theory by reporting, in the winter of 1932–1933, an investigation that proved that the inventor of the monkey wrench was not a Britisher, but an American named *Monk* (first name not given) who had been employed by Bemis & Call of Springfield, Massachusetts. In support of this accreditation is the date of Monk's invention, 1856, two years before the term *monkey wrench*, as noted in the *Oxford English Dictionary*, first appeared in print. Further, the English call a monkey wrench a *spanner*. Be that as it may, dictionaries list the origin of *monkey wrench* as obscure or unknown. Perhaps this is one bit of etymology that they don't care to monkey with.

MORTGAGE

Worm or beetle—drought or tempest—on a farmer's land may fall,
Each is loaded full o' ruin, but a mortgage beats 'em all.
                                            —Will Carleton, *Betsy and I Are Out*

In the business world death takes a holiday regarding a word in common use related to *death* (from its Latin forebear *mors,* death). That word is *mortgage*. It no longer connotes "death" in its business use, and no one thinks of it as being connected with death. The term, consisting of two elements, came from the French *mort* and *gage,* literally "dead pledge," a promise to pay upon a person's decease. Today, of course, a mortgage has nothing to do with death, that is, the demise of a living thing. It is, instead, a conveyance of property as security for a debt, one that has been contracted among the living and ordinarily expected to be discharged while the parties are still alive. (A substitute for *mortgage* is "hypothecate," from the Medieval Latin *hypothecare*. In France the word *mortgage* has been entirely replaced by *hypothèque*.)

The business custom for paying off a mortgage is through a periodic payment called *amortization,* which is a stipulated monthly charge that includes payment of current interest plus a portion of the principal. This slow but steady method of resolving a debt is, in a sense, a slow killing, since eventually it will "kill" or "destroy" the debt completely. The dictionary definition of *amortize* is "to put money aside at intervals as in a sinking fund, for gradual payment of a debt." The English word—*amortize*—can again thank the French, which assembled it from the Latin *ad,* to, and *mors,* death, and, in Old French, came up with the word's parent, *amortir,* meaning "to extinguish" or "to deaden." A mortgage that has been amortized is an extinguished debt because it has been fully paid.

MORE THE MERRIER, THE

The sense of this expression, that the more participants, the more fun for all, or that it is a welcoming greeting to an unexpected guest, seems clear. Cicero has been credited as the originator of this convivial thought. It took many centuries, however, before the idea was adopted into English and became an established idiom. In the opinion of some word hunters, but not all, Jehan Palsgrave was the first to put this thought into English. He wrote in 1530, "The mo the meryer; the fewer, the better fare." The controversy is whether Palsgrave originated the thought or simply put it into English. The doubters believe that King James I of Scotland was the first to utter this axiom. John Heywood included it in his *Proverbs* (1546): "The mo the merier, we all daie here and see. Ye, but the fewer, the better far." What he wrote, in today's language, was "the more the merrier; the fewer, the better fare," meaning the fewer mouths to feed leaves more food for the others.

MUMBO JUMBO

The combination of words *mumbo jumbo* has several lexical definitions, among which is "gibberish." And that is probably the meaning most persons would ascribe to it, "incomprehensible language." Although many word historians have tried to pinpoint the precise origin and its native meaning, there has been no consensus (the *OED* says, "Origin unknown"). However, it is generally believed that *mumbo jumbo* was derived from the Mandingo language of West Africa, and it meant "a magician who could make evil spirits depart." Mumbo Jumbo was the guardian of a village in Sudan and was represented by a masked medicine man who not only could fend off evil but also keep the women in subjection. It also is defined as a fetish, an object that has supernatural powers. With all these meanings, we wonder why Dickens, according to Holt, registered surprise that "Carlyle, who knows everything, don't [*sic*] know what Mumbo Jumbo is," and went on to point out that it was not an idol or a fetish, but a disguised man representing the combined determination of the men of the tribe to keep the women strictly in their place (apparently Mumbo Jumbo had never heard of Women's Liberation). In any event, Carlyle, you may be sure, was not the only person who did not know its "precise" meaning, whatever that might be.

MUSHROOM

The odd thing about the word *mushroom* is that it was called *mousseron* (or *moissereon*) in the North of France, influenced by the word *mousse,* which means "moss," and which has nothing to do with the edible variety of the umbrella-shaped fungus found in fancy restaurants. As is plain, neither *mush* nor *room* appears in the French word that, when anglicized, became *mushroom.* The English spelling has been attributed to the phonetic pronunciation of the French word that, to the English ear, sounded like *mushroom.* Try it before you eat it.

NAKED

> Blind and naked ignorance
> Delivers brawling judgments, unashamed,
> On all things all day long.
> —Alfred, Lord Tennyson, *Idylls of the King*

The Old English word for *naked,* meaning "fully unclothed," "bare," was *nacod.* For generations the squeamish have objected to any use of the word *naked*—it was indecent; it conjured up pornographic images. The word these genteelists preferred was *nude* (from the Latin *nudus*). They had art on their side. Renoir painted nude women, not naked women. But in other uses of *naked,* no one has remonstrated against it. For example, the *naked truth* or, as Horace put it, *nuda veritas,* meaning "the unvarnished truth," an expression founded in a fable centuries ago, has been wholeheartedly accepted even by prudes. According to the fable, Truth and Falsehood went bathing together. Falsehood left the water first and donned Truth's garments. Truth, opposed to deception, went naked. And that was the naked Truth.

NAME IS MUD, HIS

The contempt of society for a person may be summed up in a few words—*his name is mud,* which concisely expresses the revulsion society feels. And so too, but on a less vitriolic level, an employee's name is said to be mud if he is in disfavor with the boss.

No one is certain how this idiom arose. The story with the

greatest doubt attached to it involves Dr. Samuel Mudd, a Maryland physician who treated actor John Wilkes Booth after he had assassinated Abraham Lincoln. Booth, you may recall, jumped from the President's box to the stage, breaking his leg. Dr. Mudd set Booth's leg, and although no evidence was ever adduced to prove a conspiracy with Booth, Dr. Mudd was tried for the crime, convicted, and sent to prison—actually to Dry Tortugas in Key West. The second *d* in *Mudd* was dropped from the expression to give it a down-to-earth, slimy feel in keeping with the besmirching of a name.

Some authorities dispute the validity of the story and say it's pure folk etymology. They may be right, since the term *mud,* referring to something scandalous or defamatory, preceded the Civil War, which indicates a possibility that *his name is mud* also preceded the controversial act of Dr. Mudd. The first use in print of the expression was in J. Cheever Goodwin's *Wang: Elephant Song,* published in 1891. Which, as a wit might say, leaves the origin of this idiom as clear as mud. The only good thing to be said about mud is its association with a good drink: "Here's mud in your eye."

NARCISSUS

And still deeper the meaning of that story of Narcissus, who because he could not grasp the tormenting, mild image he saw in the fountain, plunged into it and was drowned.

—Herman Melville, *Moby Dick*

It's intriguing to think of the range of meanings of *narcissus* and its cognates. *Narcissus* is a beautiful flower. It was named for a handsome Greek youth who observed his reflection in a pool of clear water and became so enamored of it that he refused to leave the water's edge. He died there and was turned into a cluster of white and yellow flowers—flowers that bear his name. The Greek word for *narcissus* stands for "numbness," alluding to narcotic effects. *Narcissism,* a psychoanalytic term coined by Sigmund Freud, is morbid self-love.

NASTURTIUM

If one were to eat the leaves of a *nasturtium* (sometimes used as a seasoning in vinegar), he would find their taste so exceedingly pungent that his nose would twist. The name of this flower, historically at least, is appropriate, for it came from the Latin *nasus,* (nose) and *torquere* (to twist), which explains what happens to people who chew one of its seeds. Pliny, the Roman naturalist, said in the first century that the flower "received its name from tormenting the nose." A nasturtium might rightly be called a nose-twister.

NEITHER RHYME NOR REASON

There is *no rhyme or reason* why this phrase should have persisted since the sixteenth century. It has come to mean that something has no system or sense, that in fact it is utter nonsense. If a person fruitlessly searches for a book in a secondhand bookstore where the inventory has been shelved with no regard for subject matter, he might say, in disgust, that the books were stored without rhyme or reason. Everyone would understand the gist of that remark; however, although *reason* there makes sense, *rhyme* doesn't.

Credit for popularizing this term goes to Sir Thomas More, the Lord Chancellor of Henry VIII. It is said that an author submitted a manuscript to Sir Thomas and asked for an opinion. The work evoked no enthusiasm in him, to say the least. Sir Thomas advised the author to versify it, which he did. When the manuscript was again shown to the Lord Chancellor, he exclaimed, "Ay! ay! That will do. 'Tis rhyme now, but before it was neither rhyme nor reason."

NEW BROOM SWEEPS CLEAN, A

Anyone can take this cliché literally, because it's true in most cases that a new broom sweeps clean. But the idiom is not so used. It is used of new officeholders who zealously, sometimes ruthlessly, make many changes, sweeping away, so to speak, existing practices and some employees as well. Apparently this type of housecleaning has been going on for centuries, as witness John Heywood's proverb collection of 1546: "Some thereto said, the greene new broom swepith cleene."

This brings up another point. In yesteryear, brooms were made of green twigs or brush bound to a handle. When newly attached, the broom swept clean, but as the twigs and brush turned brown, they lost their resilience and no longer swept well. In fact, they would drop brittle pieces and thus litter what was to be cleaned. Only a new broom was sure to do a job well. With that one, to take advantage of another cliché, you can get a *clean sweep*.

The saying applies equally to any new worker who bustles about efficiently, doing a super job in the beginning (like a new broom).

NICK OF TIME, IN THE

This term implies an arrival at the last minute, at the critical moment, or just before it would be too late. Some etymologists claim that the origin of the word *nick* can be traced to Old Low German. Dr. Johnson noted it as coming from the Teutonic *nicke,* meaning "in the twinkling of an eye." In Middle English, it was spelled *nyke.* But its variant spelling was *nocke,* borrowed whole from a Middle Dutch word meaning "notch," which is what a *nick* is. The slight difference between *nick* and *notch* is that whereas a *nick* may be a shallow cut or an indentation in wood, a *notch* usually is a V-shaped cut. Possibly that difference accounts for some different uses of those words, too. For example, one speaks of being "in the nick of time" but "feeling a notch better than yesterday."

The origin of the phrase *in the nick of time* has been a puzzler for centuries. The predominant notion is that scores were kept on a tally-stick by notching (nicking). If a score was made as a game ended, it would still be in time and the tally-stick would accordingly be nicked (notched), since the score was said to be made *in the nick of time.*

NINE-DAY WONDER, A

The shortage of officers at the outbreak of World War I created a serious military problem. To remedy this lack of qualified personnel, the period to train soldiers to become officers was cut to the bone. Trainees were commissioned so rapidly that they were, according to the privates over whom they took charge, *ninety-day wonders* (the training period actually lasted ninety days). Of course, the implication was that these officers had been inadequately prepared.

The soldiers did not invent that expression. They merely resurrected a phrase that had been in use at least since the fourteenth century. Chaucer in 1374 in *Troylus* wrote: "Eh wonder last but nine nyght nevere in towne." It has been said that "in towne" implies that country folk cherish them a bit longer. In 1546, J. Heywood in *Proverbs* said: "This wonder lasted nine daies," and in 1579, Lyly in *Euphues* put it this way: "The greatest wonder lasteth but nine daies." In Shakespeare's *Henry VI* appears an interplay of conversation: "That would be ten days' wonder at the least," to which the reply is, "That's a day longer than a wonder lasts."

In current usage the phrase *nine-day wonder* is used of sensational matters that will, in all likelihood, be forgotten in a short while. Or, as one authority put it, newspaper stories that are kept alive long after their importance has died. This may be likened to an ancient proverb: "A wonder lasts nine days, and then the puppy's eyes are open." The allusion is to puppies and kittens, which are always born blind but which after a number of days open their eyes. And so, figuratively, it is with people who are blindly astonished by news but later forget it. They no longer wonder.

NIP AND TUCK

To begin with *nip*, almost all etymologists believe that its origin is so uncertain that they refuse even to hazard a guess. But one surmise is that *nip* is a clipped version of the Dutch *nipperkin,* a bottle of small capacity that holds about a half pint. (One may rightly wonder how that measure could be called a *nip.*) *Nipperkin* came from *nippertje,* a dram, which, in turn, was derived from *nippen,* to sip, and that is what one does who takes a nip. A sip and a nip are near-equivalents. Of course, *nip* has other meanings unrelated to drinking. For example, it means "to cut," as in "to nip a bud," or "to catch," as in "The pitcher tried to nip the runner off second base."

To get to *nip and tuck.* That expression, meaning "very close" or "closely contested," is another way of saying *neck and neck.* And yet there is a difference. *Nip and tuck* suggests that first one contestant is in the lead and then the other, with their positions being alternately reversed. If the competitors were neck and neck, they would be even with each other, like two horses in a dead heat. The sense of *neck and neck* is clear, but not so of *nip and tuck.* The most plausible theory concerning this assembly of words is that it relates to the sport of dueling. Duelists try to nip or prick each other. *Tuck* is an archaic word for a slender sword, from the Old French *estoc,* a tree trunk.

The query that some word historians might raise is, Did *nip and tuck,* when dueling was a common sport, mean *neck and neck*? Or is that asking to get it in the neck?

NON

The English prefix *non,* meaning "not," comes directly through Old French from the Latin *non,* which also means "not." Many English words are made negative merely by being prefixed with *non*—for example, *nonconformist* and *nonessential.* A *nonconformist* is a dissenter; a *conformist* agreeably follows the rules. That which is *nonessential* is unnecessary; that which is *essential* is vital. However, some words beginning with *non* and possessing a negative sense do not without *non* ipso facto become English words. One is *nonchalant.* A nonchalant person is unconcerned, uninterested, unenthusiastic. A concerned, interested, or enthusiastic person may not be said to be *chalant.* The word *nonchalant* stems through the Old French *nonchalois,* to be careless of, back to the Latin *non* and *calere,* to be warm. A nonchalant person, it may be assumed, feels cool toward a situation or what is being presented. *Nondescript,* meaning "undistinctive," is said of a person not easy to describe. The word is formed from *non* and the Latin *descriptus,* past participle of *discribere,* to describe. This word, if *non* is deleted, would leave *descript,* which also is not an English word. And so with the intransitive verb *nonplus,* confuse, muddle, a combination of Latin *non,* not, and *plus,* more, meaning "no further." No one is ever *plussed.*

NO NEWS IS GOOD NEWS

Quite clearly it is better to have no news than bad news. This adage in a somewhat different form was written as early as 1574 by Edward Hellowes in *Guevara's Chronicle:* "Euil newes neuer come too late." It is believed that in 1616 King James I wrote to Sir George More to persuade the imprisoned Earl of Somerset to confess to a charge of poisoning rather than to stand trial: "Let none living know of this, and if it takes good effect, move him to send in haste for the Commissioners and give them satisfaction; but if he remains obstinate I desire not that ye should trouble me with an answer, if it is no end; and no news is better than evil news."

NO SOAP

The expression *no soap* has for generations been colloquially popular, although its use is less common in recent times. It means "nothing doing" or signifies that a plan has failed. When a kid hollers to his buddy, "Didja get the money?" and the buddy hollers back, "No soap," he didn't get it.

The curious history of this phrase began in 1755 during a bit of byplay between the comic actor and playwright Samuel Foote and the Irish actor Charles Macklin. Macklin boasted that his memory was so keen and so accurate that he could repeat the most complicated passage after hearing it only once. Foote rose to the challenge and immediately improvised the following bit of nonsense: "So she went into the garden to cut a cabbage leaf to make an apple pie, and at the same time a great she-bear came running up the street and popped its head into the shop. 'What! no soap?' So he died, and she—very imprudently—married the barber. And there were present the Jabilillies, the Garyulies, and the Grand Panjandrum himself, with the little round button at top." Macklin reportedly refused the challenge, but born out of this gibberish came the phrase "no soap," which proves that the whole thing was not a washout after all.

NOISOME

> I wiped away the weeds and foam,
> I fetched my sea-born treasures home;
> But the poor, unsightly, noisome things
> Had left their beauty on the shore,
> With the sun and the sand and the wild uproar.
> —Ralph Waldo Emerson, *Each and All*

It is far from unusual for a person when entering, let's say, a discotheque or some other noisy room to say, "What a din. What a *noisome* place." The person would be speaking correctly if the complaint, in addition to the din, was that the place was disgustingly offensive; but the likelihood is against it. Probably by *noisome* was meant that the place was unbearably noisy.

Although *noisome* looks like a derivative of noise, both its meaning and its ancestry are unrelated. *Noisome* emerged from Middle English with the meaning "harmful." It was compounded by the now-obsolete *noy,* annoyance, and the suffix *-some. Noy* was a shortened form of *anoy,* from the Old French *anoi,* vexation. It and the modern *annoy* were rooted together in the Latin *in odio,* in hate, in aversion. Perhaps if the word that evolved, instead of *noisome,* was *annoyance* and had the current meaning of *noisome,* smelly, there would be less misuse and less annoyance.

NUMBERS AND LETTERS

The origins of some numbers and letters are well known. For example, *one* is from the Middle English *on, two* from *two* (no change but formerly *twa*), *three* from *thre,* and so forth. But others, particularly *eleven* and *twelve,* have a more unusual origin. During early times numbers were based on the number *ten*. The Germanic people came up with a number beyond ten (which we call *eleven*) by taking the word *ainaz*, one, and affixing *lif*, to leave. The result was the word *endleofan*, its sense being one left over after counting to ten; namely *eleven*. And so with *twelve*, a combination of *twa* and *lif*—two left over after counting to ten. The teen numbers are from Anglo-Saxon: *thriteen* or *tyneteen*, thirteen; *feower* plus *tyne* (Middle English *fourtene*), fourteen; *fiftyne* (Middle English *fiftene*), fifteen; and so on up the line.

English uses the Roman, or Latin, alphabet (the word *alphabet* comes from the Greek *alphabetos*, a combination of the first two Greek letters—alpha and beta). The letter *w*, which stands for a double *u*, but is really two *v*'s formed into a single character, came from another source. It was an English invention in the seventh century to accommodate that sound, but it was not until the fifteenth century that its first literary record was made. The letter *w* traveled to the Continent, the Engish using the runic *wyn* instead. The Normans, after their conquest in 1066 at Hastings, reinstituted the character *w*, which then became established.

The letter *z* comes from the Greek *zeta*, the sixth letter in the Greek alphabet, its last letter being *omega*, not *zeta*. The Roman alphabet dropped *zeta* because it was felt there was no need for it. With time, however, Latin found use for *zeta*, and so the letter was reinstated, but placed at the end of the alphabet, where it has remained.

O

OCTOPUS

Adopt the character of the twisting octopus, which takes on the appearance of the nearby rock. Now follow in this direction, now turn a different hue.
—Theognis, *Elegies*

Octopus (from the Greek *oktopous*) means "eight-footed." The fact is, however, that this predator has been misnamed, for it has eight arms, not feet. Its name should therefore be changed, especially since figuratively arms are implied when one says that a company invaded a small town and like an octopus grabbed control of almost everything. You grab with your hands, not with your feet. The plural of *octopus* is not *octopi,* a false Latinized plural form, but either the anglicized *octopuses* or the Greek *octopodes.*

ONION

Onions are known for their sweetly pungent taste. Some are so strong that they'll open your sinuses; others are milder. But what they all have in common is that each consists of a single bulb, unlike garlic or the shallot, which have many segments. And this singleness, this unity, gave this vegetable its name. The Romans called it *unio,* from the Latin *unus,* one, but whether the composition of the onion was the reason, no one seems to know. The root sense of *onion* is "things joined into one," a reference to the many layers that are conjoined. In any event, from the Latin *unio,* with a slight phonetic change, has sprouted the English *onion.*

Another theory is that because this vegetable resembled the shape of red pearls, which were in vogue, they called it *unio* for "pearl." As a matter of fact, the name has stuck. Chefs still serve *pearl onions,* but their color is not red; it's silvery-white.

ON ONE'S HIGH HORSE, TO BE

A person *on his high horse* is angry, overbearing, or arrogant. He's putting on airs and acting in a superior way. In times long past, however, literally *to be on a high horse* was a practical advantage—perhaps a matter of life and death. A knight who tilted with an adversary riding a low horse had a definite edge, since a downward thrust was more manageable and more effective. No prudent person would dare say to a haughty knight, "Come off your high horse," for fear of being run through.

ON TENTERHOOKS, TO BE

To be on tenterhooks is to be in a state of painful suspense or anxiety. A person awaiting the outcome of an examination might be said to be on tenterhooks; he is agonizing. This figurative use of tenterhooks is graphic, for if a person were literally on tenterhooks, he would feel the prolonged suffering of torture. The allusion is to the stretching or "tentering" of cloth. A *tenter* is a frame from which protrude hooks or nails on which stretched cloth is hung so that it may dry evenly. It resembles the old-fashioned curtain-stretcher our mothers and grandmothers used. The background of *tenter* can be found in the Latin *tendere,* to stretch. A person on tenterhooks is metaphorically racked up as though on a tenter; he's stretched tight. He is, you can be sure, under a great strain.

Tobias Smollett has been given credit as the first to use the term in print. In his *Adventures of Roderick Random* (1748), he wrote: "I left him upon the tenter-hooks of impatient uncertainty."

ONE SWALLOW DOES NOT MAKE A SUMMER

A man must not swallow more beliefs than he can digest.
—Havelock Ellis, *Impressions and Comments*

It is wise not to make a judgment based on a single experience. Not all troubles are resolved just because one of them has come to a satisfactory ending. The proverbial, and ancient, expression that says all that is *one swallow does not a summer make,* which may have come from an Aesop fable. In that story, a swallow appeared on a warmer-than-expected wintry day. A young man, spotting the swallow, immediately sold his warm coat for drink and carousing. But unfortunately for him, the next day the weather turned as cold as it had usually been at that time of year, and the carouser sadly learned that "one swallow does not make a summer." The proverb may be found in Aristotle's *Nicomachaean Ethicisma* in a slightly different form: *One swallow does not make a spring.* The season has changed, as all seasons do, but the sense remains the same. In more recent times, John Heywood in *Proverbs* (1546) said, "One swallow maketh not a summer." Unquestionably some boozers would argue that one swallow not only does not make a summer, but does not make one happy.

ORANGUTAN

The animal most closely resembling man is the *orangutan,* an anthropoid ape that lives in the forests of Borneo and Sumatra. The name of this manlike ape comes from Malay and consists of *orang,* man, plus *(h)utan,* forest. Quite clearly, the natives thought this ape to be a man of the woods. However, according to Klein the Malay term *orangutan* stands for "wild man" and was used by the natives to designate only savage tribes inhabiting the Sundra Islands. Europeans misunderstood the word and applied it to this anthropoid ape.

The fact is that orangutan and man have much in common, in addition to their general appearance. For one thing, the period of gestation of an orangutan, like that of a human being, is nine months. Also, unlike other species of apes and monkeys, the orangutan has twelve pairs of ribs, just as man has. Like man, this ape lives alone or in pairs. It can walk upright when grasping overhead branches.

Many people call this ape *orangutang*. The added final *g* converts the name (first recorded by Dr. Bontius in the seventeenth century) into a ricochet word, so that the first half rhymes with the second, a not unpleasing sound.

Those who monkey around with this spelling may be interested in knowing that the word *monkey* is of uncertain origin. Some authorities attribute it to *Moneke*, the name of the ape's son in the old folk tale "Reynard the Fox." *Moneke* is a German surname which may have come from the old Italian *monna*, female ape. *Monna* is a corrupt form of *madonna*, my lady, my mistress. Of course, no disparagement is intended.

ORION

Every Boy Scout learns astronomy sufficiently well to identify the constellation *Orion*, the hunter. One star marks his right shoulder and another, a blue star, his left. His belt, outlined by three bright stars, has dangling from it a sword punctuated by three fainter stars. Orion was known for his powerful physique and notable beauty. He fell in love with Merope, the daughter of the King of Chios. When the King refused to give him his daughter's hand in marriage, Orion tried to kidnap her, for which offense the king blinded him. Orion regained his sight by exposing his eyes to the rays of the rising sun.

According to another legend, Apollo was indignant at his sister's affection for this handsome hunter. Apollo challenged his sister, Artemis (the Roman Diana), to test her archery prowess by shooting at a distant point bobbing in the water. Artemis took aim, the arrow hit the mark, but much to Artemis's astonishment, the target turned out to be the head of her lover. Artemis's sorrow at Orion's death was so profound that she converted him into a constellation and placed him in the sky with his belt and sword. *Orion* we can see nightly; the story behind it we can merely imagine.

ORNERY

Some English words are born out of wedlock; that is, they have no progenitors, developing on sloppy semantic pathways until reaching full maturity. These words may surface from misspellings, but more often from mispronunciations. The word *ornery* is a case in point. It had no forebears. It simply was a dialectal pronunciation of *ordinary*, which of course means "common," "normal," "regular," "according to custom." With time, during the nineteenth century, *ornery* became a substitute for *ordinary* in regional areas.

Poor shotes that ye couldn't persuade us to tech,
Not in ornery times, though we're willin' to feed 'em
With a nod now and then, when we happen to need 'em....
—James Russell Lowell, *The Bigelow Papers*

The sense of *ornery* became "contemptuous," as voiced by Huck Finn in Mark Twain's *Huckleberry Finn* (1884): ". . . seeing I was so ignorant, and so low-down and ornery"; but then the word took on a more pejorative meaning: bad temper, uppity, cantankerous, difficult, and downright unpleasant. And this word *ornery*, a corruption of *ordinary*, although an informal term, is still with us and listed in all respected dictionaries. Illegitimate children have a right to a full life, too.

OUNCE

There is no *z* in *ounce*. Yet its symbol is *oz*. Why that? someone might justifiably ask. The answer is obscure, but authorities offer two theories. (No clue, however, can be found through its ancestry. The immediate ancestor of *ounce* is the French *unce;* its ultimate ancestor is the Latin *uncia,* twelfth part.) One theory, advanced by the *Oxford English Dictionary,* is that *oz* was a fifteenth-century abbreviation of the Italian *onza,* ounce. The abbreviation became so widespread that it was accepted into English as a symbol. Other authorities believe that during the Middle Ages many printers used a terminal sign resembling a *z* to symbolize contraction. It particularly was used in words ending in *et*. Hence *videlicet,* Latin for "it is easy to see," was set in type *viz,* the first two letters plus the terminal sign (the modern meaning of *viz* is "namely" or "to wit"). And so with *ounce,* a combination of its initial letter and the sign of terminal contraction. Take your pick.

OVER A BARREL

The interesting thing about this term is that it has, to borrow another cliché, turned turtle. When we speak today of a person being *over a barrel,* we mean that he's helpless because he is in someone's power. We may say, for example, "The finance company has my neighbor over a barrel," meaning if he doesn't square things with it, he will be subjected to a lawsuit and his mortgage may be foreclosed. The expression *to be over a barrel* in current lingo implies clearly that a person is at a serious disadvantage. Raymond Chandler in *The Big Sleep* (1939) wrote: "We keep a file on unidentified bullets nowadays. Someday you might use that gun again. Then you'd be over a barrel." The implication was that if you used that gun, you would be apprehended because the bullet expended would be evidence against you, much to your disadvantage.

According to speculation by the *Oxford English Dictionary,* the expression originated in the practice of trying to revivify a person rescued at sea. By placing him or her over a barrel head down and then rolling the barrel, the person's lungs might be emptied of water. The resuscitation did not work in every instance, but the helplessness of the victim was plain in every instance. And so the thought of helplessness—to be over a barrel—has persisted from the rescue of watery victims to the metaphorical position some of us find ourselves in today.

OXYGEN/NITROGEN

Any beginning chemistry student learns quickly that the air that animals and plants breathe consists primarily of *oxygen* and *nitrogen.* Oxygen was discovered by Carl Wilhelm Scheele of Sweden about 1772, and independently by the English scientist Joseph

Priestly in 1774. It is both the life-saving gas and a chemical element. About eight-ninths of the weight of water consists of oxygen. It supports combustion; without it, fires would not burn. Previously it had been supposed that all combustible substances contained an element called *phlogistos* (from a Greek word meaning "inflammable"), which during combustion was released as flame (*flame* is Greek *phlogos*).

The French chemist Antoine-Laurent Lavoisier, who interpreted the role of oxygen in respiration, named it *oxygen* from the French *oxygene* (Greek *oxus,* acid, plus *genes,* born, a misinterpretation of *genes* to mean "producing"). Lavoisier believed that oxygen was an essential part of all acids. Although mistaken, by the time the error was discovered, the name *oxygen* had been set, and so it has remained.

Nitrogen occupies about four-fifths of the earth's atmosphere. In the early 1770s chemists concluded that air is a mixture of two gases. Scheele named one "fire air," because it supported combustion, and the other "foul air," because it was the residue after the "fire air" was consumed. Clearly the "fire air" was what was later termed *oxygen,* and the "foul air," *nitrogen.* No name for the latter element, however, was generally accepted until 1790. It had been called *azote* by Lavoisier because of its inability to support life (from the Greek *a,* not, and *zote,* life). The French chemist Jean-Antoine-Claude Chaptal, whose experiments established a relationship between the new gas and niter—in fact that it could be used to produce niter—called it *nitrogen,* a coinage now universally adopted.

P

PADDLE YOUR OWN CANOE, TO

A person who is independent and self-reliant is said to be pad-
dling his own canoe. This expressive phrase first appeared in 1802,
according to Ciardi, about the time settlers began their westward
trek. Captain Frederick Marryat used it in 1844 in his *Settlers in
Canada*. The phrase became the title of a sparkling song composed
by Dr. Edward P. Philpots, published in May 1854 by *Harper's
Monthly*. The seven stanzas of the song end with the same refrain.
Here are two:

> Voyager upon life's sea,
> To yourself be true,
> And whate'er your lot may be,
> Paddle your own canoe.
>
> . . .
>
> Leave to heaven, in humble trust,
> All you will to do;
> But if you succeed, you must
> Paddle your own canoe.

The idea that one must succeed on his own was conceptualized
a long, long time ago by Sextus Propertius (54 B.C.–A.D. 2) who,
although using entirely different words, may have been the progen-
itor of *paddle your own canoe*. He said: "Let each man have the
wit to go his own way."

PAJAMAS

A student of word histories may rightly ask, Is it possible, when going to bed, to wear only the pajama tops? The answer is, perhaps sartorially, but not etymologically, despite the Broadway hit *The Pajama Game,* in which the trousers were considered a nuisance. The word *pajama,* meaning a loose Oriental trouser of cotton or silk, came from the Persian *pai,* leg, and *jama,* clothing, and adopted by Britons in the nineteenth century. Originally pajamas were worn just in harems (see *Hue and Cry and Humble Pie,* "petticoats"), but then men decided to wear them, too. Britons had added a matching top during the colder British weather. All this has bastardized the word, since the pajama (pluralized to match other garments—*trousers, breeches, pants*) properly refers only to a leg-garment.

PARASITE

We all know what a *parasite* is, and I'm referring to the social animal. He's a hanger-on. He flatters you for the sake of what you can give him without making any contribution of his own, a human sponge who soaks up whatever he can. The ancestor of *parasite* is the Greek *parasitos,* which meant "eating at another's cost," although literally it meant "one who sits near the food." Dinner guests, usually priests and government officials invited to eat with a wealthy host, were *parasites.* But with time, the abuses of these parasites, taking advantage of their host's hospitality, caused the word to take a downturn, and it acquired the pejorative sense of "one who lives at another's expense," its present-day meaning. With more time, *parasite* acquired a general sense so that the term now applies to any organism that feeds on another and depends on it for its existence. The term is often used in biology, for example, *host parasite.*

The most cogent definition of *parasite* was a remark by Ed Wynn, radio's "perfect fool." He said, "A parasite is the guy who goes through the revolving door on your push."

PARTING SHOT, A

There are many kinds of *shot*. For example, there's a *big shot*, an important person (sometimes self-styled), and *a long shot*, a remote chance. Then *to have a shot at*, to have an inexperienced try at something, possibly *a shot wide of the mark*, completely wrong. We sometimes get *a shot in the arm*, to enliven or give us enthusiasm, which makes us move ahead *like a shot*, rapidly and willingly.

But the shot that is different is the *parting shot*, historically the final shot of the ancient Middle Eastern warriors, the Parthians, who, when in fight, discharged arrows and other missiles at their pursuers and then wheeled out of range. This maneuver gave their enemy, to use another idiom, not even a short shrift. Hence *a parting shot* has come to mean hurling an insult at an adversary or making a final thrust in an argument with no chance for reply. It is the last word or the exit line.

PATTER

In Latin, *paternoster* (*pater* plus *noster*) means, with the sequence of the words reversed, "our father." It is the Latin name for the Lord's Prayer, taken from its first two words: "Our father which art in heaven." From this ancestor has come the English word *patter*, meaning "gibberish chatter," and later "the jargon of magicians or any profession or class" and "the glib talk of pitchmen."

The odd derivative from *paternoster* evolved during the medieval era, when the prayer was required to be recited many times by priests, who, knowing the prayer from memory, would rush pell-mell through it, mechanically mumbling words spilled out atop each other. Clearly the garbled recitation made no sense to them. From this mumbo-jumbo came (from *pater*) the word *patter*, to describe the muttering one would hear at prayer time.

Do not confuse this word *patter* with the one that means "to make a succession of quick, light, soft taps." This latter *patter* is a frequentative of *pat*, to strike gently, reproducing the sound produced by the action, like raindrops against a windowpane.

Longfellow immortalized that *patter* in his *Children's Hour:* "I hear in the chamber above me/The patter of little feet." This patter may be called *pitter-patter.*

PENGUIN

Penguin? What is it? Is it a flightless bird? Is it a publishing house? Or is it both? If you said "both," you're right. Penguin USA is a division of Penguin Books Ltd, Harmondsworth, Middlesex, England.

The *penguin,* the bird that inhabits the Antarctic, appears in formal dress regardless of the time of day. Its name came about in an unusual way. During the seventeenth and eighteenth centuries Breton and Welsh seamen sailing the North Atlantic saw birds with webbed feet and heavy bodies that couldn't fly. The birds fed themselves by diving into the water for their food. The seamen named the birds, in Welsh, *pen gwyn* because they had white heads—*pen,* head, and *gwyn,* white. What the seamen did not know was that the bird they saw was the great auk.

Some time later Sir Francis Drake, while sailing through the Straits of Magellan, noticed flightless birds that resembled the ones seen in the northern latitudes. Hence he dubbed them *penguins.* Drake was so impressed by their appearance that he even named an island in their honor. But one mistake was made. The birds he saw had black heads, not white. The birds incorrectly named by the Breton and Welsh seamen are now an extinct species, the last of the auks having disappeared in the mid-nineteenth century. The birds mistakenly named by Drake are thriving, their black heads proudly topping their tuxedo-like dress.

PHAETON

A *phaeton,* a light open carriage drawn by a pair of horses, is designed to accommodate two persons. It was also the name of the son of Apollo, the sun god.

According to legend, Apollo attempted to prove his paternity of Phaeton by telling his son that any wish he asked would be granted. Phaeton thereupon asked that he be permitted to drive the chariot of the sun for one day. Apollo, knowing how tremendously difficult it was to control the highly spirited steeds who pulled this chariot, tried to dissuade his son from this dangerous venture, but to no avail. Apollo reluctantly yielded. Phaeton, weak and inexperienced, did drive the chariot, but came so close to the earth as almost to set it afire. As it was, he scorched Libya and much of Africa (whose people were blackened). To prevent complete disaster Zeus (Jupiter) hurled a lightning bolt against the charioteer and killed him. Phaeton's sisters, who had yoked the horses to the chariot, were changed into poplar trees and their tears into amber.

The following appears in Shakespeare's *Romeo and Juliet:* ". . . such a waggoner/As Phaeton would whip you to the west,/ And bring in cloudy night immediately."

PICAYUNE

Something trivial, petty, or cheap—that is, a small object of little value—may be called *picayune*. And it may be that word historians have felt that *picayune* was too trivial and unimportant to come up with a definite history of its origin. The best that can be said about it in this regard is that there are hypotheses, that its genesis remains obscure.

The word may have derived from French dialect, which used the word *picaillon* to represent a small copper coin of little value, worth about a farthing. The Spanish *pequeño,* Italian *piccolo,* and French *petit* may be cognates. Another surmise is that the word came from the Latin *pecunia,* wealth, property, but that evolution has not been clarified. Others have pointed to the source as the eating habits of woodpeckers. These birds drill holes in trees to find insects to eat, from which came *picus,* meaning "to pierce." This verb gave way to another—*pica*—which, among many other meanings, meant "to jingle, jangle," as loose coins do in someone's pocket. From the sound of the coins arose the word *picaio,* money. It was a small step to come up from "money" to *picayune,* "small money that jingled," a step taken by the French in Louisiana. The natives there have been so enthralled with the word that in New

Orleans their newspaper is named *The Picayune,* its original sense being "trivial," that is, small talk, gossip.

And so we might say that something not worth a picayune is, to borrow another cliché that bears the same meaning, not worth a rap or a tinker's dam. Or is all this lost in a jingle?

PIG IN A POKE, TO BUY A

> Though he love not to buy the pig in the poke.
> —John Heywood, *Proverbs*

From the countryside has come the bucolic expression *pig in a poke,* which means "to buy something without examination." Generations ago, when county fairs were the region's most exciting social events, so much so that they attracted large numbers of the local gentry, all kinds of tricks were played on unwary visitors to extract their money. One usual ploy was to offer for sale a suckling pig already bagged and ready for delivery. If a rustic accepted the poke without examining its contents, he got nothing for his money—except a mangy cat, which is what the cheat was palming off. The bumpkin, making a purchase sight unseen, was said to be "buying blind." And that is what a *pig in a poke* has come to mean. (A *poke* is a small bag, from the French *poche,* pocket or bag.) Of course, a cautious buyer would have opened the bag to examine the pig, which no doubt would disclose the deception.

This scheming practice has led to a related expression—*to let the cat out of the bag,* meaning "to reveal a secret." A cautious buyer upon opening the bag would do just that, since the cat in all probability would leap out and dart away, which would show up the cheat for what he was. Perhaps, and this has not been attested, the expression *left holding the bag* may also be related to this slick trick, for it would only be the bag that the cheat would have left as the fruit of his scheme.

PIN MONEY

Today when we speak of *pin money,* we don't mean money to be spent on pins, but money to be spent on trivials. That practice, however, was not always so. At one time pin money was given to a wife for the sole purpose of buying pins—and from that custom the compound word *pin money* has continued until this day.

In the fourteenth century pins were invented. The convenience and effectiveness they provided over wooden skewers, which was what had been used to that time, had a tremendous impact on the lives of women, especially since almost all of them spent many hours sewing. The manufacturer of pins, however, was not allowed to sell them whenever he desired. His selling days were restricted. Pins could be sold only on the first and second of January of each year. Hence on those days husbands gave their wives money with which to buy pins, which, quite naturally, came to be called *pin money.*

Small personal allowances (and some not so small) are still referred to as *pin money,* although the chances are that not a cent of those allowances is ever spent on pins.

PIKER

Although everyone knows that a piker is a tightwad, no one knows how that allusion developed. Diverse opinions abound, but no proof. The theory with the greatest following attributes the term to migrants from Pike County, Missouri. When these people, seeking employment, arrived in California, they were so ragged and poverty-stricken that they appeared to be worthless and shifty. They were, so to speak, good for nothing. Another belief is that a *piker* was a tramp who "hit the road," in this case a *pike,* a shortened form of turnpike.

Turnpikes became common after the Norman Conquest. The word *turnpike* is a compounding of the verb *turn* and the noun *pike,* a barrier—hence a pole or pike to halt vehicular traffic until the toll is paid.

One who traveled by foot down a pike was called a *piker.* The theory that a *piker* was a soldier in a regiment commanded by

Z. M. Pike during the War of 1812 has not been given much credence, despite the argument that Pike's soldiers were so poorly armed that they trained with pikes. Through the years, *piker* meant a poor sport, a cheap gambler, or a fourflusher, among other things. But these senses have all given way to one. Today a *piker* is a cheapskate.

PLAIN SAILING

When a person says he's had some problems but that from now on it will be *plain sailing,* it is clear that he means there'll be no further hitches. Nothing will be stopping him; there will be no barriers; and he'll be moving right along. The correct phraseology according to authorities, however, is *plane sailing,* which makes *plain sailing* a corrupted form. The art of determining a ship's position, when considering the world to be flat rather than spherical, is *plane sailing.* This kind of navigation, by a plane chart, is reasonably accurate for short distances. But if you use this expression and spell it right—*plane sailing*—the chances are that most people will think you misspelled it. To sail the semantic sea smoothly, take no chances. Spell it *plain sailing.*

PLAY FAST AND LOOSE, TO

In sports, a player said to be *fast and loose* may be in tip-top shape and playing his best. For example, a baseball pitcher who feels loose and can throw fast is at his peak. But the cliché *to play fast and loose* does not allude to baseball or any other sport except possibly to one played between a man and a woman, a trifling with one's affections. The expression signifies unreliability, inconsistency, loose morals, and generally refers to an unscrupulous character.

An old cheating game, popular in the sixteenth century, or possibly even earlier, was named "fast and loose." It was played at fairs with a belt and a stick. Here's how James O. Halliwell described it in his *Dictionary of Archaic and Provincial Words, Obsolete Phrases, Proverbs and Ancient Customs, from the*

Fourteenth Century (1847): "A cheating game played with a stick and a belt or string, so arranged that a spectator would think he could make the latter fast by placing a stick through its intricate folds, whereas the operator could detach it at once." The fact is that the customer's efforts were directed toward an impossible feat. The term was often used by Shakespeare, including in *Antony and Cleopatra*: "Like a right gipsy, hath, at fast and loose, beguiled me to the very heart of loss." The notion of loose morals, of infidelity, has often been signified by the term. This saying appeared as early as 1547 in *Tottel's Miscellany*: "Of a new married student that plaied fast and loose." William Thackeray in *Love the Widower* (1860) was equally direct: "She had played fast and loose with me."

PLAY POSSUM, TO

To play possum is to pretend ignorance or to feign sleep or illness or to lie low while trouble is brewing. Or it may be said of anyone who in any way dissembles.

The phrase comes directly from the possum's ability to simulate death when approached by a predator. The possum goes limp, closes its eyes, and shows no signs of life. The point behind this ploy is that some predators will not eat an animal they have not killed. It is said that no amount of handling will cause a possum to exhibit signs of life. To make a possum active, it would have to be thrown into water.

The true name of this animal, a small arboreal marsupial, is *opossum,* which derives from the Algonquian term *apasum,* a white animal. The appearance of an opossum can be best summed up in the words of Captain John Smith: "An opossum hath an head like a Swine, and a taile like a rat, and is of the bigness of a cat." *Possum,* from *opossum,* is an example of aphesis, the loss of an unstressed vowel at the beginning of a word, like *squire* from *esquire* and *cute* from *acute.*

PLAY THE SEDULOUS APE, TO

This term (*sedulous* means "diligent in application," "persistently and carefully maintained," "persevering in effort"), often used of writers and artists, indicates an aping of the style of another. The expression may apply to anyone in the creative arts who models his or her works on that of another so faithfully that it may be said to be imitative. Robert Louis Stevenson in his *Memories and Portraits* (1887) coined the phrase. He wrote: "I have played the sedulous ape to Hazlitt, to Lamb, to Wordsworth, to Sir Thomas Browne, to Defoe, to Hawthorne, to Montaigne, to Baudelaire, and to Oberman. That, like it or not, is the way to learn."

POLKA DOT/POLONAISE

One might imagine that the origin of the phrase *polka dot,* a dot repeated to form a pattern, would be clearly documented. After all, everyone knows what a *polka* is and a *dot* stands for. Regardless, how the word developed is a matter of dispute among etymologists.

To start at the beginning, a lively dance, dubbed the *polka,* said to have been invented in Bohemia in 1831 by a servant girl, became popular in Poland and then spread to other countries. Some word sleuths ascribe the origin of the word *polka* to the Czech word *pulka,* a half-step. A *polka* is a pattern of three steps and a skip or hop, which, in a sense, is a half-step. And so this theory makes sense. But others, equally authoritative, maintain that the dance was named after the female partner. In Polish, *polka* means "woman"; "man" is *polak.* This theory too makes sense.

But even if the latter idea is correct, it does not make the *dot* in *polka dot* feminine, although one belief is that polka dots were first woven by Polish women. Another thought advanced, but one not enjoying much support, is that *polka dot* is a re-spelling of *poke a dot.* Still another is that *polka dot* became a common design on dresses, hats, umbrellas, and so forth because of the wide popularity of the polka in the 1800s. As more and more dancers took to the floor in double time, so did more and more garments and accessories appear decorated in dots as a tribute to the popular dance.

Another Polish dance, a stately marchlike dance, the *polonaise* (it also refers to a dress worn by Polish women in the eighteenth and nineteenth centuries, and hence taken to mean "women of Poland"), did not receive the distinction of having dots named after it.

Incidentally, in French, *polanaise* means "Polish," a derivative of *Polonia,* the Latinized name of Poland.

POMPADOUR

A popular hairstyle of the 1940s was the *pompadour,* a fancy coiffure in which the front hair is brushed straight up from the forehead. The originator of this towering mass was Madame de Pompadour, the favorite mistress of King Louis XV of France. This beautiful and radiant court intimate was known not only for her ornate hairstyle but also for her profligate lifestyle.

Privileged by the king to spend unlimited sums of money from the royal treasury, she did just that and soon became a target of intense hatred by the impoverished French people.

Unrepentant and undaunted, Madame Pompadour replied to her critics, *"Après moi, le déluge,"* literally, "After me, the flood." Although this statement has also been attributed to the king, it seemed rather to encapsulate her philosophy of life: live today to the fullest and let tomorrow take care of itself.

During her stewardship of the royal boudoir, Madame de Pompadour received from her benefactor three châteaux and the entire village of Sèvres, where she established the celebrated and highly successful national porcelain factories. It seems that she was as good at this business as she was at her other.

POPLIN

The Pope does not fabricate cloth, yet his name, advanced by one theory, is associated with a ribbed material of lustrous texture called *poplin.* According to the story with a large following, the Roman Church from 1309 to 1377 (some authorities give different dates) had two Popes, one in Rome and one in Avignon, France. The shrewd French merchants took advantage of a Pope's presence in Avignon and advertised a strong, plain-woven fabric, to be used especially for clothing and curtains, as "the Pope's linen" because it was made at papal Avignon. The phrase, slightly fused and the last syllable dropped, became *poplin.*

Others have theorized that the French, because Avignon was the seat of the papacy, called the town *papeline,* a dubious alteration of the Italian *papalina,* papal. (In Italian the word for *pope* is *papa,* and the word for *skullcap,* the kind worn by popes, is *papalina.*) From the French corruption, this belief holds, evolved the name of the fabric made in that town. Still another surmise is that the fabric derived its name from that of a Flemish textile city, Poperinge, which in French became *papeline* and then *popeline.* This last theory has been generally discredited.

PORCUPINE

> And each particular hair to stand on end,
> Like quills upon the fretful porpentine.
> —Shakespeare, *Hamlet*

A *porcupine* is a gnawing animal about thirty inches long with stiff quills on its back. The quills, with their sharp barbs, are raised only when the animal is fearful or excited. One is advised to stay clear of them. A blow from a porcupine can be painful.

The porcupine is a rodent; it is unrelated to the swine family except by name. The Romans thought that this burrowing animal resembled a small pig, and so they named it *porcus,* pig, plus *spina,* thorn—a thorny pig. The French, adopting but altering the name slightly, called it *porc aspin,* spiny pig. Middle English called it *porkepin,* a small step to its present spelling, which, however, had several variations at its inception into modern English. Shakespeare, for example, called it *porpentine.*

Another pig word, *porcelain,* a highly glazed ceramic, is a derivative of *porcus* but is not related to "swine." How so? Portuguese traders got the idea that a cowrie shell was shaped like the back of a pig and that its side contained an opening resembling a female genital organ. The Italians borrowed that idea and gave *porcus* a double meaning—"young pig" and "vulva." The shell itself they called *porcellana,* from *porcella,* a little pig, and from that word came the expensive porcelain dinnerware that graces the banquet tables as well as the dinner tables of Mr. and Mrs. America.

PORTLAND CEMENT

Many people are familiar with the term *Portland cement.* But the question they might raise is: Why Portland? Of one thing they may be sure, the cement (the word *cement* comes from Latin *caementum,* meaning pieces of rough uncut stone) is not made in Portland, Oregon, or in Portland, Maine, or, for that matter, in any city named Portland. In fact, the *Portland* part has no connection with cement at all. The term derives from the Isle of Portland in England, and yet cement was never made there either.

Portland cement was invented in 1824 by a stonemason named Joseph Aspdin, of Leeds, England. He called his product *Portland cement* because it resembled Portland stone, limestone quarried on the Isle of Portland.

For the technically minded, Portland cement is a hydraulic cement made by heating a mixture of limestone and clay, containing oxides of calcium, aluminum, iron, and silicon, in a kiln and pulverizing the resultant clinker.

PRIVATE

Among the definitions of *private* found in dictionaries are "limited to one person" and "not in a public position." Of course, these definitions apply to the adjective *private.* As a noun, *private* refers to a soldier of the lowest rank. Certainly the adjective could not rightly be applied to such a soldier, since a *private* is not holding a position limited to one person and he is, in fact, serving the public. But etymologically a *private* is both deprived of rank and separated from civilian life. The Latin *privo,* from which the word *private* comes, means "to separate or to deprive." Which raises a query: May a private, *separated* from his family, justifiably gripe that he's being *deprived* of life's pleasures?

PRIZE

A *prize* is something given for winning. This meaning of *prize* would indicate that the loser in a prizefight got nothing except a severe headache and a few other pains. That is generally true, except in a professional prizefight. But note that a prizefight through the seventeenth century was with swords, not with fists. In other categories, where a trophy is offered, only the winner walks off with the prize. What is strange about the word *prize* is that literally it means "of price," not something given as an award. The fact is that the word *prize* did not exist before the seventeenth century, at which time it emerged as a doublet of *price*. The immediate ancestor of *price,* the French *pris,* a derivative of the Latin *pretium,* reward, value, price, represented the idea of an equivalent of a thing.

Price had several unrelated meanings, but when the word entered the English language, it contained one sense of *pris*—money paid for something, the cost. Another meaning of *price* was "the victor in a contest." When *prize* was spun off from *price* as an independent word, it came to represent the reward given to a victor, a reward which might be only a trophy. The orthographical change from *price* to *prize* is said to have been influenced by the unrelated French word *prendre,* to take, to seize. This *prize* is something captured in war, especially an enemy's ship and its cargo taken at sea. Today the most common prize is one won by chance—in a lottery.

PSYCHE

Fair Psyche, kneeling at the ethereal throne,
Warmed the fond bosom of unconquered love.
—Darwin, *Economy of Vegetation*

The terms *psychology* and *psychiatry,* respectively, designate the science of the mind and the branch of medicine dealing with the treatment and prevention of mental illness. In each case, the base word is *psych,* from *psyche,* a Greek word meaning "breath" or "life." The English word *psyche* refers to the spirit as distinguished from the body, but it has been extended to include the mind, the sense in which it is now used.

Psyche, in classical mythology, was a beautiful maiden with whom Cupid became enamored. He transported her to a magnificent palace where he spent his nights making love to her, all the while shielding his face, lest she recognize the God of Love. He warned her not to try to find out who he was, but simply to trust him. However, she allowed herself to be swayed by her jealous sisters who, wishing her ill, kept telling her that she might be sleeping with a monster. And so one night, impelled by both curiosity and fear, she secreted a small lamp on her person—and at a propitious moment lit it and beheld the handsomest face she had ever seen. Unfortunately, a drop of oil from her lamp fell upon Cupid's shoulder, awakening him. Cupid upbraided Psyche for her lack of trust and fled. Psyche's lovely palace then disappeared, and she became so desperately saddened that she tried to drown herself. But, fortunately for her, after suffering many hardships and much humiliation in her wanderings, through the beneficence of Cupid—his love for her had not diminished—she was made immortal and united with him forever. And so ends a true love story.

PULL SOMEONE'S LEG, TO

A person who says "Stop pulling my leg" thinks he's being teased, tricked, or fooled humorously. Although the term is well known, its origin is unknown. All the etymologists can do, if they don't want to pull a person's leg, is conjecture.

The most arresting, but possibly apocryphal, story concerning this expression is said to involve public hangings, which during the nineteenth century were great spectacles. Many people so thoroughly enjoyed watching the grisly end of those condemned that they even held "hanging parties." Charles Dickens was a notorious giver of such parties. Hanging as a method of putting to death was cruel and merciless. It did not immediately kill all the victims; some would writhe in agony. As a humane gesture toward these poor souls, their friends and relatives were allowed to pull on their legs to hasten death, and thus end their suffering. Which should give a person a moment of pause before asking someone to stop pulling his leg.

PUNDIT

A *pundit* is not one who writes puns. To the contrary, what he says or writes more likely will be serious, learned, and worthy of critical attention. The word's origin lies in *pandit,* a Hindustani word, which in India means "learned and versed in Sanskrit," but its ultimate core is the Sanskrit *pandita,* meaning "a scholar," one with skill, understanding, and learning. According to Safire, "the term is widely applied to almost any member of the newspaper and radio-television fraternity encompassed in Eisenhower's 'sensation seeking columnists and commentators.' " Today a *pundit,* as we use the term, is not merely a learned person but also an authority. Nevertheless, that person need not know Sanskrit. But some references to a pundit are made with tongue in cheek. They're not meant to be complimentary.

PUT ON THE DOG, TO

The expression *to put on the dog* means "to put on airs" (another cliché), "to make pretensions of grandeur," "to act in a conceited manner," or "to dress flashily." Why a dog was chosen to be the key mover rather than a parrot, a cat, or even a skunk (a skunk wouldn't even need a white tie if it were "putting on the ritz") is hard to say. Or is it that dogs sometimes appear to be showing off? One theory is that the onset of lapdogs after the Civil War— pampered as they were and looking snootily at strangers—gave birth to the expression *putting on the dog.* Another is that it became college slang on the campus of Yale University during the early years of the Civil War. What is known is that in 1871 it was incorporated into a text written by L. H. Bagg, *Four Years at Yale:* "To put on the dog is to make a flashy display." Further known is that the phrase not only permeated American college campuses but also spread into general usage, becoming as common or possibly commoner on the street than on the campus. This homely saying is now here to stay as an established idiom, even by those who don't own a mutt.

PUT THE CART BEFORE THE HORSE, TO

> This methinks is playnely to sett the carte before the horse.
> —Early English Tract Society, *The Babees Book*

The most preposterous word in the English language is *preposterous*. It is a combination of *pre,* before, and *post,* after, which is, as the Germans say, "putting the horse behind the carriage." Its root sense is back and frontward, and that's absurd. But that is what *preposterous* means: "absurd."

This brings us to the proverbial expression *to put the cart before the horse,* a common saying even before Cicero penned it in 61 B.C.: *"Currus bovem trahit praepostere"* ("The plow draws the oxen in reversed position"). Whether one uses the Latin version, with an ox, or the English version, with a horse, the idea is the same: the usual order of things has been reversed. Many languages have borrowed this thought. The French say, *"Mettre la charrette avant les boeufs,"* and the Germans, *"Die Pferde hinter dan Wagen spannen."* Which shows that there can be mix-ups in many languages.

PUT THE KIBOSH ON, TO

To put the kibosh on means "to put an end to," "to squelch," "to dispose of." Dickens in *Seven Dials* spelled it *kye-bosk,* but its sense of "finishing off" something was the same. The word's origin is controversial. Some authorities theorize that it is a Yiddish expression that evolved from the Middle High German *keibe,* meaning "carrion." Others believe that it was founded in the Gallic *cie bas,* which means "cap of death." No matter which viewpoint is accepted, the present sense of *kibosh* is clear and unmistakable, that something has come to a sad end—*carrion,* of course, is dead or decaying flesh and the sense of "cap of death" is self-evident.

PUT UP YOUR DUKES

If one hasn't learned it early in life, he certainly will when he has a grandson. The *it* being referred to is the phrase *put up your dukes.*

Augustus Frederick lived in the early nineteenth century. He became the Duke of York by royal appointment. The Duke's interests were many and varied, but his favorite pastime was pugilism. He was so devoted to the prize ring and counseled so many prizefighters that they named their fists after him—"Dukes of York," which was later abbreviated to *dukes.* Today, one who challenges another to fisticuffs need not be in a ring to be understood when he says, "Put up your dukes."

Phrase sleuths have come up with several other theories concerning the origin of *dukes,* all of which are unrelated and remain what they are, pure conjecture. One notion concerns the habit Cockneys had of rhyming their cant expressions. The phrases need not make sense so long as they rhymed. For example, forks consist of fingers, and so mentioning the word *forks* might lead to "Duke of Yorks." From this, it has been suggested—although it does not logically follow in American minds—came *dukes,* meaning "hands." Another idea that has been advanced is that the troops of the Duke of Wellington, in deference to the magnitude of his nose, called all noses *dukes.* Since primary targets in a free-for-all were noses, *dukes* became associated with the object that struck them, the fist. It became a *duke-buster.* But, with time, simply a *duke.*

PYGMALION

The delightful musical *My Fair Lady,* based on George Bernard Shaw's *Pygmalion,* published in 1912, has made the name *Pygmalion* a somewhat common word. But what should be remembered is that the name *Pygmalion* does not appear in the play and that the play is not the story of Pygmalion. Only by implication do the feelings and accomplishments of Henry Higgins, a professor of speech, and Liza Doolittle, a Cockney flower peddler, resemble that of Pygmalion and the woman he ultimately married.

In Greek mythology Pygmalion, a king of Cyprus, was a misogynist or woman-hater. Although he disliked all women, he carved out of ivory a statue of a woman that was of such unmatched beauty that he fell in love with it. He prayed to Aphrodite, the goddess of love, to infuse it with life. She answered his prayers. Pygmalion married the maiden and by her became the father of a son, which clearly proved that Pygmalion enjoyed caressing warm flesh more than sculpting cool ivory.

PYTHON

A *python* is a large snake that, like the boa, coils around and kills its prey by crushing. Several kinds of pythons make up this genus of reptiles. Originally the word *python* was spelled with a capital *P* because, according to Greek mythology, it was a particularly enormous serpent or dragon. It was hatched from the slime of the earth after the Flood and, when grown, lurked in the caves of Mount Parnassus, spreading terror among the inhabitants. When Apollo, the god of the sun, arrived in Delphi to establish his oracle, he learned about Python, found the monster serpent, and slew it with an arrow from his silver bow. It has been said that this non-venomous snake was named after the state it was in after Apollo killed it—rotting in the sun. The Greek verb meaning "to rot" is the source of the name *python*.

QUARRY

And let me use my sword, I'd make a quarry
With thousands of these quartered slaves. . . .
                    —Shakespeare, *Coriolanus*

The noun *quarry* may refer either to an object of pursuit or to a place from which building stone is obtained. The first *quarry*, the prey of the huntsman, came to mean an animal being pursued by hunter and hounds. With time, *quarry* took on a broadened meaning—any object, perhaps a customer or a female companion. But this was not so centuries ago when *quarry*, from an altered Old French word, *cuirée*, from *cuir*, hide, and ultimately from the Latin *corium*, skin, meant "entrails," and entered Middle English as *querre* (two syllables). The *querre* was that part of a slain animal which, after its flaying, was placed on the animal's hide as a reward for the hounds after the hunt. It was, in simpler language, what the dogs were given to eat. With more time *querre* became *quarry*.

The word *quarry*, the place in which stone is dug out, comes from the Old French *quarriére*, presumably from *quarré*, squared stone, ultimately from Latin *quadrare*, to square. During Roman times, cut stones were squared on the spot. The first record of the use of *quarry* in this sense was in 1420. Certainly neither a hunter hoping to eat his quarry nor a street urchin seeking a square meal is looking for a square stone.

QUARTER

A *quarter* (from the Latin *quartus,* fourth) is the fourth part of anything, but *quarter* (from the Latin *quadrus,* square, its sense being "four-walled") is a district of a town—the native quarters; the Latin Quarter. In this usage the plural *quarters* is commoner. All of this raises a question. How are these words related to such phrases as *to cry quarter,* meaning "to beg for mercy," or *to grant quarter,* meaning "to spare the life of an enemy"? Unfortunately, as to the origin of these idioms, no phrase sleuth has come up with even a single clue. One suggestion was that the expression *to grant quarter* originated with Dutch and Spanish diplomats during the eighteenth century, when they agreed that prisoners could be ransomed for one quarter of their pay. This notion, quite obviously, was mere folk etymology. The pay of a soldier at that time was so meager that it could hardly cover the cost of a bullet. Imagine receiving one fourth of that salary as ransom! The originator of such unconvincing surmises, one might say, deserves no quarter.

QUEEN

> I would not be a queen for all the world.
> —Shakespeare, *Henry VIII*

Traditionally, a *queen* was a female monarch or the wife of a king. But currently more queens are male homosexuals, usually transvestite, passive feminine partners. No matter which queen is meant, the word is homegrown (not American English, of course, but Old English). During those ancient days the word *cwen* meant "queen" as well as "wife or woman." The word *quean,* a word of contempt for a disreputable woman, came from the same root. In Middle English *cwen* became *quen* because, after the Norman Conquest in 1066, French scribes changed all English words that began with *cw* to *qu*; hence *queen* (the extra *e* was added later), *quick, quell, qualm,* and so on.

One more point. *Cwen* is related to *gyne,* Greek for *woman,* which has given us the combining form *gyne,* now used in the word *gynecology,* the study of diseases of women, and *gynecolo-*

gist, a physician specializing in gynecology. Which leads us to the conclusion that a queen is etymologically related to her gynecologist.

QUEER

One may punningly, but with justification, say that *queer* has a queer ancestry. Its traditional meaning—"deviating from the normal or the expected," "strange"—is clear, but where the word *queer* came from is not. Some dictionaries say its origin is unknown, some say it's obscure, and some say it's conjectural. One authority surmises that its ancestor probably lay in the German *quer,* cross, oblique. That which is oblique is not straight, and is away from the norm. Another theory is that its root can be found in the Latin *torquere,* to turn, the follow-up thought being that something turned is twisted and hence not normal. An even less attested conjecture is that *queer* derives from the Latin *quaero,* inquire, a notation made alongside the names of customers with a dubious financial history. Probably more often than its dictionary denotation, *queer* is used as a slang term for "feeling ill at ease," "queasy." It is also used of a transaction or a plan that is upset, a deal that has been *queered.* And in its most abrasive use, it is applied to those who prefer sexual activity with members of their own sex, homosexuals. All this makes it, one might say, a really queer word.

QUEUE

When a group of people are told to queue up, they may not realize that, figuratively speaking, they have been told to form a tail. What they will be doing, of course, is forming a line. This figurative sense, however, is of recent origin. In Middle English a *queue* meant only the tail of a beast. *Queue* came from the Old French *coue,* whose forebear was the Latin *cauda,* tail. It wasn't until the middle of the eighteenth century that *queue* acquired a secondary meaning, "a plait of hair worn hanging down behind," a pigtail. In 1777, W. Dalrymple wrote: "They came not out . . . in the morning till their hair was queued." This sense of *queue* evolved from the resemblance of a braid of hair hanging down the back of the neck to the tail of an animal. In modern times the line of people standing before a box office or waiting for a bus came to be called a *queue* because, like a tail, it too was long and tapering.

Punsters like to ask the question: "What five-letter English word can drop its last four letters without affecting its pronunciation?" The answer, of course, is *queue*. And "What English word has four vowels in a row?" Again the answer is *queue*. For those who wonder about the word *pigtail,* a synonym of *queue,* its earliest metaphorical references were not to a plait of hair, but to a strip of tobacco so twisted that it resembled a pig's tail. The word first appeared in print, and in this sense, in 1688.

QUINSY

Quinsy is a severe inflammation of the tonsils. The word is lineally descended from the Latin *cyanchia* and the Greek *kunanche,* which means "dog strangulation." It was believed that persons afflicted with inflamed tonsils threw their mouths wide open like dogs, especially mad dogs. From *kunanche* came *kuansy,* whence *quinsy.* The term, now rare, was in common use through the nineteenth century as a general term for any sore throat.

RAGAMUFFIN

> I have led ragamuffins where they are peppered.
> —Shakespeare, *Henry IV, Part I*

A *ragamuffin* is a ragged, disreputable fellow or a ragged child. The ragged part in *ragamuffin* is easy to understand. But why *muffin*? Unfortunately, no one has been able to answer that question. Brewer says a *ragamuffin* is "a regular muff," a sorry creature in rags. The word *muff*, of uncertain origin, refers, according to Klein, to a clumsy fellow. Today we speak of a bungler as one who has muffed the ball. A theory with some acceptance is that *ragamuffin* comes from the French *Ragamoffyn*, the name of a demon in old mystery plays, which first appeared in 1393 in Langland's *Piers Plowman*. There the demon was described as being dressed in rags, a common description during medieval times. From that usage came the sense "shaggy" and "unkempt." Everyone agrees that ragamuffin's second element is unrelated to the word *muffin*, a small, round cake. Until satisfactory evidence is unearthed, we who use the word *ragamuffin* must do so ignorant of its source.

RAINBOW

A colorful English word, from Old English *renboga*, which first appeared in print in 1000, is *rainbow*, a solar reflection that exhibits the colors of the spectrum in concentric bands. A sister word, one associated with rainbows, is *iridescence*, a play of colors producing rainbow effects. The root of this English word can be traced to Greek mythology, in which the messenger of the gods, Iris, appeared in the form of a rainbow. When she needed to convey a message from a god in heaven to a mortal on earth, she took a convenient stairway down—a rainbow. It must have been particularly pleasing for her to descend on a rainbow, for her name was derived from the Greek word for "rainbow"—*Iris.* In 1634 T. Johnson in his book on surgery, when referring to an ulcer, used both *Iris* and *rainbow:* "about the circle of the Iris or rainbow." Today the best-known use of the word *iris* is of the colored portion of the eye (a term originated by Benjamin Winslow, a Dane, in 1721). It also is a herbaceous plant with sword-shaped leaves and large showy flowers, which in French is *fleur-de-lis,* or lily-flower. One more, and not to be forgotten: *Iris* is a pretty female name. The combining form *irid* is used in other words—*iridescence,* previously mentioned, and *iridium,* a metallic element of the platinum group that, when combined with other elements, forms a substance of various colors.

RAINING CATS AND DOGS, IT'S

> What woulds't thou have of me?
> Good king of cats, nothing but one of nine lives.
> —Shakespeare, *Romeo and Juliet*

Many expressions center on the word *cat.* For example, a *cat-o'-nine-tails,* which possibly got its name because a cat is thought to have nine lives. There have been other guesses. A *cathouse* is a cheap brothel. The term is of uncertain origin, but it may have come from an old word for prostitute—*cat*—or from the sexual behavior attributed to cats.

Tennessee Williams's celebrated play *Cat on a Hot Tin Roof* has popularized that phrase with recent generations. But its history goes back at least to the beginning of the century. Its implication, that a cat on a hot tin roof would surely be nervous and jumpy, has given rise to its figurative sense of ill at ease, a feeling of not being "at home" in the situation.

But the most common expression is one made during a thunderstorm: *it's raining cats and dogs.* Of the many conjectures that have been advanced concerning the origin of this phrase, the one that makes the most sense is that in times past the gutters, after a cloudburst, would overflow not only with filth and debris but also with dead cats and dogs. Something about the phrase must have struck a responsive chord, since it is still widely used, even though it is not now customary to see dead cats and dogs floating in the rivulets emptying into sewers.

RANKLE

To *rankle,* everyone will agree, is to inflame with anger. The dictionary definition given *rankle* is "to cause continued irritation, anger, or bitterness."

Uncovering the parentage of this word requires such patience and ingenuity as to make the search seem almost impossible. In Greek, *drakon* means "snake"—a large crawling thing with piercing, terrifying eyes. The Romans called their serpents or dragons by a similar word, *draco.* From its diminutive form, *dracunculus,* came the meaning "a festering sore," since (farfetched as it seems) these ulcers were thought to resemble small serpents and to burn like a snake bite.

Through a series of sound and orthographic changes, *dracunculus* landed in English as *rankle* (not too dissimilar from the Latin if the *d* is dropped). Today when someone feels offended or rankled, he feels as though he is suffering from the bite of a dragon or the burning sensation of an ulcer.

RAP

If one says it's not worth a tinker's dam or it's not worth a rap, he means the object is valueless or the idea is useless. The question that therefore arises is, What is a *rap?* The logical answer that comes quickly to mind is a rap of the knuckles or a sharp knock on a table or a desk, since such a rap is certainly nonproductive and worthless. But phrase historians think otherwise. For one thing, a small copper coin minted during the reign of George I (1714–1727) and widely used in Ireland was called a *rap* (the source of its name is unknown). This coin had little value, about half a farthing. However, it often passed as a bogus halfpenny owing to the scarcity of genuine money. In 1724, Jonathan Swift mentioned this practice in *Drapier's Letters* when he wrote: "Copper halfpence or farthings have been for some time very scarce, and many counterfeits passed about under the name of raps."

Another possible source for the word *rap,* but also unestablished, is the German *rappe,* a counterfeit penny circulated in the fourteenth century on the Continent and said to have been brought to the British Isles by Irish freebooters. The supposition that *rap* was an acronym from the first letters of *rupee, annas, pice,* the Indian money units, has no historical evidence to support it. All this might lead to the conclusion that the ancestry of *rap* is unverifiable, possibly because etymologists felt that to learn its origin, as the saying goes, wasn't worth a rap.

RED HERRING

Many common expressions contain the word *red—to be caught red-handed,* meaning in the very act; *won't give up even a red cent,* meaning not to expect any contributions; *to see red,* to become enraged like a bull.

Another "red expression," centuries old yet very much alive, is *dragging* (or *drawing*) *a red herring across the trail.* This saying originated among hunters who would drag a red herring across a fox's trail as a means of misleading hounds while they were being trained. The smell of a herring would destroy the fox's scent. In sportsmen's jargon, this practice was known as "setting the hounds at fault." Incidentally, the herring was red because it was salted and smoked, a process which gave the herring that color.

The figurative use of the expression today implies evading an issue or diverting someone's attention by raising a side issue or dragging in something irrelevant. We now use a shortened form— *let's not have* (or *do not give us*) *a red herring* or simply *that's a red herring.*

REST ON ONE'S LAURELS, TO

> And the myrtle and ivy of sweet two and twenty
> Are worth all your laurels, though ever so plenty.
> —Lord Byron, *Stanzas Written*
> *on the Road Between Florence and Pisa*

To rest on one's laurels is to be satisfied with one's position or success, to be content to relax in the knowledge of past achievements, and to find no need to strive for further glory. Laurels, during ancient days, were wreaths of leaves and twigs used as a mark of honor to crown heroes, poets, great athletes, leading statesmen, and other distinguished members of the community. The laurels were sometimes made of evergreens to symbolize everlasting fame.

The term *laurel* has, in addition to *to rest on one's laurels,* generated other common expressions. One is *to look to one's laurels,* a warning to be alert to encroachment of one's position by competitors and not to underestimate rivals. Another is *to win laurels,* to win honors and acquire glory. The term *laureate* is probably today's most universal reminder of the ancient custom involving laurels. The honorific *poet laureate* (*laureate* meaning "worthy of laurels for one's achievements," from the Latin *laureatus,* crowned with laurels) was first bestowed on John Dryden in the seventeenth century. The Nobel Prize has made the term *laureate* a household name. The recipient of a Nobel Prize is now known as a *Nobel laureate,* an honored person.

According to Greek mythology, the beauty of Daphne, a daughter of the river god, so charmed Apollo that he pursued her avidly but fruitlessly, because just as he was about to overtake her, she prayed for aid and immediately turned into a laurel tree. Apollo loved the *laurel* ever after. But how that satisfied all his cravings we'll never know.

RIGMAROLE

> In that manner vulgarly,
> but significantly, called rigmarole.

Rigmarole refers to disjointed, confused talk, speech that is rambling, foolish, nonsensical, or, in the words of Maury Maverick, long-winded gobbledygook. But that current usage bears no connection to the history of the word. In fact, the essence of *rigmarole,* when it emerged as an English word, was not talk but documents.

In 1296, Edward I invaded Scotland to extract oaths of allegiance from the Scottish noblemen. Since they were in no position to refuse his demands, they presented him with individual deeds of fealty called *ragman roll* (*ragman* is a word of uncertain origin). The documents were numerous, and the list of names exceedingly long. Eventually the *ragman roll* was consolidated into one document that measured forty feet. To quell any resistance, the King sent messengers throughout Scotland to read to the populace from the *Ragman Roll.* Since the couriers read too quickly to allow these ordinary people to understand what they heard, the name *Ragman Roll* became slurred into *rigmarole,* and acquired the sense of incoherent speech or jumble of words which is the word and meaning that have survived to this day. *Rigmarole* has also come to be spelled *rigamarole,* which, in the opinion of some people, makes for easier pronunciation and a pleasanter sound.

RIOT ACT, TO READ THE

If an employee tells a fellow employee, "The boss is mad; he's going *to read the riot act,*" the words are not to be taken literally, but the message is clear. The employees are going to be bawled out, reprimanded.

This idiom, *to read the riot act,* originated in 1714 when a riot act was enacted during the reign of George I, an unpopular, domineering German (the first of the Hanoverian line) who despised the English language and refused to learn it. To protest the King's insensitive indifference to the English language, some people gathered and a few got out of hand. Riot acts, designed to prevent riotous gatherings, had existed prior to the one enacted in 1714, but that one was the first comprehensive law. Its provisions specifically described the acts prohibited and the penalties that could be imposed. To disperse an unruly crowd of twelve or more persons, a competent authority would read the following from the act: "Our sovereign Lord the King chargeth and commandeth all persons being assembled immediately to disperse themselves, and peacefully to depart to their habitations or to their lawful business, upon the pains contained in the Act made in the first year of King George for preventing tumultuous and riotous assemblies. God save the King." If during the hour following the reading of this proclamation the crowd had not disbanded, those remaining could be arrested and found guilty of a felony, and jailed for not less than three years.

The effect of this act was so telling that from it the expression *to read the riot act* caught on and has stayed, with its less drastic current meaning of "to warn" or, at the least, "to scold vigorously."

ROOK

A person who has been *rooked* has been cheated, duped. It is as though he had been attacked by a bird of prey, for, in one sense, he has been gouged out of his lawful property.

There is a semantic analogy between a bird of prey and a cheat. The black crows that plagued the American colonists, feeding on other birds, farmers' seeds, and tender shoots, shrieked as they descended for their prey. Writers who have tried to characterize these harsh sounds came up with the word *hroc* (with a long *o*, supposedly imitative of the birds' noisy cries). In Middle English *hroc*, with the *h* silenced, became *rok* and eventually *rook*. In time these thieving birds lent their name to human beings who defrauded others; that is, *to rook* a victim.

ROUÉ

A *roué* is a debauchee, a profligate. The word's ancestor was the Latin *rota*, which means "a wheel." Its original sense, there fore, had no connection with dissoluteness. The French converted the Latin noun into a verb, *rouer,* meaning "to break on the wheel," referring to an instrument of torture designed to extract confessions from criminals.

About 1720 the Duc d'Orleans (after whom the city of New Orleans was named) was appointed Regent of France to serve until Louis XV attained his majority. The Duc was a reprobate and his companions were equally dissolute. They were so wanton that they deserved, he jestingly insisted, to be broken on the wheel. He therefore called them *roués,* a name they proudly assumed as a badge of loyalty—such devotion as to be willing to be tortured on the wheel. Today we would say that their badge should have read "worthless."

ROUND ROBIN

A *round robin* was a petition or a protest with the signatures written in a circle so as to disguise the order in which the subscribers signed. Since it was impossible to tell who signed first, no one appeared as the ringleader. This device saved many a seaman from being thrown into the brig and many a courtier from being beheaded. The practice during the seventeenth and eighteenth century was to punish severely a man whose name appeared on a petition as the originator of a protest. But with a round robin, to mete out a punishment, the ship's captain would have to punish the entire crew and the king would have to execute all his courtiers because the instigator could not be known.

Robin (in *round robin*) does not refer to a bird but to the French word *rond,* round, which makes *round robin* redundant—a combination of English *round* and French *rond,* or "round round." The original full expression was *rond ruban,* meaning "round ribbon," because the signatures were written on a ribbon placed in a circle on the petition or protest. It doesn't take too much imagination to see that the French *rond ruban,* when slurred, became English *round robin.*

RUBÁIYÁT

Many American students are familiar with the work called the *Rubáiyát of Omar Khayyám*. They probably know that Omar, who lived during the eleventh century, was a Persian epigrammatist, but they may not know that he also was a famous philosopher and mathematician. His work on algebra was known throughout Europe in the Middle Ages, and his research in astronomy helped reform the Persian calendar.

Although Omar wrote few verses that can be definitely attributed to him, those proven to be his poignantly reflect admiration for a gentle nature and the pleasure of love. His work was brought to the attention of the West by the classic translation of Edward FitzGerald, published in 1859.

Omar was the son of Khayyám, a name that in Persian meant "tentmaker," which probably was the occupation of Omar's father. What in all likelihood is less known is the meaning of *Rubáiyát,* a word of Arabic origin. It means "something made of four parts." The word's singular form is *rubai,* a collection of four-line stanzas, or quatrains.

These pearls of thought in Persian gulfs were bred,
Each softly lucent as a rounded moon;
The diver Omar plucked them from their bed,
FitzGerald strung them on an English thread.
—James Russell Lowell,
In a Copy of Omar Khayyám

RULE OF THUMB

The idiom *rule of thumb* has come to signify any rough guess or measurement based on practice rather than scientific measurement or an exact formula. An opinion or an estimate made by rule of thumb is founded solely on one's experience. The expression, it is believed, became general from the habit of clothiers and carpenters of measuring with the lower part of the thumb (that part of an adult's thumb measures approximately one inch). Another use of the thumb as a measuring device was common among brewers.

They didn't measure length, however; they measured temperature. During the days when sanitary requirements were not so demanding as those of today, brewmasters customarily tested the temperature of the beer by thrusting a thumb into the vat. The beer so tested was called *thumb brewed*. Of the two theories of the origin of *rule of thumb*, a jury of word historians would probably favor the former, thus proving that it's hard to beat experience. As to the second, unlike the thrust of the brewmaster's thumb into the vat to see that all is fine, jurors turn their thumbs down to say the very opposite. The thumb, incidentally, at one time could save a life or be a symbol for death. The life of vanquished Roman gladiators depended on the vote of the spectators by thumb. If they wished the gladiator to be slain, they turned out their thumbs, *verso pollice*; if to live, they turned their thumbs out but within their fists.

RUMINATE

> He chew'd
> The thrice-turn'd cud of wrath, and cook'd his spleen.
> —Alfred, Lord Tennyson, *The Princess*

To think that a person who ruminates at length and a cow chewing a cud have something in common. A cow's stomach is divided into four separate chambers. The cow does not thoroughly chew the food being eaten, but passes it along to a section known as the paunch. Later, at the cow's leisure, the food is regurgitated, chewed up, and reswallowed. The returned food, the bolus, is the cud, the thing we always talk about as being chewed by a cow. What the cow is doing, as is the man pondering, is ruminating. To *ruminate* means both "to chew the cud" and "to meditate." The word derives from the Latin *rumino,* from *rumen,* throat, gullet. The wit who applied the word *ruminate* to a person who is meditating believed that bringing to the mind ideas being worked on was similar to a cow's bringing up food from its stomach and chewing it all over again. They both were ruminating.

Incidentally, many animals are ruminants; that is, they have three or more cavities in the stomach and chew the cud. Among them are antelopes, camels, deer, giraffes, goats, and sheep.

SACKCLOTH AND ASHES, TO BE IN

One experiencing penitence and contrition, or simply being distraught over something he or she has done, may be said *to be wearing sackcloth and ashes.* This term is an allusion to the ancient Hebrew custom of donning sackcloth covered with ashes to express humbleness before God when attending certain religious ceremonies. *Sackcloth* is a coarse, dark haircloth from which sacks are made. The Bible contains this passage:

> And I set my face unto the Lord God,
> to seek by prayer and supplication,
> with fasting, and sackcloth, and ashes...."
> —Daniel 9:3

SAGA/SAGACIOUS

> What this country needs is a good five cent *saga.*
> —Groucho Marx, paraphrasing the punchy statement
> made by Vice-President Thomas R. Marshall

Although the word *saga* can be clearly seen in the word *sagacious,* the words are unrelated. *Saga* is a Scandinavian term meaning "tale." *Sagacious,* meaning "wise," comes from the Latin *sagire,* to perceive keenly or quickly.

Originally a *saga* was a medieval Icelandic prose narrative recounting the traditional history of kings or other important people. It then came to embody the story of heroic deeds and legendary events, and later, as in Galsworthy's *Forsyte Saga*, a detailed account of a family's life. In loose usage *saga* has many synonyms—*tale, story, epic.*

The noun form of *sagacious,* which is *sagacity,* refers to qualities of keen perception. Many years ago this keenness referred only to animals that exhibited particular success in catching their prey. This, of course, is no longer so. *Sagacity* now pertains to human shrewdness and sound judgment in the affairs of man.

A *sagacious* person may be regarded as a *sage,* but the origin of these italicized words can be found in different ancestors. The English word *sage,* "a very wise man," comes from the Latin *sapere,* to be wise, and was absorbed into Old French as *sage,* the same form used in English. The Latin ancestor of *sagacious* was mentioned in the first paragraph.

SALAD/SAUCE

> Salt seasons all things.
> —John Florio, *Second Frutes*

We all know that salt, sodium chloride, a white crystalline substance, is used in almost every meal. (The word *salt* comes from Latin *sal.*) What is less well known is that from the Latin adjective *salsa,* "things preserved in salt," came the common dish called *salad.* And so did the word *sauce.* Further, the dish that holds the sauce (the Latin *salsarium*) became, via the French *saucière,* the English word *saucer,* which holds a cup more often than a sauce.

Salt is usually applied through a *saltcellar,* a container for salt, which in Middle English was spelled *salte-saler. Salte* means "salt." The second element, *saler,* from the Old French *salier,* means "salt box," which makes the word *saltcellar* tautological, since the word *salt* appears twice. The *cellar* part of the English word has no reference to a room built below ground. It is simply an alteration of *saler.*

SARDONIC

The word *sardonic,* which conjures up a picture of a habitual doubter, means "bitter, cynical, scornful." Its genesis can be found in a poisonous plant called *sardonia,* a growth native to Sardinia. The acrid plant was reputed to be so very bitter as to cause convulsions that distort the face of one who eats it and to make that person seem to be grinning. But actually his twisted face reflected the throes of death. The poor souls, it might be said, died laughing.

SCHIZOPHRENIA

The so-called split personality has been popularized in cinematic portrayals as a weird, though a not too unusual, condition. A person suffering from *schizophrenia* (New Latin, "split mind," from the Greek *schizein,* to split, plus *phrenia,* mind) in the popular belief alternates between personalities. But this is not so. A person suffering from dissociated states may have multiple personalities.

The strange condition involving a dual personality—one usually completely good and the other usually completely bad, there being no gray area—was dramatically brought to the public's attention in Robert Louis Stevenson's famous story *The Strange Case of Dr. Jekyll and Mr. Hyde,* published in 1886. Dr. Jekyll, a respected physician, discovers a drug that can change a placid, beneficent person into an odious, depraved creature. The good doctor experiments on himself, drinks the potion, and becomes a vicious brute. Calling himself Mr. Hyde, he commits various crimes and, eventually, a murder. With time, the effect of the drug becomes so potent that Dr. Jekyll can no longer restore himself to the person he once was. He is trapped in the Hyde personality. In desperation he takes the only solution open to him: he commits suicide. Fortunately, most people having multiple personalities are not governed by such excessively bizarre behavior.

SCRATCH ONE'S BACK

A *scratch,* a light cut, is not painful but is nonetheless unwelcome. The itching of one's back, however, is so annoying that a person most likely will scratch it or rub his back against a wall to relieve the itchy feeling. This need to be soothed by back-scratching has entered the political arena as a phrase to describe the actions of two politicos who have agreed to help each other—"You vote for my bill and I'll vote for yours," which in idiomatic language is, "I'll scratch your back if you'll scratch mine." The idiom has passed from the field of politics to almost anything else where the reciprocation is based on selfish interests—"I'll speak well of you if you don't criticize me" becomes "I'll scratch your back if you'll scratch mine."

SCRATCH, TO START FROM

A person who is unexpectedly scratched may start from the surprise or the pain, or both. But the expression *to start from scratch* is not related to any form of skin-cutting. It came from a cutting on the ground that marked the starting point for runners in a race. The runners were said to *start from scratch,* the usual starting point. Handicapped competitors were given an advantage. They did not "start from scratch," the scratched line, but were placed ahead of it. In current usage the idiom, which may refer to almost any beginning, has retained its original sense of starting with no advantage, without having a head start over others.

SEPARATE THE WHEAT FROM THE CHAFF, TO

This saying has been proverbial for distinguishing the good from the bad, the wanted from the unwanted, the superior from the inferior, the valuable from the worthless. The term emerged from the age-old farming practice of winnowing, exposing wheat to the wind so that the chaff would blow away, leaving the grains. A record made in 1729 by Peter Walkden in his diary read: "Winnowed my wheat the chaff out of it." The idea was metaphorically expressed by John the Baptist of the one "that cometh after me" (Matthew 3:12): "Whose fan in his hand and he will thoroughly purge his floor, and gather his wheat into the garner; but he will burn up the chaff with unquenchable fire." The term is unquenchable, too, for it is alive today, even in urban areas where the agricultural practice of winnowing is unknown. G. B. McCutcheon expressed the thought succinctly in *Anderson Crow* (1920): "They separated the wheat from the chaff."

SERENDIPITY

One who goes to Sri Lanka in search of *serendipity* goes to the right place. Sri Lanka was formerly called Ceylon, and before that—long before that—Serendip.

Serendipity is a nonce word coined by the British author Horace Walpole to mean "the making of discoveries that one is not seeking." He claimed that he had based the word on the title of a Persian fairy story, "The Three Princes of Serendip," whose heroes, according to a letter he wrote on January 28, 1754, "were always making discoveries, by accident or sagacity, of things they were not in quest of." The classic example, from the Bible, is the story of Saul, "who set out to find his father's asses but instead found a kingdom." That's serendipity one can't beat.

SESQUIPEDALIAN

A word of many syllables may be termed *sesquipedalian,* a combination of the Latin *sesqui,* half, plus *ped,* foot, and the suffix *ian,* which makes the word mean "a foot and a half long." Of course, the word is not so long as all that, but it is longer than what we're accustomed to using. Holt points to Winston Churchill's famous remark, "a terminological inexactitude," as a sesquipedalian substitute for "inaccurate charge," used in reference to the word *slavery* as applied to Chinese labor in South Africa. The word's forebear can be pinpointed because it first appeared, dressed in its Latin form, in *Ars Poetica,* "The Poetic Art," published just before the death, in 8 B.C., of the man who coined that long-living, yard-long term, which he used to mean "great, stout, and lofty words," the Roman poet Horace.

SET ONE'S CAP FOR, TO

Women of today seldom wear hats or caps. Perhaps they don't know what they're missing—a hat might attract a beau. At least, that was the belief during Victorian days, when the wearing of caps indoors (usually of muslin) was de rigueur. (Remember Whistler's mother?) But younger women wore fancier ones, placed at a fetching angle, to gain the attention of a man. A lady expecting to see a gentleman who has set her heart aflutter would don her prettiest cap. She was said to be *setting her cap at him.* Goldsmith, in 1773, in *She Stoops to Conquer,* used the idiom this way: "Instead of breaking my heart at his indifference, I'll . . . set my cap to some newer fashion, and look for some less difficult admirer." In 1832, Byron said: "Some, who once set their caps at cautious dukes." Today a man takes his hat off to a woman who may figuratively set her cap for him.

SEVENTH HEAVEN, TO BE IN

To be in *seventh heaven* is to be blissful, perhaps ecstatically so, for, according to one theory, the seventh ring of stars is the highest, the farthest away from Earth, and must, this reasoning holds, surely be God's abode.

The Muslim belief is not far different but more detailed. According to that account, man goes through seven stages, or heavens, in his ascent to God. The seventh—the highest—is where rapture is a daily portion. "Each of its inhabitants," it is said, "is bigger than the whole Earth. Furthermore, each person acquires 70,000 heads with as many mouths and tongues, and each tongue speaks 70,000 languages—all forever chanting the praises of Allah."

Today we speak of *seventh heaven* as a state of ecstasy, without religious significance, as in Sir Walter Scott's *St. Ronan's Well* (1824): "He looked upon himself as approaching to the seventh heaven." And so with a crapshooter who keeps throwing sevens. He's enraptured—and enriched, too. If he keeps throwing them one after another, he's likely to be in seventh heaven.

SHORT SHRIFT, TO GIVE

In earlier times prisoners to be executed for the crime of murder or assassination were denied the last rites of the Roman Church. But others condemned to death—for example, military captives—were shown a semblance of consideration. They were permitted a visit by a priest to hear confession and grant absolution. However, the time allowed the prisoner was brief, just a few minutes; those about to be executed apparently did not deserve much priestly attention. Since the sacramental confession had to be short, it came to be called *a short shrift* (*shrift* is from the Anglo-Saxon *scrifan*, to shrive, to absolve a penitent). In modern English the phrase *short shrift* has no religious significance. It is used to mean to give little or no time or consideration to a person or to summarily dismiss something unpleasant. In all its senses, *short shrift* is to give quick and unconcerned treatment of a person or proposal.

In Shakespeare's *Richard III,* the Duke of Gloucester (later to become Richard III) has ordered the beheading of Lord Hastings. Sir Richard Radcliff, assigned to see that the execution was done, says to Hastings, who is bemoaning his fate: "Come, come, dispatch; the duke would be at dinner:/Make a short shrift; he longs to see your head."

SHOT HIS BOLT

Long as a mast and uprighte as a bolt.
—Chaucer, "The Miller's Tale"

The *bolt* in this phrase is an arrow with a heavy head, a bullet-like knob, and not the bolt on a door. And since arrows are shot from bows, the expression *shot his bolt* logically follows. The figurative sense, which has made the phrase a popular one, is that anyone who has tried and done whatever he could, but to no avail, has expended all his resources and has therefore shot his bolt.

The word *bolt* has given birth to other *bolt* phrases, *bolt upright* for one. A person sitting bolt upright is sitting as straight as an arrow. A *bolt of cloth* is so called because of its straight, long narrow shape. The idea of speed is inherent in the flight of an arrow, and so *to bolt* is to move quickly. A person who bolts for the door walks straight to it as fast as possible.

SHREWD

In today's usage the word *shrewd* has a "smart" connotation: calculating, cunning, sharp. A shrewd person is admired as being ingenious, possibly astute, but these senses are of comparatively recent times. Although the etymological origin of *shrewd* has never been fully established, it is believed that its remote progenitor was a mouselike animal called a *shrew,* in Old English *screawa.* This animal was reputedly the meanest mammal in animaldom. It was said to have the power of harming cattle while scurrying over their backs and was even fabled to have a venomous bite. It would fight another animal to the death over a scrap of food, and when victorious would eat the victim to boot. From these beliefs in Middle English emerged the word *shrewede,* accursed, depressed, hence malicious; and so *shrew,* a vile-tempered, scolding woman, which was popularized in Shakespeare's *Taming of the Shrew.* A shrew was said *to shrew,* that is, to curse, to beshrew. From its past participle, *schrewen,* was formed the adjective *shrewd* with its weaker sense of malicious cunning. And, as though going from the ridiculous to the sublime—one extreme to another—*shrewd,* as previously mentioned, is no longer a word of perjoration but of grudging admiration. We feel complimented when told by our wife, after dealing with the car salesman, that we were *shrewd.*

SKELETON

Greek has been our most prolific source of medical names. One common term is *skeleton,* which refers, of course, to the bony structure supporting an animal body. The word *skeleton* in this sense was brought into the English language in 1578 by a London surgeon, John Banister, during the reign of Queen Elizabeth I. Since English law prohibited the dissection of human bodies, many physicians had no intimate knowledge of a body's framework and had to depend for their information on European sources. Banister published a book on anatomy—*History of Man*—which primarily contained material he had acquired from the works of other anatomists. But what to call this bony framework was a matter to be decided. Banister recalled that in Greek the word for "mummy" was *skeletos,* which literally means "all dried up," as all mummies were. The term seemed appropriate, but he made a slight variation in spelling—*skeleton*—a spelling that had occasionally appeared in foreign texts.

This all means that someday we will all become mummies, even the poppies.

SKELETON AT THE FEAST

He was the general skeleton at all banquets.
—Vizetelly, *Glances Back*

An Egyptian practice, according to Plutarch in his *Moralia,* "Dinner of the Seven Wise Men," was to place a skeleton in a prominent seat at the banquet table to remind the merrymaking guests that all men are mortal and that a person had better mend his ways while he still had a chance. Or, in a less morbid sense, pleasures are theirs but so are responsibilities. Of course, a skeleton as a dinner companion (or as now more commonly put, *a skeleton at the feast*) is bound to create a somber atmosphere and depress everyone's spirits. However, some feasters might react otherwise to this symbol of death, and instead become galvanized into enjoying all kinds of merriment—carousing, singing, dancing, lovemaking—adopting the ancient proverb, "Eat, drink, and be merry, for tomorrow ye die."

Despite this centuries-old Egyptian custom, the saying *a skeleton at the feast* did not enter English literature until the mid-nineteenth century. Longfellow set the phrase in cement in his "The Old Clock on the Stairs":

> The stranger feasted at the board;
> But like the skeleton at the feast,
> That warning timepiece never ceased—
> Forever—Never
> Never—Forever!

The metaphor when used today implies that someone's presence dampens the spirit and gaiety of others.

SKELETON IN THE CLOSET, A

It is said that almost every family has a hidden worry or a shameful secret that at any cost must be concealed from the public. The expression that represents this predicament is a *skeleton in the closet,* which was brought into literary use by William Makepeace Thackeray in 1845 through *Punch in the East:* "There is a skeleton in every house."

Who gave birth to this cadaverous saying has never been established, but surmises abound. One is an allusion to a closet in Bluebeard's Castle, where Bluebeard kept his murdered wives. Another tells of a woman found by the town fathers to be completely carefree and trouble-free. They had been searching for such a person. Happily, they presented an award to her at her house, whereupon she led the committee to an upstairs closet which she opened, revealing a human skeleton. She then explained that her husband compelled her to kiss the skeleton, the remains of her husband's rival, killed in a duel. Still another is that since dissection was prohibited by law in England until the passage of the Anatomy Act of 1832, a physician who before that date bought a corpse from a ghoul would be likely to protect his prize by concealing the skeleton in a closet, away from prying eyes.

Regardless of its genesis, one must agree with Farquhar in *The Beaux' Stratagem:* "There are secrets in all families"; and with the unknown author of *Italian Tales of Honor, Gallantry and Romance:* "There is a skeleton in every closet."

SLEEP LIKE A TOP/LOG, TO

> I shall sleep like a top.
> —Sir William Davenant, *The Rivals*

A person who has had a good night's sleep might exult, "I slept like a top; nothing awakened me." The simile is very old. Sir William Davenant used it in *The Rivals* (1668): "I shall sleep like a top." Yet it may be asked, How does a top sleep, and why is a spinning top likened to a sleeping person? A top doesn't sleep, of course, but when it spins rapidly, when it is at the height of its gyrations, it does seem to be motionless, which justifies the analogy to a person sleeping. Perhaps a better analogy, as given by one wit, lies in the noise they make—a top hums and a person snores.

Those ingenious etymologists who have fancied the word *top* as coming from the French *taupe*, mole, have been scoffed at by other word lovers on the grounds that the French expression is *dormir comme un sabot*, "to sleep like a wooden shoe," and not *comme une taupe*, like a mole. Which raises a Gallic question, What makes a wooden shoe particularly somnolent? On the other hand, the American saying "I slept like a log" has the same sense. A wooden thing, whether a shoe or a log, is dead to the world.

SLOGAN

Dictionaries list the many meanings of a word, some of which may seem or even be completely unrelated to the other meanings. Take the word *slogan* as an example. Its primary meanings are "a phrase expressing the aims or nature of an enterprise or organization" or "a catch-phrase used in advertising or promotion," such as "We love to fly and it shows," "When you care enough to send the very best," "Don't leave home without it." Madison Avenue spends much of its time dreaming up slogans for clients who want catch-phrases that will energize the public to buy their products or services. The second definition usually given harks back to the origin of the word *slogan* and gives us a better undersanding of the aggressive need for commercial slogans. It is "a battle cry of the

Scottish clans," a corruption of the Gaelic *slaugh*, host, and *gairm*, shout.

In the business world of today, slogans are commercial battle cries. They "shout" at us from radios, television, periodicals, from any means that can drum their message into our heads. Which makes some people wonder whether the public should have its own battle cry: "Down with slogans."

SMALL FRY

The term *small fry* is a humorous reference to a considerable number of children. The allusion evolved logically from its ancient base, the Old Icelandic *frjor*, seed. Anglo-Saxon picked it up through the Old French *frai*, spawn, and spelled it *frei*, which became present-day *fry*. It is now defined as both "young fish" and "offspring." Originally *fry* was applied only to the eggs of fish, such as herring, pike, and salmon, but later to the small fish themselves, particularly the progeny of salmon. It was so used in Dampier's *Voyage* (1697): "This small Fry I take to be the top of their Fishery." At that level it was a small step to pick up this phrase to mean "small children." Harriet Beecher Stowe did just that in *Uncle Tom's Cabin*. She wrote: "Mrs. Bird . . . followed by the eldest boys, the smaller fry having by this time been safely disposed in bed." Although the expression is generally used of a number of small children, it has been used in certain situations of a single child, as in Shakespeare's *Macbeth*, in which a murderer in the presence of Lady Macduff calls her son *a young fry of treachery* as he stabs him, inflicting a mortal wound.

SMALLPOX

Although *smallpox* (the Old English *smael*, small, and *pox*, the plural form of *pock*) has been a dread disease, today it is no longer contracted. In the past it brought millions to an early death. King Henry VIII took note of this widespread killer. He said: "They do die in these parts . . . of the small pokkes and mezils." Epidemics of smallpox recurred regularly in Europe and then became commonplace in the New World with the coming of the Spaniards.

The disease was virtually controlled, thanks to an invention of an ingenious, observant medical student. In 1796 Edward Jenner noticed that milkmaids seemed free of this disease. He determined, after investigation, research, and experimentation, that a person inoculated with cowpox (a mild infection) would become immune to smallpox. Jenner's first inoculation, given to an eight-year-old boy, was of cowpox vesicules obtained from the hands of a milkmaid. Months later he inoculated the boy with smallpox, but no disease developed. The effectiveness of the vaccine (from Latin *vacca,* cow) was proved. Since then untold numbers of people have received vaccinations, eliminating this scourge from mankind.

SMELL A RAT, TO

> Do you smell a fault?
> —Shakespeare, *King Lear*

Rats have been unwelcome intruders in homes and palaces since ancient times. In fact, it is said that many towns harbored more rats than people. To get rid of these pests, rat-chasing animals—terriers, cats—were housed, especially in the more opulent dwellings. It would not be unusual for a family dog, while the family was resting during the evening hours, to jump up and start for a wall or a portion of a floor, whining and scratching. The assumption was that the dog *smelled a rat.*

In 1550, John Skelton in his *Image of Hypocrisy* wrote: "Yf they smell a rat/They grisely [means fearfully] chide and chant." And so the expression *to smell a rat* evolved—and has remained in the cliché corner ever since as a homely way of saying a person suspects that something has gone wrong, that there is a dangerous or disgraceful cover-up.

SNEEZE

An old nursery rhyme reads:

> If you sneeze on Monday you sneeze for danger,
> Sneeze on Tuesday, kiss a stranger,
> Sneeze on Wednesday, sneeze for a letter,
> Sneeze on Thursday, something better,
> Sneeze on Friday, sneeze for sorrow,
> Sneeze on Saturday, see your sweetheart tomorrow.

Sneezing through the centuries, beginning with the ancient Greeks and Romans, was bound up with superstitious beliefs. It still is, to a certain extent, considering the knee-jerk remark made, even by strangers, when someone sneezes—*Gesundheit! Crisce sant!* But very few people would now take those pious hopes seriously.

The word *sneeze,* an involuntary expulsion of breath caused by irritation of the mucous membranes, has a semantic history of a spelling change with no noticeable concomitant change in pronunciation. In Old English the forebear of *to sneeze* was *fneosan,* to blow. The factors causing this drastic change were (1) the similarity of the appearance of *s* and *f* (without the crossbar, an *f* looks like an initial *s*); (2) The combination *fn* was a rarity in English at the beginning of a word; (3) The sounds that *f* and *s* represented were similar. In the fifteenth century *snesen* appeared in print, whereas William Caxton a decade earlier had printed *fnese* in the same text. And so with another orthographic alteration, modern English has come up with *sneeze.* Those interested in delving into this aspect of etymology and its consequences on today's orthography may rightly say, to borrow a cliché, "This is nothing to sneeze at."

SNIDE

Because word historians are unable to come up with sensible etymology in every case, some people make *snide* remarks about them. Of course, the remarks are mindless. In many instances there is no evidence at all of a word's development. The word might have just "grow'd" like Topsy. *Snide* is a case in point. Its origin is unknown, but not its meaning: "derogatory in a malicious, superior way." It is said of a person who makes nasty, sarcastic, or cutting remarks.

The theory that *snide* came from the German *schneiden,* meaning "to cut" or "to make cutting or sarcastic remarks," and entered the language as a slang term has received less than lukewarm acceptance by etymologists. And yet a *schneider,* a tailor, is one who cuts. And so it's possible that there's a connection between a snide remark—a cutting remark—and a cloth on a tailor's table about to be cut.

SNUG AS A BUG IN A RUG

Probably what has kept this idiom alive is the appeal of similar sounds, the rhyme factor, since the allusion is farfetched. And what kind of bug was meant? Perhaps a beetle, but no one knows for certain. The phrase was used by an unknown playwright in 1769 in *Stratford Jubilee,* in which appeared this line: "If she has the mopus's, I'll have her, as snug as a bug in a rug." At that time *mopus* meant "money." But the idiom had been preceded by similar phrases, even by Shakespeare, who occasionally used the word "dog" instead of "bug" and "safe" instead of "snug." The idiom means "safe," "comfortable," "the very utmost in contentment."

SOCRATIC IRONY

Perhaps the most practical legacy this world has received from the renowned Socrates is a method for obtaining information. Socrates elicited his information by framing questions so carefully as to make the responses coincide with conclusions he intended. He did this by pretending ignorance concerning the matter at hand, as evidenced by the question, thus luring the responder into displaying the little knowledge he might possess.

The technique of apparent self-denigration—encompassing a willingness to adopt the opponent's view but really dissembling to expose his flaws—is called *Socratic irony.* It has often been said that by reason of this stratagem, Socrates drove his enemies to distraction, but, as everyone knows, they drove him to drink.

SOMERSAULT/SAUTÉ

It may be hard to believe that the disparate terms *somersault* and *sauté* are cognates—words derived from a common ancestor. The word that gave rise to both those terms is the Latin *salire,* to leap. A *somersault* is an acrobatic stunt in which there is a leap and turn in a complete circle, the heels going over the head, ending with the head up. The word was a borrowing from the French *sombresault,* a variant of *sobresault,* from *sobre,* above (Latin *supra*), and *sault,* leap (Latin *saltus*). The cooking term *sauté,* another French word borrowed into English, means "to fry lightly in a shallow pan in a small amount of fat." The French connection with these words lies in the action of jumping or leaping that is common to both. Such action is obvious in a somersault. It is also clear with *sauté* if a dish is being heated with a little fat, for the droplets of fat will be seen to leap about.

There are, of course, several English words that honor *salire* as their ancestor *(assault, sally, salient),* but an unexpected one is *salacious,* lustful. That word was originally sired by the Latin *salax,* meaning "exciting lust," through which came its progeny *salire,* to leap. That leap, unlike the jumping about of droplets of fat, is not due to heat from a stove.

SOP

The word *sop* is not a slang term; it merely sounds like one. It has, in fact, an ancient background. During Roman times a sop was a bribe. The politicians gave a form of bribe, *panem et circenses,* bread and circuses, to the Roman populace—to control them and keep them reasonably happy.

The mythological Cerberus, Pluto's three-headed dog with the tail of a serpent who guarded the gates of Hades, was regularly offered a sop by those seeking to pass without molestation. It was a custom of the Greeks and Romans to place in the hands of the deceased a piece of cake or other morsel of food to serve as a bribe to Cerberus. This *sop,* spelled *sopp* in Anglo-Saxon and *soppe* in Middle English, came to mean "dipped bread," that is, bread dipped in wine or another liquid. With time this sense of "soak" has come to be applied in other cases of saturation. An unprotected person coming out of a thunderstorm is said to be *sopping wet.* The Roman sense of *sop,* a bribe, is still current, but it is of secondary importance to the sense of soaking, perhaps because no one believes in Cerberus.

SPICK-AND-SPAN

This cliché means "neat," "spotlessly clean," "in perfect order," and referring generally to something new. Although the origin of the expression is obscure, what the words represent is clear. A *spick* (from the Swedish *spik*) is a spike or nail; a *span* (from the German *spannau*) is a chip. A ship being launched was said to be *spick-and-span;* that is, every nail was new as well as every chip of timber. Originally the expression was *span-new,* later *spick and span new,* and then, with *new* dropped, *spick-and-span.* The word *span* is a cognate of *spoon.* In former times chips of wood were used as spoons. For those wondering about the connection between the noun *spoon* and the verb *spoon,* to make love, there is none. The latter *spoon* came from *spoony,* meaning "silly," an outgrowth of *spoon,* meaning "simpleton," a bit of eighteenth-century slang. And although simpletons are not the only ones who make love, from the noun *spoon (simpleton)* came the verb meaning "to make love," or "to spoon."

SPINSTER

The odd word *spinster* first appeared in print in 1362, but with a meaning different from what it is today. A spinster was one who spins (from the Middle English *spinnen,* to spin), a common occupation of an unmarried woman in earlier times. In fact, it was then believed that no woman was fit to become a wife until she had spun a set of linens for her body, table, and bed. Shakespeare used the term *spinster* in several plays—"The spinsters and the knitters in the sun" *(Twelfth Night);* "The spinsters, carders, fillers, weavers" *(Henry VIII).* Beginning in the seventeenth century, the term *spinster* was added to a woman's name to designate a state of celibacy. An unmarried woman's name would appear in official documents thus: "Johanna Hunt, spinster."

The meaning of *spinster* today is "an unmarried woman, especially one beyond the usual age for marriage." Such a person is euphemistically called *a maiden lady* or derisively *an old maid.* J. Roberts in 1719 first wrote about spinsters in this sense: "As for us poor Spinsters, we must certainly go away to France also." Charles Dickens in *Pickwick Papers* spoke of "Tupwan and the spinster aunt."

A spinster may be said to be on the distaff side of the family— that is, the female side. In Anglo-Saxon, *distaff,* then spelled *distaef,* literally meant "a bedizened staff." Its first element, from *diesse,* a bunch of flax, is appended to *staff,* which came from the Sanskrit *stha,* stand, entering Old English as *staef,* stick or staff. The English prefix *be,* according to Shipley, is often used to denote the act of, as in *besmirch* or *belittle.* The association of *distaff* with *female* evolved simply because the spinning of thread was an accepted occupation or pastime among women. Nowadays, of course, spinsters have stopped spinning, but for another reason: they're no longer in the social whirl.

SPITTING IMAGE, THE

A boy who is a *spitting image* or *the spit and image* of his father resembles him closely. But more than that, according to the expression, he is his father's exact likeness, his very image. Many languages have a similar expression. For instance, the French say, *"C'est son père tout craché"*—that is, "He's the living image of his father," but literally, "He is his father completely spat."

Some authorities disagree with that interpretation, however, and believe that the original expression was *spirit and image.* Their contention is that *spit* is simply a slurring or a regional pronunciation of *spirit.* And there's no way of telling who's right.

ST. VITUS'S DANCE

The medical name for an affliction involving uncontrollable movements of the muscles of the arms, legs, and face is *chorea,* a Greek word meaning "dance." (From it English has derived the word *choreography* and the more evocative *chorine,* a chorus girl.) In layman's language it is known as *St. Vitus's Dance,* a neurological disease attributed to earlier rheumatic fever.

The popular name for this condition comes from the name of a Roman saint who suffered martyrdom at the hands of Emperor Diocletian. For some unknown reason a belief arose that this saint was associated with good health. In the late Middle Ages followers of St. Vitus became convinced that dancing around his statue, invoking his curative power, would protect against disease. The dances sometimes reached a degree of frenzy, but there are no attested reports of beneficial effects. However, the name of the disease—*chorea*—has become established as St. Vitus's Dance. The Dance, it might be said, has danced itself into a permanent niche in the English language.

STEAL ONE'S THUNDER, TO

> Thunder is good; thunder is impressive;
> but it is lightning that does the work.
> —Mark Twain,
> Letter to an Unidentified Person

A person who *steals one's thunder* is, according to today's popular speech, acting as though another's accomplishments are his own. He simply has not the grace to acknowledge that the idea he's taking advantage of was conceived by someone else.

The interesting thing about the expression is that basically it is true—in one sense someone's thunder was stolen. It all started in 1709 when a play written by John Dennis called *Appius and Virginia* was produced at the Drury Lane Theatre in London. Dennis, for this play, introduced a device to simulate thunder, which turned out to be more realistic than any that had been heard before on a stage. Dennis's play was a tragedy, and the critics thought it a tragedy in other ways. The play was a financial flop, and the theater's manager soon withdrew it. Dennis later attended a performance of *Macbeth*. When the witches' scene came on with thunder and lightning, Dennis recognized that his invention to produce the sound of thunder was being used. He rose and shouted: "That's my thunder, by God! The villains will not play my play, and yet they steal my thunder."

STEVEDORE/LONGSHOREMAN

In the minds of most people the words *stevedore* and *longshoreman* are synonymous. They refer to a dockside worker who loads and unloads ships. This belief that the words are interchangeable is reinforced both by their etymology and by their dictionary definitions.

The noun *stevedore* comes from the Spanish *estivador,* meaning "a packer or stower." Its verb form, *estivar,* to stow cargo, was derived from the Latin *stipare,* to compound, to stuff, to unpack. Therefore, quite clearly, a stevedore is a person employed to load or unload cargo.

A *longshoreman* works along the shore, as the name implies, loading and unloading ships. The word is simply a contraction, and therefore a variant, of *along-shore-man.* Such a person may also be rightly called a *stevedore.* However, it should be borne in mind that a stevedore may be an employer of longshoremen, whereas a longshoreman is always a laborer on piers to which ships are moored.

STICK IN ONE'S CRAW, TO

The phrase *to stick in one's craw* is said to have been first used by hunters who noticed that some birds would occasionally swallow a stone larger than their craw. Since the stone couldn't go down, it would not reach their digestive tract. And so this saying entered general usage, meaning that when you can't swallow something, that is, when it is too difficult or repugnant to accept, it sticks in your craw, especially if you have no choice but must abide with it. Instead of *craw,* one might substitute *gizzard.* A *craw* is a bird's crop, a "preliminary stomach" or a sort of "storage place." A *gizzard* is a bird's active stomach, the one in which food is ground fine. For those concerned that a bird might be made ill if it swallowed a stone, be assured that birds regularly swallow pebbles, sand, and gravel, which stick to the walls of the gizzard to help grind the food. These ingredients keep the bird healthy.

According to Mark Twain's *Huckleberry Finn*, "sand in one's craw" fosters courage, the thought being that sand eaten by a chicken gives it endurance.

STICK ONE'S NECK OUT, TO

This idiom means "to invite trouble," "to take a risk," or, at the least, "to be conspicuous." The provenance of this proverbial saying may have been a barnyard. Chickens, when on the beheading block, are known to thrust out their necks, a move which fortunately makes their beheading easier. Hence a person exposing himself to danger, deliberately taking chances, is like a chicken sticking out its neck. And if he sticks it out far enough, he too may "get it in the neck." As Fluellen in Shakespeare's *Henry V* said to Williams, whom he thought a traitor, "Let his neck answer for it." In more recent times, Raymond Chandler (1936) in the *The Black Mask* wrote: "You sure stick your neck out all the time."

STIFF-NECKED

A willfully obstinate or defiant person is said to be stiff-necked. This saying was derived from Hebrew and was applied to stubborn oxen. Oxen were man's source of plowing power. When an ox became stubborn and stiffened its neck muscles, no one would be likely to budge it, and all plowing would cease. The ox would not, the saying goes, answer to the reins. Although ox power has long been abandoned, the expression survives, possibly because there are as many stiff-necked people today as there were stiff-necked oxen in ancient times. The scriptures contain a number of references to *stiff-neck,* among which are Psalm 75—"Speak not with stiff neck"—and Jeremiah 17—"They obeyed not, but made their necks stiff." For those who dislike the sound of the phrase, the same result can be reached through another cliché, the simile *stiff as a board.*

STRAW THAT BROKE THE CAMEL'S BACK, THE

This saying is as common as any expression in general usage. It of course means that the limit or the breaking point in expense, in endurance, or in what have you has been reached and that any more will ruin or destroy. What may not be so widely known, however, is its origin. It was invented by Charles Dickens and appeared in his *Dombey and Son* (1848), in which he wrote: ". . . as the last straw breaks the laden camel's back." It is thought by some authorities that the older proverb " 'Tis the last feather that breaks the horse's back" may have inspired Dickens. How old this latter phrase is is unknown, but Thomas Fuller (1608–1661) recorded it in his *Gnomoloia.*

In any event, the moral behind the saying is not to overdo, not to place too much of a burden or responsibility on anyone, not to weaken a financial structure to the point that one more move will be ruinous.

STYMIED, TO BE

A person who is *stymied* has been frustrated, thwarted, blocked in his or her efforts to accomplish an objective. Clearly, one who is stymied—hindered from proceeding according to plan—is disconcerted and downhearted. The sense of *stymie* may be too severe to apply to a game like golf, but, strange as it may seem, the term originated on the golf course. If a player's ball fell in a line toward the hole and close behind the opponent's ball, the player's ball was said to have *laid a stymie.* The choice the player had was to try to loft the ball over the one in front or else lose a stroke. And from this dilemma has emerged the word *stymie,* now used in general speech to mean "to block or impede."

SWORD OF DAMOCLES, THE

> Uneasy lies the head that wears a crown.
> —Shakespeare, *Henry IV, Part II*

If a person who covets someone's lofty position is then placed in the other's seat of authority, he may be shocked to learn how precarious a seat it is to occupy. This, in a general sense, is the gist of the story behind *the sword of Damocles,* an expression that has come to typify a threatening peril, an imminent danger.

According to this myth, Damocles, a companion of Dionysius the Elder, the king of Syracuse, always extolled the felicity of the king in that he enjoyed both wealth and power. Dionysius decided that his sycophantic courtier should be made to learn at first hand that a king's life consisted of more than privilege, that it was also hemmed in by continuing danger. To this end, Dionysius invited Damocles to a sumptuous banquet and placed him on the royal seat. Damocles was delighted and felt honored until he discovered that above his head was an unsheathed sword suspended by a single horsehair. It has been said that Damocles lost his appetite.

T

T, TO A

To a T is an expression that grew out of the draftsman's T-square, a T-shaped ruler used to draw parallel lines. *To fit to a T* has come to mean "to fit exactly." If a *T-square* is placed on a drawing board, it will fit like a T, so precisely and accurately that it can be the base for a *set square*, "a flat triangular instrument with one right angle and the other angles set at various degrees." Without these architectural instruments, the buildings that architects design would not be set square nor would they fit to a T. The metaphor is used in other senses. We say that the suit fits to a T, the pie was baked to a T, and the steak was done to a T.

One discordant note—some etymologists believe that the expression *to a T* preceded the invention of the T-square, as witness the prestigious *Oxford English Dictionary,* which says the original sense of *to a T,* meaning "exactly" or "properly," has not been ascertained. Suggestions that it was the *tee* at curling, or at golf, or a T-square appear on investigation to be untenable. One more: the *OED* added that the idea from which the expression arose, that the proper completion of a *t* is by crossing it, has not been established.

The name *T-square* appeared in print in the eighteenth century, possibly shortly after its invention, but the term *to a T* predates it by more than a hundred years. The *OED* has a record of its use in 1693. In George Farquar's *Love in a Bottle* (1699) appeared the following: "He answered the description . . . to a T, sir."

TAKE THE CAKE, TO

To take the cake is proverbial for "to win the prize." In general usage, however, it signifies a thing done preeminently well. A person who excels at something or says something witty might be praised by being told, "You take the cake." Of course, he gets no cake, but the fact is that when this saying was first used, in the final quarter of the nineteenth century, an actual cake was given, but under different circumstances. In the South, blacks, to entertain themselves, held contests in which couples were judged by the grace and style of their movements as they walked around a cake. Those couples whose steps were the fanciest or the most appealing were adjudged the winners and received a prize—the cake they had just walked around. As they were about to leave, they were told, "Don't forget. You take the cake." And, as can readily be imagined, the popular dance before the coming of jazz, the *cakewalk,* developed from these very contests.

TAKE THE WIND OUT OF SOMEONE'S SAILS, TO

It doesn't matter whether you're an old salt or a landlubber, you've probably said on some occasion or at least heard someone say, "I took the wind out of his sails." What was said metaphorically was that that someone had figuratively or literally been stopped, placed at a disadvantage, or had his ego deflated. In any event, that person has been nonplussed. This saying reflects an old maritime maneuver, one during the days of sailing vessels, whereby a vessel, to impede the progress of another, sailed to the windward of it so that it was becalmed and helpless. What was done was that the covering vessel's sails acted as a barrier and prevented any wind from reaching the other vessel. On land, the saying was of course used only figuratively, as witness this statement by Sir Walter Scott in *The Fortunes of Nigel* (1822): "He would take the wind out of the sail of every gallant."

TAKE WITH A GRAIN OF SALT

Salt is an additive that makes food more palatable. A pinch of it can convert a dull dish of food into one that is truly tasty. Dating back to Roman times, the expression *to take* (something—a promise, a protestation of love, or whatever) *with a grain of salt (cum grano salis)* implies skepticism or even out-and-out distrust. Just as salt may improve the taste of an unappetizing meal, so one presented with a proposal that is unappealing or an improbable story, if he wishes to accept it, had better take it with a figurative grain of salt. He'll be able to "swallow" it more easily.

There's an ancient and often-repeated story, supposedly first told by Pliny the Elder, that concerns Pompey and Mithradates, King of the Persians, whose palace Pompey had seized. Pompey, as the story goes, found the king's antidote for poison. The instructions concluded by saying: "to be taken fasting, plus a grain of salt" *(addite salis grano).* Some word sleuths doubt the facts in the Pliny story; others say it is apocryphal. Take your pick, but take it with a grain of salt.

TALK TURKEY, TO

The turkey is a much more respectable bird (than the bald eagle), and withal a true original native of America.
—Benjamin Franklin, Letter to Sarah Bache

The idiom *to talk turkey* has been a part of American speech ever since the turkey was first spotted in the New World. Some authorities attribute the phrase to the ability of colonial hunters to imitate the sound of a turkey—to talk turkey—which enabled the hunters to lure the fowl within shooting distance. But according to a charming bit of colonial legend, a white man and an Indian decided one day to go hunting. They agreed to divide the spoils equally between them. Their marksmanship netted four crows and four turkeys. When it came time to divide the spoils, the white said, "You take this crow and I'll take this turkey." The white man repeated the same thing until the Indian found himself with four crows. At which point the Indian protested. "Ugh," he said, "you talk turkey for you but not for me. Now I talk turkey." He then proceeded to get his rightful share. This story has variations, but from it, according to the belief of many word origin detectives, the phrase *to talk turkey* entered the English language as an expression meaning "let's talk plainly and seriously" or "let's get to the point," or, more in the vernacular, "let's get down to brass tacks."

TARGET

The word *target* can be traced to an early French word, *targe,* a light shield, which was borrowed whole into the English language in the thirteenth century, spelled and pronounced just like that of the French. We find the word in Chaucer's *Canterbury Tales* ("The Knight's Tale," 1387), in which the knight remarked: ". . . the rede statue of Mars, with spere and targe." A century later English adopted the diminutive French form, *targette:* a small target or shield. Shakespeare in the latter part of the sixteenth century used the term in *Henry VI,* when Henry's son, Edward, declares: "Whate'er it bodes, henceforward will I bear/Upon my target three fair-shining suns." The eighteenth century saw an extension—an object to be shot at for practice, its primary current sense. But it may be noted that Samuel Johnson omitted it from his *Dictionary.* Nevertheless, its meaning remained and its sense kept evolving, so that today it may be applied figuratively as well as literally. Alfred Lord Tennyson in "Locksley Hall" (1842) wrote: "Hark, my merry comrades call me, sounding on the bugle-horn./ They to whom my foolish passion were a target for their scorn." We might conclude by saying that this is a word that's on target.

TARIFF/SARDINE

Many common terms in English come from foreign words. The words had nothing to do with English as such, but they described a practice or a thing for which no English word existed. The words were therefore borrowed, and then anglicized. Two such were the words *tariff* and *sardine.*

The English word *tariff* means "a list of charges" (a hotel tariff, a railroad tariff), but it may mean "any duty itself." *Tariff* derives from Arabic *'arafa,* to notify, and *ta'rif,* a notification. In the sixteenth century English borrowed the word to mean "a schedule of customs duties."

The island of Sardinia near Italy was known for a little fish that, when packed in oil, made a delectable food. The name given the fish, as might undoubtedly be surmised, was *sardine.*

TEDDY BEAR

A *teddy bear* is a child's toy, but one some adults enjoy playing with. Although no one is certain of the source of this name, the story that has made the most frequent rounds, though possibly apocryphal, makes sense to some authorities. Theodore Roosevelt, who was our President at the turn of the century, was an inveterate hunter. It is said that in 1902 Roosevelt, who was affectionately called Teddy, was hunting bear in Mississippi. He was given a chance to shoot a bear cub, but he refused to do so. A stuffed bear, to commemorate this act of compassion, was manufactured by a Brooklynite and placed on the commercial market. Sales of the bear, dubbed *Teddy Bear* after the President, soared in volume and the name *teddy bear* became a household term. It still is. But jokesters continue to guffaw at their wit when they ask the riddle: "If you see T.R. as the President when he's dressed, what do you see when he's undressed? Hah! Hah! Teddy bare!"

TEETOTALER

> I'm only a beer teetotaler, not a champagne teetotaler.
> —George Bernard Shaw, *Candida*

A *teetotaler* is a person who abstains from the use of alcoholic liquors. The word has been attributed to Richard Turner, an Englishman, but whether he coined it or stumbled into it has not been established. According to the story, in 1833 Turner, after a lecture on temperance, spoke to a small group on total abstinence. But he stuttered as he spoke the word *total.* It came out "t-t-t-total abstinence." About the same time in America, pledges against imbibing intoxicating liquor were made to the New York Temperance Society in 1837. Those members who had previously pledged wrote on their pledge cards "O.P." (for Old Pledge) alongside their name. Their promise was to abstain from drinking distilled liquor. Those promising total abstinence added the letter "T" (for Total). Since "T-total" was mentioned so often, it came to sound like a word and, in fact, became one—*teetotal*. No one is certain whether to credit the word *teetotal* to Turner or to the use of *T-total*. Among authorities, it may be said, there is no to-to-total agreement.

TEMPEST IN A TEAPOT, A

How much of a tempest can be raised in a teapot? A *tempest* is a violent windstorm or a furious commotion. A *teapot* is a small container from which tea is served. Quite clearly the reference to a tempest is figurative; it means much ado about nothing or making a fuss over a trifle. The notion of a *tempest in a teapot* originated with Cicero when he wrote his *De Legibus: "Excitabat enim fluctus in simpulo,"* which translates into "He used to raise a tempest [or a storm] in a teapot." It has been said that the saying was introduced in England by Lord North when he referred to the Boston Tea Party, an uprising of American colonists against the tea tax. Lord North undoubtedly underestimated the severity of the tempest or the size of the teapot. The storm it generated must have caused King George III, like a tempest in a teapot, to boil over.

TESTIMONY

That part of the male organ of regeneration, the testicles, has been a source of several common English words, each unrelated to the other. The most surprising word coming from that source is the name of a flower, milady's favorite, the *orchid*. A species of this flower was observed by Pliny the Elder, Roman author and naturalist, during one of his investigative walks. He said, *"Mirabilis est orchis herba, sine serapias gemina radice testiculis simili,"* which, as paraphrased, means that he thought it remarkable that the twin roots of the flower resembled hairy testicles. Pliny did not name the flower, however. It was dubbed *orchid* in Landley's *School of Botany* (1845) in England. The Latin term *orchis* is now a relic except in botany and medicine.

An *avocado* is a pear-shaped fruit from the avocado tree. The original Mexican name for the fruit was *ahuactl,* which meant "testicle" and which was so named because of the shape of the pear. The Spaniards found that name hard to pronounce, and so through popular etymology came up with *avocado.* It is doubtful that the Spaniards had associated "lawyer" in their language (spelled *abogado,* but the *b* is sounded almost like a *v*) and *avocado* meaning "testicle," although lawyers are known to get things all balled up. It is believed that *testicle* is a word that evolved eventually through *testis,* with its sense of "witness," for since Roman times, men took an oath on their testicles, and what they said became their *testimony.*

THERE BUT FOR THE GRACE OF GOD GO I

There but for the grace of God go I has been said and resaid ad nauseam, yet no one can attest to its origin. The meaning of the phrase is clear—because of my good fortune, though I have committed the same follies or misdeeds as the person I see being condemned or facing disaster, I have nevertheless been lucky enough to avoid the consequences. I am yet free, unpunished.

The saying has been attributed to many men: John Bunyan (1628–1688), John Wesley (1703–1791), John Newton (1725–1807)— all, quite naturally, pious and zealous. But most word and phrase historians think that the likely inventor of the phrase was John Bradford, a religious martyr by the grace of Queen Mary I. But that is getting ahead of the story.

According to legend, John Bradford once remarked, as he watched a condemned criminal being carted to the gallows, "There, but for the grace of God, goes John Bradford." Unfortunately for Bradford, however, the favor of God did not last long. During the reign of Queen Mary (the infamous Bloody Mary), Bradford was tried as a heretic and convicted. On July 1, 1555, he was burned at the stake. The published works of the Dean of Canterbury, Frederic

W. Farrar, famous for his sermons entitled "Eternal Hope," contained a reference to this saying, crediting it to Bradford. If this attribution could be authenticated, the purpose of the religious bigots to exterminate him and his freedom of thought would not have been entirely reached. They wantonly destroyed his body, but they could not obliterate his name.

THERE'S MANY A SLIP 'TWIXT CUP AND LIP

The saying *there's many a slip 'twixt the cup and the lip* is proverbial. It means, of course, that nothing is certain until it is actually possessed. The expression, a very ancient one, was nurtured in Greek classics. According to legend, Ancaeus, son of Poseidon and helmsman on the ship *Argo,* took great pains with his vineyards and gloried in their growth. But his treatment of his slaves was abominable. He was cruel. One slave had the audacity to tell Ancaeus that he would not live to enjoy his wine. After the harvest, Ancaeus, to show the slave that he was wrong, summoned him and held up a cup of fresh wine, which he said he would now drink. The slave, undaunted, said, "There's many a slip 'twixt the cup and the lip." Just then a messenger arrived and informed Ancaeus that a wild boar was destroying his vineyard. Ancaeus put his cup down with the wine untasted and immediately left to find the boar, but was himself slain by it. The slave turned out to be a prophet. Perhaps he should have toasted himself with that cup of wine.

THERE'S THE RUB

We sometimes had those little rubs which Providence sent to enhance the value of its favours.

—Goldsmith, *The Vicar of Wakefield*

To understand this curious idiom, one must know that at one time *rub* was a noun meaning "impediment or obstacle." An obstruction or a hindrance was called a *rub.* The expression was derived from a term used in the game of bowls in which anything that interfered with the free movement of the ball (the bowl), that diverted its intended course, was called a *rub*. But the use of the word *rub* as we know it today is credited to Shakespeare, from the famous soliloquy of Hamlet:

> To die, to sleep;
> To sleep; perchance to dream: ay, there's the rub:
> For in that sleep of death what dreams may come,
> When we have shuffled off this mortal coil,
> Must give us pause . . .

THICK AS THIEVES

This peculiar idiom is fairly new, about two hundred years old. Its sense is conspiratorial intimacy or, at the least, a very close friendship. If Jane and Mary see each other frequently, shop together, vacation together, and play games together, they may be said to be *as thick as thieves*. Theodore E. Hook in 1833 put it this way in *The Parson's Daughter*: "She and my wife are as thick as thieves, as the proverb goes." The expression more anciently was *those two are very thick*. But *to be thick* also meant to be a slow thinker, a not very bright person. The alliterative *thick as thieves* eliminated that problem. Evans points out that this cliché has many suitable companions, *as thick as hail, as thick as hops, as thick as huckleberries,* and to emphasize profusion, *as thick as porridge,* and for chumminess, a fine old Scotch simile, *as thick as three in a bed.* But perhaps some of those are putting it on too thick.

THREE/THIRD

> With lokkes crulle as they were leyd in presse.
> —Chaucer, Prologue to *The Canterbury Tales*

Did you ever stop to wonder why we say *three* and *third* instead of *three* and *third*? It would certainly seem more logical if the ordinal number *third* corresponded to its original cardinal counterpart *three*. The ultimate ancestor of both those words was the Indo-

European *trei-*. In Anglo-Saxon the ordinal form was *thridda,* which continued into Middle English. During that period, through a process known as *metathesis* (the transposition of a letter or syllable within a word), the *r* changed places with the *i,* making *third.* In fact, it really became *thirde,* but later the final *e* was dropped. The interchange of position of letters within a word was not an uncommon happening in the English language, witness *aks* to *ask, brid* to *bird, clapse* to *clasp, crulle* to *curly* (see Chaucer above) and *thirl* to *thrill.*

THREE R'S, THE

The basis of all education is generally considered to be *the three R's*—reading, writing, and arithmetic. It is said that the originator of this phrase was an illiterate Lord Mayor of London, Sir William Curtis, who, in the early nineteenth century, proposed a toast—"To Reading, Riting, and Rithmetic." He didn't know it then, but we know it now—his illiteracy has been immortalized.

THROUGH THICK AND THIN

It might be that *through thick and thin* is the oldest idiom currently in use. It appeared in *The Exeter Book,* which antedated Chaucer's *Canterbury Tales* (1386) by hundreds of years. This ancient saying means "despite all difficulties, disregarding all obstacles and impediments, through fair weather and foul, steadfast." In "The Reeve's Tale," Geoffrey Chaucer wrote: "And whan the hors was loos, he gan to goon/Toward the fen ther wilde mares renne,/ Forth with 'wi-he!' thurgh thikke and eek thurgh thenne." The origin of this expression is made clearer by Edmund Spenser in his *Faerie Queene* (1590):

> His tyreling Jade he fiersly forth did push
> Through thicke and thin, both over banck and bush,
> In hope her to attain by hook or crook.

The *thick* in the idiom is an abbreviated form of *thicket,* a dense growth of underbrush or small trees. Riding a horse through a thicket was unpleasant and sometimes precarious. *Thin,* of course, means open and clear ground.

THUMB THE NOSE, TO

Thumbing the nose, a common practice among children, is a sign of disrespect. Mockery—"Janie is a crybaby"—is belittling or ridiculing. Although one does not mock with the nose, the word *mockery* comes from the Late Latin *muccare,* which means "to wipe the nose," sometimes done as a gesture of scorn. No sound theory has been advanced as to why the nose should play such a prominent part in gestures of derision, although *to turn up one's nose* has a sound foundation in fact. When a person sneers, he curls his upper lip, a movement that turns up the nose, giving him a look of contempt. Persius in *Satires* warned against this facialism in these words: "You are scoffing and use your turned up nose too freely." Nevertheless, that a person's nose is an exceedingly important organ in ways other than its designed purpose was made clear by Blaise Pascal: "If Cleopatra's nose had been a little shorter," he said, "the whole face of the world would have been changed."

In French, the gesture *to thumb your nose* is called *pied de nez,* nose-foot. It shows defiance or disrespect.

THUNDERSTRUCK

> And thou, all-shaking thunder,
> Strike flat the thick rotundity o' the world.
> —Shakespeare, *King Lear*

Although the expression *thunderstruck* goes back for centuries, no one is known to have been struck by thunder. The fact is that thunder is a loud noise accompanying a flash of lightning; it is not a striking force.

From the Old English *tunor* evolved the Middle English *thunor,* later to become "thunder." Why the *d* was added has not been established, perhaps to approximate more closely the sound of the growl or bang of the expanding air that frightens so many people. No doubt the supposed consequent effect of thunder instilled as much fear as lightning, even though the devastating effect of lightning on barns and other buildings was visible. As early as 1400 Maundev wrote: "We ware . . . stricken doune to the earth with great hidous blastez of wind and of thouner." In modern discourse a person made temporarily speechless, whether from fear or surprise, is said to be *thunderstruck.*

The fifth day of the week, *Thursday,* was named after Thor, the Norse god of thunder, who, it was believed, hurled thunderbolts at the earth. And so did Jupiter (the Roman counterpart of the Greek Zeus), usually depicted with a scepter in his left hand and a thunderbolt in his right. Thunderbolts, of course, are mythological missiles. Shakespeare spoke of them in *Julius Caesar,* when Brutus said: "Be ready, gods, with all your thunderbolts,/Dash him to pieces!"

TILT AT WINDMILLS, TO

It is always satisfying to know the origin of a phrase so well known as to have become a cliché. *To tilt at windmills* is one whose provenance is solid. It was a creation of Cervantes in his famous *Don Quixote* (1605). Quixote, with his lance ready for attack, rode his gallant steed throughout the countryside to destroy the giants, which were really windmills. Here is an excerpt from Cervantes's book:

At this point they came in sight of thirty or forty windmills . . . as soon as Don Quixote saw them he said to his squire, "Fortune is arranging matters for us better than we could have shaped our desires ourselves, for look there, friend Sancho Panza, where thirty or more monstrous giants present themselves, all of whom I mean to engage in battle and slay, and with whose spoils we shall begin to make our fortunes, for . . . it is God's good service to sweep so evil a breed off the face of the earth."

The expression has come to mean attacking imaginary foes, fighting with nonexistent enemies, or warding off dreamed-up dangers.

TIMEPIECE

In the Middle Ages people told time by the number of bells sounded from a clock tower. They didn't look at a clock; they listened to it. This, considering the etymology of the word *clock,* was the right thing to do. The English word *clock* comes from the French *cloche,* which in turn had come from the Late Latin *clocca,* "a bell."

After faces were put on clocks so that people could read the time, timepieces came to be made much smaller, some so small that they could be placed in a small pocket. This timepiece was dubbed a *watch,* and for a simple reason—the instrument was watched. Strangely enough, today "watch watchers" are a rarity but "clock watchers" are a common breed.

TOE THE MARK

This common expression needs no explanation, yet for the record it must be stated that, as widely used today, it means, figuratively, "to conform to standards of discipline," "to be up to snuff," "to come up to scratch." A person required to live up to a strict course of conduct is being made "to toe the mark." Literally, the term has been the starter's call at racetracks, where the runners stood with the tip of their toes touching a line, the mark from which the race was to begin. From childhood we have heard the starters bark the signal: "On your mark, get set, go!" Bear in mind that since the mark is really a line, the expression *toe the line* is also in common usage in the sense of "having to follow strict orders." The *Westminister Gazette* reported in 1895: "The phrase 'toeing the line' is very much in favour with some Liberals."

The phrase *toe your mark* was born in a prizefighting ring, but initially wore different clothing. Its meaning was first expressed by *come to the scratch* or *toe the scratch.* A long time ago boxing rings were divided into two equal parts by a distinct line. The boxers had to come to this line before starting to battle. Holt points out that during those times, when pugilists fought almost to the death, the referee would require the battered hulks to come to the center of the ring to see whether they could "toe the line" under their own steam.

TORPEDO

A *torpedo,* almost anyone would say, is a self-propelled under-water projectile. It is fired from ships, submarines, or aircraft car-riers. Imagine the surprise of some people when told that a *torpedo* is not only a destructive engine but also a fish. With its tapered tail and slender body, this *torpedo* was allied to the ray, a fish that emitted an electric charge. The shock from a grown torpedo could stun a man. In 1520 appeared this statement by someone named Andrewe: "Torpido is a fisshe, but who-so-handleth hym shalbe lame & defe of lymmes that he shale fele no thyng." That one so struck by a ray "shale fele no thyng" is borne out by the Latin def-inition of *torpedo,* "numbness, lethargy, listlessness," from *torpere,* to be sluggish or numb. By the eighteenth century the sense of *torpedo*—stiffness, numbness—had spread to everyday activity and applied to many things where promptness or agility is not dis-played. Witness these lines from the *Life of Johnson,* by James Boswell, written in Italy in 1743: "Tom Birch is as brisk as a bee in conversation; but no sooner does he take a pen in his hand than it becomes a torpedo to him, and benumbs all his faculties."

The first self-propelled torpedo was launched in 1866. It was put together by Robert Whitehead, a Scottish engineer, who was given a plan for a torpedo by Captain Luppis of the Austrian Navy. The torpedo was improved with time both as to accuracy and as to the distance it could travel. During World War II the torpedo was a dreaded missile. Like the fish, it could "sting."

TOWER OF STRENGTH

Everyone would like to think that a member of his family, usu-ally the father, can be called on in any case, a person the family can always rely on for assistance or guidance no matter what the problem. That person is, idiomatically, a *tower of strength,* a sense given this phrase in the Bible. During the days of medieval urban development, the phrase took on a literal meaning with the erection of fortified towers to which people could go if the outer walls of the city were breached by invaders. A most prominent tower is the Tower of London, today a refuge for the Beefeaters and a sightseeing attraction for visitors. Lord Tennyson in 1852 set this idiom in cement in his *Ode on the Death of the Duke of Wellington:*

> O iron nerve to true occasion true,
> O fallen at length, that tower of strength
> Which stood four-square to all the winds that blew.

TUMBLER

A *tumbler,* as we know it, is a flat-bottomed glass having no handle, foot, or stem. It therefore is a receptacle that is unlikely to fall or tumble. Which makes one wonder whether it has been misnamed. The fact is that the term *tumbler* is no longer an accurate designation for this type of drinking glass, but it was originally. In the seventeenth century drinking glasses were made with a rounded or pointed bottom to make them tumble if set down on a table. It was dangerous, therefore, to set them down before they were entirely empty. The idea behind the odd bottom was to make sure that the drinker left nary a drop—that he emptied his glass. Perhaps the slogan of the times was "Waste not, want not." But surely it had to be "Bottoms up."

TURKEY

A Thanksgiving dinner would not be complete without a turkey. This fowl was discovered in America by early Spanish explorers and, when brought to the continent in the sixteenth century, created quite a sensation. The bird was unnamed; apparently no one thought to ask the Indians what it was called. And so the American bird came to be named by Europeans, who dubbed it *turkey.* How this name was arrived at, however, has not been fully attested, although some authorities have strong views on the subject. One conjecture is that the bird was brought into Europe from the New

World through Turkey, hence its name. Another is that Europeans called it *turkey* because it so very much resembled an African bird that had been introduced into England by Turkish traders. The confusion surrounding these names has been cleared. We have now learned that the African bird came from the coast of Guinea, and it has been given its rightful name, *guinea fowl.* The habitat of the turkey has been established as being in America. It seems that, no matter how you look at it, when Americans sit down to carve the turkey, they will have to call it by its European name.

Another favorite of Americans named after Turkey is a bluish-green mineral, the gemstone *turquoise.* Its full name, bestowed by the French, was *la pierre turquoise,* which means "the Turkish stone." It was so named because the stone was brought to Europe from the Sinai peninsula through Turkey.

TURNING A HAIR, NOT/WITHOUT

It is not uncommon, when referring to someone who looks composed, showing no signs of distress in the face of an agitating problem, to say, "He hasn't turned a hair." This phrase may have arisen on a bridle path, for it is a horse that is alluded to as *not having turned a hair.* Jane Austen in her *Northanger Abbey* (1818) dreamed it up. Referring to a horse, she wrote: "He had not turned a hair till we came to Walcot Church." The idea is that a horse has a glossy coat of hair unless it sweats, which horses do when in distress. Then their hair roughens up. A horse that is no longer cool no longer has smooth, unruffled hair. And no longer may it be said that the horse "hasn't turned a hair," or, as put by Richard D. Blackmore in *Dariel* (1898) of an unruffled person, "She never turned a hair ... as the sporting people say."

TURTLE

> Rise up, my love, my fair one, and come away.
> For, lo, the winter is past, the rain is over and gone;
> The flowers appear on the earth; the time
> of [the] singing [of birds] is come, and the voice
> of the turtle is heard in our land.
>
> *The Song of Solomon,* 2:10–12

The harbinger of spring, the *turtle* referred to in the Bible, is not the turtle we know, a tortoise, but a *turtledove,* a fowl known for its soft cooing sound. The Romans called the bird *turtur,* said to be a repetition of *tur,* imitative of its mournful coo. The Latin word *turtur,* as anglicized, became *turtle.* Until the discovery of the New World, all references to *turtles* were to the birds we now call *turtledoves.*

The other turtle, the one children like to play with and the one we sometimes eat in soup, was given its name by Spanish sailors, who called it *tortuga.* The French version was similar: *tortue.* These names had a Latin ancestor, *tortus,* meaning "twisted," "crooked," possibly because these marine reptiles had twisted feet and legs. To English sailors the Spanish name sounded like the one originally given to a "turtledove," *turtle.* And so they called these sea creatures *turtles,* although they could not fly nor coo a single *tur.*

UNCLE SAM

I'm a Yankee Doodle dandy,
A Yankee Doodle do or die;
A real live nephew of my Uncle Sam's
Born on the Fourth of July.
—George M. Cohan, *Yankee Doodle Dandy*

The initials U.S. are often used to mean the United States, but they also may stand for *Uncle Sam,* a nickname for the United States Government. That lanky, goateed All-American who wears a red, white, and blue top hat and swallowtail coat is known to everyone, but no one is certain how his name originated.

To word historians, who by and large support either of two versions (but there are others), the more likely account is that it was first used during the War of 1812. Opponents of the war equated the letters *U.S.* stamped on war supply containers with "Uncle Sam," an eponym they sneeringly used as representing an object of waste and foolishness. The derisive sense evaporated with time, and *Uncle Sam* emerged in a favorable light as a personification of the United States. The theory with greater support, however, is that during this war an army inspector in Troy, New York, stamped *U.S.* on food containers approved for shipment, but because his first name was Samuel (his last was Wilson), he jokingly came to be called "Uncle Sam." From one of these hazy beginnings, Uncle Sam grew to be a nationally recognized—and officially adopted—symbol.

URANUS

A slight sound at evening lifts me up by the ears, and makes life seem inexpressibly serene and grand. It may be in Uranus, or it may be in the shutter.

—Henry David Thoreau, *Journal 10–12, 1841*

An ancient Greek god, *Uranus,* the god of heaven and the husband of Gaea, the goddess of earth, was immortalized through a discovery in the sky and another one in the earth. (He was also castrated by his son Cronos with a sickle, at the instigation of his mother.)

In 1781, Sir William Herschel, a British astronomer, spotted a new planet, the first such discovery since ancient times. Up to that moment man had observed six planets: Mercury, Venus, Mars, Jupiter, Saturn, and Earth. (The last, of course, was not only observed but stood on.) In honor of the god of the sky, Herschel named his discovery *Uranus.*

In 1789, not long after the discovery of Uranus, Martin Klaproth, a German chemist, was experimenting with pitchblende when he found within it an unusual new metallic element, one that was radioactive. In honor of the new planet, Klaproth coined a name for his find, *uranium,* which sounds like a modern Latin term but is not. *Uranium* contains forms of a chemical element, *isotopes,* used as a source of atomic energy.

UP TO SNUFF/PAR

The chief difference between *up to snuff* and *up to par* is that the former phrase refers to a desired level of quality or performance or to one's state of health, whereas the latter refers to what is typical. A person who is *up to par* (*par* meaning a normal standard) is managing as usual, the way it should be.

The current sense of *up to snuff* is entirely different from what it had been through the centuries. Before pointing out the change, it should first be borne in mind that *snuff* is not here referring to powdered tobacco, which was habitually inhaled by courtiers and others pretending to elegance, but is, instead, an Anglo-Saxon word cognate with the Middle Dutch *snuffen,* to snuffle out the filth from one's nose, and the German *schnuffeln,* to smell. *Snuff* subsequently became the equivalent of *sniff,* both meaning "to draw air through the nose." It has long been thought that a person alive to scent is wide awake and wise. A sharp sense of smell, figuratively speaking, therefore came to signify acuteness or alertness, as implied in other analogous "smell" expressions—*to smell a rat* and *to be on the right scent.* Nowadays, however, *up to snuff,* rather than referring to a person who is alert—that is, not easily deceived—is used of one's physical condition. A person in normal health is said to be *up to snuff.*

Up to par is a borrowing from golf. In fact, the full expression is *up to par for the course. Par* is the number of strokes allotted to play a hole as a standard, one not often reached. The term is sometimes reversed, *to be below par,* meaning "unsatisfactory or in poor health." C. E. Montague (1867–1928) in *Fiery Particles* wrote: "I was born below par to the extent of two whiskies."

UPPER HAND, TO HAVE THE

This expression, an old one, refers to someone who dominates the policies or structure or operation of an organization. This person is the one in control. The idiom was born on a broomstick. Children for generations past, and perhaps until the present time, have played a game in which one of them puts a hand at the bottom of the broomstick and the next person puts one of his or her hands on top. Each thereafter takes turns until there is no broomstick left to put a hand on. The hand on top, the upper hand, wins. It is said that this was an ancient gambling game, but the truth of that theory has not been determined.

UPSET THE APPLECART, TO

> I have upset my apple-cart; I am done for.
> —Lucian, *Pseudolus*

A person who spoils another person's carefully laid plans may be accused of *upsetting the applecart*, a metaphor that has been with us for many centuries. The Romans said: *"Plaustrium perculisti"* ("You have upset the applecart"), which means that now everything is ruined because of your stupidity. But why, someone might ask, was the word *apple* joined to *cart*? No one knows. It has been a matter of speculation for many years. One guess is that it was simply a childish reference. Another is that some student, when translating the Latin, mischievously converted *cart* into an *applecart*. Still another theory is that medieval roads were full of ruts and to get a cartload of produce to the market was tricky. If the cart was caught in a rough area and toppled, the common expression was, "There goes his applecart," no matter what was spilled. It is unlikely that the true source of this expression will ever be known. It was first recorded in 1796 in Grose's *Classical Dictionary of the Vulgar Tongue*. Thomas G. Fessenden used the phrase around 1800 in a poem attacking Thomas Jefferson: "He talketh big words in Congress and threateneth to overturn the apple-cart." But George Bernard Shaw made it universally prominent through the title of his play *The Apple Cart*. Nowadays apple-carts are no longer seen, but the cliché persists.

VENT ONE'S SPLEEN, TO

A *spleen* is a ductless, glandlike organ at the left of the stomach in man, and near the stomach and intestines in other vertebrates. It stores blood and helps filter foreign substances from the blood. The spleen was once believed to cause low spirits. It was regarded as the seat of morose feelings, bad temper, and spite. When a person is said *to be venting his spleen,* he is melancholy or being spiteful. No matter which, he has ill feelings. John Tatham wrote about it as early as 1641: "Did you e'er hear spleen better vented?" Denis A. McCarthy offered a philosophical concept that the world has waited for but has never attained: "This is the land where hate should die,/ No feuds of faith, no spleen of race."

VICIOUS CIRCLE

A *vicious circle* is defined as "a chain of circumstances in which the solving of one problem creates a new problem which makes the original problem more difficult of solution." Or, to state it in other, simpler words, it is a bad situation that grows worse and worse because dealing with one problem creates another. Even the solution of one problem creates other problems. This concept comes from formal logic. It is the fallacy of relying on a statement to prove another that depends on the first one for proof. The *Encyclopedia Britannica* (1792) says: "He runs into what is termed by logicians a *vicious circle.*" George du Maurier, in 1892, not only used the term *vicious circle* tellingly, but also upstaged the Surgeon General. He wrote: "The wretcheder one is, the more one smokes; and the more one smokes, the wretcheder one gets—a vicious circle."

WALK ON AIR, TO

It would be fascinating for a person to be able to walk on air or to fly through the air. But science has not as yet discovered the secrets of personal aerodynamics. Nevertheless, some people on occasion do *walk on air,* figuratively speaking; that is, at the moment they are elated, ecstatic, exuberantly joyful, possibly because of some good fortune. They have a feeling of having been lifted from the ground and are now floating. It is what is assumed to be a heavenly feeling. Such a sensation was described by Robert Louis Stevenson in *Memories and Portraits* (1887): "I went home that morning walking upon air." John Keats, with his feathery touch, in his poem "Isabella" pictured two lovers as "Parting they seemed to tread upon the air,/Twin roses by the zephyr blown apart to meet again more close."

Shakespeare in his *Sonnets* took a different tack. He wrote: "I grant I never saw a goddess go./My mistress when she walks, walks on the ground."

WALLS HAVE EARS, EVEN

When one is whispering a secret to someone, not unusually the person is cautioned to speak still lower because *even walls have ears.* What is meant, of course, is that others might be listening—so be careful. This warning has been with us at least since the time when the Louvre was built in Paris. Catherine de Médicis, the Queen, was suspicious of her royal courtiers and advisers. She therefore had the building so constructed that she could hear in one room what was being said in another. And no doubt she learned of state secrets and plots to destroy her. The probabilities are that some of these loudmouths lost their heads because they didn't know that even walls have ears.

WARM THE COCKLES OF THE HEART, TO

> It is a cockle, or a walnut shell.
> —Shakespeare,
> *The Taming of the Shrew*

The word *cockle,* referring to a part of the heart, as in *to warm the cockles of the heart,* is not listed in modern dictionaries. Although the allusion to something that gratifies one's deepest feelings, that evokes a glow of pleasure, is well known and widely accepted, the part of the heart called *cockles* may have been a figment of someone's imagination when first uttered centuries ago, which, of course, was long before anatomy became the science as we know it. In fact, in *Gray's Anatomy* under "heart," you will find no mention of *cockles.*

Cockles are small saltwater shellfish whose divided shell is heart-shaped; that is, according to the popular conception of the shape of a heart as is often seen on a St. Valentine's Day card. It may be that *cockles* in *cockles of the heart* was derived from that supposed resemblance to heart ventricles. But it should be pointed out that in Latin "ventricles of the heart" is *cockleae cordis.* Perhaps therein lies a clue.

WEAR ONE'S HEART ON ONE'S SLEEVE, TO

To wear one's heart on one's sleeve is to expose secret hopes, wishes, or intentions. But when this saying first appeared in Shakespeare's *Othello,* it referred to a lady's token of devotion actually worn by her love on his sleeve. It meant that everyone could now take notice of the secret that had been ensconced in the wearer's heart. Here's the way Iago put it in *Othello:*

For when my outward action doth demonstrate
The native act and figure of my heart
In compliment extern, 'tis not long after
But I will wear my heart upon my sleeve
For daws to peck at.

The practice of wearing a token of love on a sleeve antedated Shakespeare by centuries. Knights were accustomed to attaching to their sleeves favors given them by their ladies so that everyone could know of the knight's formerly hidden attachment.

WEEK

Doomsday is the eighth day of the week.
—Stanley Kunitz, *Foreign Affairs*

Although everyone is aware of the number of weeks in a year, no one knows exactly how the division of time called a *week* came about. A *week,* of course, is any successive seven days, which is what the ancient Hebrew week consisted of. According to the book of Genesis, the world was created in six days, and the seventh day was a day of rest and worship. West Africans had a four-day week and Central Asians a five-day week. The Assyrians added another day; their week lasted six days. The Babylonians adopted a seven-day week, relating their time to the phases of the moon, of twenty-eight days. The number *seven* was sacred to them, and so they established four seven-day weeks, which, roughly, became the length of the month. (More accurately, the moon's phases take approximately twenty-nine and a half days.) The Scandinavian week consisted of five days. Under Roman influence the week was increased by two days—the Sun's day and the Moon's day—to make it seven days.

The English word *week* can be traced to the Middle English *weke, wike.* Many languages had similar-sounding words. The original sense seems to have been "a change in time, a regularly recurring period," and is related to the Old English *wice,* succession. And so it is that week follows week unendingly.

WET ONE'S WHISTLE, TO

To wet one's whistle is to moisten the windpipe by taking a drink. One cannot whistle easily with dry lips. Rather than lick the lips, it is better to have a drink. The idiom *to wet one's whistle* is traceable to the thirteenth century. In *The Battle of the Wines* appears this ditty:

> Listen now to a great fable
> That happened the other day at table
> To good King Philip, who did incline
> To wet his whistle with good white wine.

Chaucer, in *The Canterbury Tales* ("The Reeve's Tale"), has this to say: "So was hir joly whistle wel y-wet."

WHAT THE DICKENS

What the dickens would seem to be an emanation from the name of the well-known novelist Charles Dickens. But that exclamation and the novelist's name had nothing to do with each other. In fact, the term preceded Dickens by centuries. Shakespeare used it in 1598 in *The Merry Wives of Windsor,* in which Miss Page, struggling to recall Falstaff's name, says, "I cannot tell what the dickens his name is." Conjectures regarding the origin of *dickens* have ranged from *Old Nick* to Niccolò Machiavelli to *devilkins* or *devil,* and there have been others. Most authorities, but not all, think the most plausible is that *dickens* is simply a euphemism for *devil.* The *Oxford English Dictionary* agrees, for it says that *dickens* is apparently a substitute for *devil,* "as having the same sound." Others suggest that *dickens* is a worn-down version of *devilkin* or *deilkin,* imps, but nothing to substantiate this idea has been found. With all this confusion, one may rightly say, "How the dickens am I to know?"

WHEN IN ROME, DO AS THE ROMANS DO

When in Rome, do as the Romans do is such a common saying that it needs no explanation. Its history is interesting, however, because, unlike today, when the saying is used only figuratively (do as others do with whom you live), it was advice to be followed literally. The advice came from St. Ambrose and was given to St. Augustine regarding the proper day of the week on which to fast. St. Augustine's mother had come to Milan and, learning that fasting was not observed on Saturday as it was in Rome, questioned her son. He thought it best to consult St. Ambrose, who said, according to the *Epistle to Januarius,* "When I am in Rome, I fast on a Saturday; when I am at Milan, I do not. Follow the custom of the church where you are." Which stated proverbially is, "When in Rome, do as the Romans do."

WHEN MY SHIP COMES IN

The cliché refers to hoped-for success so that a fortune will be made. A person might say, "When my ship comes in, then I will pay all my bills" or ". . . then I will buy that stately house up on the hill." Originally the term was widely used during seafaring days, but in two different ways. An investor on land was concerned about the safety of the ship and cargo in which he had invested his money. He would feel much better, and breathe a sigh of relief, when his ship came in. This state of worry was phrased by Henry Mayhew in *London Labour and the London Poor* (1851): "One [customer] always says he'll give me a ton of taties [potatoes] when his ship comes in." The wives of the seafarers had other anxieties—the safety of their husbands. When merchant commerce was a chief means of transportation, ships traveled slowly and communication was so poor that no one knew precisely when to expect the ship's arrival. All the wives could do was wait and hope. The term came to be used figuratively as well. William Morris, editor-in-chief of *The American Heritage Dictionary,* mentions a bit of dialogue from a celebrated novel of the nineteenth century, *John Halifax:* "Perhaps we may manage it sometime." "Yes, when our ship comes in." Brewer says the allusion is to the *Argosy* returning from foreign wars laden with rich loot, which will enrich the merchant or investor who sent the ship forth.

> And I have better news in store for you
> Than you expect: unseal this letter soon;
> There you shall find three of your argosies
> Are richly come to harbour suddenly.
> —Shakespeare, *The Merchant of Venice*

This expression has been obsolescent because transportation is no longer dependent solely on ships. But it has recently experienced a revival by those who are so dejected that they're sure nothing will go their way. They put it this way: "When my ship comes in, in all probability I'll be waiting at the airport."

WHISTLE IN THE DARK, TO

When a person is in a frightening situation, the chances are that he will try to call up his courage by acting cheerfully. One way is by whistling, a practice particularly applicable in the dark or in a lonely place. Hence this idiom, which goes back a long way. John Dryden, in *Amphitryon* (1690), had this to say: "I went darkling and whistling to keep myself from being afraid." Robert Blair in *The Grave* (1742) wrote: "Schoolboy . . . Whistling aloud to bear his courage up." Whistling to show unconcern or lack of fear when confronted with a difficult situation is a habit that has stayed with us.

WHITE ELEPHANT, A

No one wants a *white elephant*. The expression, which gained prominence in the latter part of the nineteenth century, refers to a burdensome gift that must be kept for fear of offending the donor. More often, however, the expression refers to a foolish purchase, one, as it turns out, that is useless. In Siam, now Thailand, all white elephants were sacred and were the property of the king. They were, in one sense, an expensive burden, a luxury that no one, except the king, could afford because, being sacred, these elephants were not allowed to be put to work and therefore could not earn their keep. A rajah, when he disliked one of his nobles and wished to ruin him, would present him with a white elephant. The gift was a serious form of punishment. Considering the cost of its maintenance, it would not be long before the supposedly enriched courtier would find himself impoverished.

P. T. Barnum, the famous circus entrepreneur, has been the subject of several stories concerning his exploits with white elephants. In one, Barnum in 1863 bought a white elephant from Siam. When he received a bill for the shipping charges, which were incredibly high, he declared, "I really bought myself a white elephant." According to another version, a competitor bought a white elephant, which attracted much attention. Barnum, showman that he was, didn't want to be outdone, but he didn't want to invest in a white elephant either. So he whitewashed a gray garden-variety elephant and paraded it about as a white elephant. What has not been told is whether that elephant was ever caught in a heavy rain.

WHOLE HOG, (GO) THE

> Frogs Eat Butterflies. Snakes Eat Frogs.
> Hogs Eat Snakes. Men Eat Hogs.
> —Wallace Stevens, Title of poem

To go the whole hog means "to go all the way," "to do the thing completely, thoroughly," "to commit oneself without reservations." How this idiom arose has not been attested. But there are theories. One, to which some authorities subscribe, is that a *hog* was a coin, a shilling during the seventeenth century. It may have had a hog stamped on its obverse side. Since a shilling was a goodly amount of money in those days, to spend or bet it all was an expensive step to take. But a spendthrift might say, "Shucks, I'm going the whole hog," just as someone in the United States might say, "I'm going to spend the whole buck." Another theory, which is less convincing, is that the expression is attributable directly to a 1779 poem by William Cowper, "The Love of the World Reproved; or Hypocrisy Detected." According to this poem, Mohammed forbade his followers from eating some unspecified part of the hog. The hungry Mohammedans, not knowing which part was intended, decided to experiment on a hog, but they could not agree on the portion to be excepted. Each Mohammedan strove to prove that the part of the hog he preferred was not the forbidden part:

> But for one piece they thought it hard
> From the whole hog to be debar'd;
> And set their wit at work to find
> What joint the prophet had in mind.
> Much controversy straight arose,
> These choose the back, the belly those;
> By some 'tis confidently said
> He meant not to forbid the head;
> While others at that doctrine rail,
> And piously prefer the tail.
> Thus conscience freed from every clog,
> Mahomedans eat up the hog. . . .
> With sophistry their sauce they sweeten,
> Till quite from tail to snout 'tis eaten.

WILD-GOOSE CHASE, A

A *wild-goose chase* is a worthless errand, a senseless pursuit, a harebrained scheme. It is, to quote Dr. Samuel Johnson, "a pursuit of something as unlikely to be caught as a wild goose." A wild goose is exceedingly hard to catch, and furthermore, if caught it is of no value. It is inedible. So why catch it? In the sixteenth century a game played on horseback was known as a *wild-goose chase* because the play resembled the V formation of geese in flight. In *Romeo and Juliet,* the game is referred to by Mercutio when he says, "Nay, if thy wits run the wild-goose chase, I have done; for thou has more of the wild-goose in one of thy wits than, I am sure, I have in my whole five. . . ." To which Romeo replies, "Thou wast never with me for anything when thou wast not there for the goose."

WINDOW

> I remember, I remember
> The house where I was born,
> The little window where the sun
> Came peeping in at morn.
> —Thomas Hood, "I Remember, I Remember"

Window, an opening, especially in a building to admit light, is a word that presents a fascinating image. Working backwards, the word *window* in Middle English was a near spelling, *windowe.* But in Old Norse, its forebear, it was *vindauga,* literally "windeye," a combination of *vindr,* wind, and *auga,* eye. A *window,* therefore, was an eye for the wind or an aperture through which one's eye could see the wind. Today windows may not serve to see the wind, but they remain the eyes of the building. Dr. Johnson defined *window* humorously as an "orifice in an edifice."

WITHOUT BATTING AN EYELID

The word *bat* appears in many everyday expressions. In *right off the bat,* the allusion is to a baseball, which, when struck by a *bat,* flies off quickly. Figuratively the idiom means "without hesitation or deliberation." In the phrase *like a bat out of hell,* the *bat* referred to is a nocturnal flying mammal. The idea behind the idiom is that since bats loathe light, they would fly as rapidly as possible away from hell to escape its fiendish eternal fires. Figuratively it means "with great speed" or "recklessly." But in the saying *without batting an eyelid,* there is no reference either to a bat used in a sport or to a nocturnal creature. It refers to a fluttering or a blinking of the eyelids, a spasmodic, uncontrollable movement. In this sense *bat* comes from French *battre,* to beat, its sense being a fluttering of wings. *Batting,* as it first appeared in 1615 in Latham's *Falconry,* was the fluttering or flapping of the wings of a bird striving to get away. Metaphorically, *without batting an eyelid* means betraying no surprise or emotion. A girl who bats an eyelid is winking; a man who does not bat an eyelid in return is not heeding the signal.

WORLD IS MY OYSTER, THE

This curious saying means that the world is the place in which we must take advantage, extract profit, as one would extract a pearl from an oyster. It has become the watchword for ambitious youth who, full of hope and dreams, naturally look to the future. The metaphor came from the pen of William Shakespeare. In *The Merry Wives of Windsor,* the buffoon Sir John Falstaff asks a braggart named Pistol for a favor, but is turned down. Later Pistol asks Falstaff for a loan, which he turns down, saying, "I will not lend thee a penny." Pistol's retort, made while he is brandishing a sword, has been used so often as to become a cliché. He says: "Why then the world's mine oyster,/Which I with sword will open." As Evans remarked: "O. Henry observed a sword is a far more suitable instrument than a typewriter for opening oysters."

WOULDN'T TOUCH IT WITH A TEN-FOOT POLE

A person objecting to a proposition or wishing to avoid a situation that is distasteful, repugnant, or dangerous might say, "I wouldn't touch it with a *ten-foot pole*" (*pole* comes from the Latin *polus,* a pole or stake), a figurative sense that developed midway through the nineteenth century. What was meant was that on no account would there be any interest. If instead of a ten-foot pole one of eight or twelve feet were mentioned, would the expression lose its effectiveness? It would not. The same point would be made. But what would be missing is the historical accuracy behind the size of the pole. The fact is that a *ten-foot pole* was the standard size used by boatmen who hauled merchandise in poleboats with flat bottoms. Hence to measure the depth of the water, boatmen cut their poles at ten-foot lengths. The poles then served both as a measuring rod and as the propeller with which the boatmen pushed. When people in these river communities found reason to avoid a matter, they expressed their objection by saying, "I wouldn't touch it with a riverman's ten-foot pole." Poleboats went out of existence, and so did the word *riverman's* in the phrase, but the rest of the expression survived. It is still very much with us today. Anyone can see why accuracy will not accept any length other than ten feet.

X RAY

An *X ray* is a photograph taken with X rays (for the technical-minded, it is "a relatively high-energy photon, with wavelength in the approximate range from 0.05 to 100 Angstroms"). Almost everyone—certainly those who have sat in a dental chair—has been X-rayed.

The development of the X ray, an extremely useful aid to the healing arts, was a lucky discovery, not an invention. The discovery came about in 1895 when a German physicist experimenting with a vacuum tube on the conduction of electricity through gases noticed that a fluorescent screen near the tube had become luminous, even when shielded from the light of the tube. Further study made the physics of this strange behavior clearer, but since the nature of the luminosity was uncertain, the discoverer called it *X-Strahl* (*X* since the days of Descartes has designated the unknown; *Strahl* in German means "ray"). These rays are sometimes called *roentgen rays,* and a medical specialist in the field is known as a *roentgenologist.* The physicist discoverer was Wilhelm Konrad Roentgen (also spelled Röntgen), the first Nobel prizewinner for physics.

YOU CAN'T MAKE A SILK PURSE OUT OF A SOW'S EAR

Many sayings, proverbs, and axioms tell us what we can't do. For example, "You can lead a horse to water but you can't make him drink," "You can't fight City Hall," "You can't take it with you," "You can't win 'em all," "You can't make an omelet without breaking eggs," and so forth. But one that clearly makes no sense and one on which no one needs advice is "You can't make a silk purse out of a sow's ear." And of course the fact that you can't is so obvious that no explanation is needed. And yet this proverbial warning has been with us since the sixteenth century and is still in circulation, even in metropolitan areas where probably some who use the term don't know what a sow is, and may have never seen one. For the record, a *sow* is an adult female hog. The sense of the proverb, of course, is that you cannot make something good or of value out of what by nature is bad. If you don't have the right material or idea to begin with, you'll end up with something unsatisfactory. Although said in different words by Alexander Barclay in *Certayne Eglogues* four hundred years ago, the thought is still the same: "None can . . . make goodly silke of a gotes fleece"; and Stephen Gosson in *Ephemerides* (1579) wrote: ". . . seekinge . . . to make a silke purse of a Sowes eare." Jonathan Swift in *Polite Conversation* (1738) recorded it the way it is used and spelled today.

ZEST

> I shall grow old but never lose life's zest.
> —Henry Van Dyke, *The Zest of Life*

Everyone admires spirited enjoyment, wholehearted interest, that which, in a word, is called *zest*. Such a lively word, one would imagine, should have a clear, vivacious ancestor. But this is not so. In fact, its origin is uncertain. The word's genealogy can be traced to the French *zeste*, but beyond that no ancestral background has surfaced. The meaning of *zest*, in French, bore no relationship to that which appeared in the first line. It meant "orange or lemon peel." A *zest* was an additive to food or drink to give it flavor or to make it spicy. Geoffry Blount, in 1674, said of *zest*: ". . . Orange, or such like, squeezed into a glass of wine, to give it relish." The meaning of *zest*, an orange or lemon peel to add flavor, shifted to the food or drink itself. It was the comestible that came to have zest—an exciting flavor or piquancy. At the beginning of the nineteenth century the word took an even more dramatic turn; *zest* came to mean "keen enjoyment." A belly dancer at a bachelor's shindig might add zest to the party.

ZEUS

The Greek god *Zeus,* the king of the gods in the Greek pan-
theon, found that turning people into animals was an effective
disguise of a person's true identity. No one would think that the animal was really a person. For example, he once turned himself into
a bull so that, when mingling with the king's herd, he could be
close to Europa, the king's daughter.

In another case—from which geographical names evolved—
Zeus, again enamored by the beauty of a maiden (this time a
nymph named Io), had to dig deeply into his bag of tricks so that
he could make love to her away from the watchful eye of his jealous wife, Hera. He did this by changing Io into a cow. But since
Hera knew Zeus to be crafty, she sent Argus, who had a hundred
eyes, to see what was happening. Zeus killed Argus. Hera, not to
be outdone, and now sure of her husband's infidelity and the true
identity of the cow, sent a fly with a large stinger to molest her and
to give her no rest. Io, still in the form of a cow, fled the land and
went from place to place to avoid the fly. On one occasion she
crossed the straits near Istanbul, which, in honor of the event, was
named *Bosporus,* meaning, in Latin, "cow crossing"—*cow* in Latin is *bos.* (For geographic precisians, the *Bosporus* connects the
Sea of Marmara and the Black Sea.) In desperation Io jumped
into the sea between Greece and southern Italy. This event was
memoralized by the name given the sea—the Ionian Sea. And for
those who think this story is a lot of bull, who is there to argue
with them?

References

Brewer, Cobham E. *Dictionary of Phrase and Fable*. New York: Harper & Row, 1964.

Ciardi, John. *A Browser's Dictionary*. New York: Harper & Row, 1980.

Evans, Bergen, and Cornelia Evans. *A Dictionary of Contemporary American English*. New York: Random House, 1957.

Freeman, Morton S. *Hue and Cry and Humble Pie: The Stories Behind the Words*. New York: Penguin Books, 1992.

Holt, Alfred H. *Phrase and Word Origins*. New York: Dover Publications, 1961.

Klein, Ernest. *A Comprehensive Etymological Dictionary of the English Language*. New York: Elsevier, 1986.

Mencken, H. L. *The American Language*. New York: Alfred A. Knopf, 1963.

OED: The Oxford English Dictionary. London: Oxford University Press, 1935–1988.

Partridge, Eric. *A Dictionary of Slang and Unconventional Language*. New York: Macmillan, 1950.

Shipley, Joseph T. *Dictionary of Word Origins*. New York: The Philosophical Library, 1945.

Index

abet, 1
a bird in the hand, 27–28
abode, 97
a bolt from the blue, 33
aborigines, 1–2
aboveboard, 2
absence, conspicuous by his, 72–73
absurd, 2–3
a busman's holiday, 47
according to Hoyle, 3–4
a chip off the old block, 62
acute, 79
adolescent, 4
adult, 4
Aegean Sea, 4–5
Aesop, 5
a feather in one's cap, 109–10
a fine kettle of fish, 172
a fool and his money are soon parted, 116
a fool's paradise, 116
aghast, 113
a horse of a different color, 153
air, to walk on, 299
Aladdin's lamp, 5–6
alcove, 6–7
a lick and a promise, 183
a little bird told me, 186–87
all balled up, 8
all over but the shouting, it's, 8–9

almighty dollar, the, 9
alphabet, 212
alto, 165
amortization, 202
an ax to grind, 16
anecdote, 8–9
a nine-day wonder, 208
answer, 9
Antarctic, 11
antibiotic, 17
A-one/A-1, 9–10
ape, to play the sedulous, 229
applecart, to upset the, 296
apple-pie order, in, 10
arctic, 10–11
Arctic bear, 10–11
arena, 11–12
Argentina, 12
arm, shot in the, 222
around the bush, to beat, 22
asbestos, 12
ashes, to be in sackcloth and, 253
a skeleton in the closet, 262
assay/essay, 13
asset, 13–14
a tempest in a teapot, 281
Atlantic Ocean, 14–15
Atlantis, 15
a tree, up, 18
at the drop of a hat, 95
at the end of one's rope, 101–02

automobiles, 15
average, 15–16
avocado, 282
a white elephant, 304–05
a wild-goose chase, 306
ax to grind, an, 16

bacillus, 17
back, scratch one's, 256
bacon, to bring home the, 39–40
bacteria, 17
badger, 17–18
bag, left holding the, 225
bag, to let the cat out of the, 225
balled up, all, 7
baritone, 165
Barkis is willin', 19
bark up the wrong tree, to, 18
barnacle, 19
barnacle, goose, 19
barrel, lock, stock, and, 188
barrel, to be over a, 218
base, 164
bass, 164–65
bassinet, 20
batting an eyelid, without, 307
bay, to hold at, 150
bayonet, 20–21
bear, teddy, 280
beard the lion, to, 21
bear it, grin and, 137
bears, bulls and, 44–45
beat around the bush, to, 22
beat/flog a dead horse, to, 83
beat the rap, to, 22–23
beef, to, 23–24
bee in one's bonnet, to have a, 23

before you can say Jack
    Robinson, 24–25
behind the scenes, 26
bell, book, and candle, 25
bell the cat, who will, 25–26
belt, hitting below the, 149
berry, brown as a, 41
better part of valor is discretion,
    the, 186
beware of Greeks bearing gifts,
    135–36
big shot, 222
billiards, 26–27
bird in the hand, a, 27–28
bird told me, a little, 186–87
bite off more than you can chew,
    to, 28
bite the bullet, to, 28–29
bite the dust, to, 29
black book, in one's, 29–30
blacksmith, 30
blatherskate, 59
blockhead, 31
blood, cold-, 68
bloody but unbowed, 31
blue, a bolt from the, 33
boat, to be in the same, 163
bodice, 32
bogus, 32–33
bolt, shot his, 259–60
bolt from the blue, a, 33
bolt of cloth, 260
bolt upright, 260
bones about it, to make no, 194
bonnet, to have a bee in one's, 23
book, in one's black, 29–30
book, and candle, bell, 25
boomerang, 34
boot, 34

boot, to give someone something to, 129
bootlegger, 35
bootless, 34
Bosporus, 312
boss, 35
boulevard, 35–36
Braille, 36
brasilwood, 37
bravado, 87
bravo, 165
Brazil, 37
bread, 37
break the ice, to, 38
brick, 38–39
bring home the bacon, to, 39–40
broom sweeps clean, the new, 206–07
brouhaha, 40
brown as a berry, 41
brown study, in a, 41–42
browse, 42
bucket, to kick the, 173
buckle, 42–43
buckram, 64
bug, 43–44
bugaboo, 43
bugbear, 43
bug in a rug, snug as a, 267
bullet, to bite the, 28–29
bull in a china shop, like a, 44
bulls and bears, 44–45
bull story, cock and, 67
bulwark, 36
burning ears, 45
burn the candle at both ends, to, 45–46
bury the hatchet, to, 46
bush, to beat around the, 22

bushed, 47
bushel, to hide one's light under a, 147
busman's holiday, a, 47
bust, 48
butter won't melt in his mouth, 48–49
buxom, 49
buy a pig in a poke, to, 225
buy for a song, 49–50
by hook or by crook, 50–51
by the skin of one's teeth, 51

caboodle, kit and, 173–74
Caesar, 52
Caesarean section, 52
cake and eat it, you can't have your, 145
calculate, 53
calculus, 53
caldron, 63
calico, 64
call a spade a spade, to, 53–54
camel's back, the straw that broke the, 273–74
canapé, 152
candle at both ends, to burn the, 45–46
candle, bell, book, and, 25
candles, 54
canoe, to paddle your own, 220
cap, a feather in one's, 109–10
cap for, to set one's, 258
caracul, 64
cart before the horse, to put the, 236
Casanova, Lothario: Lover Boys, 55

Cassiopea, 55–56
cat, who will bell the, 25–26
catastrophe, 85
Catch-22, 56
cathouse, 244
catnaps, 119
cat-o'-nine-tails, 244
cat out of the bag, to let the, 225
cats and dogs, it's raining,
    244–45
cat's paw, to be made a, 57
cattycorner, 57
cellar, 254
Celsius/Fahrenheit, 107
cement, Portland, 232
centigrade, 107
chaff, to separate the wheat from
    the, 256–57
chaos, 99
character, 57–58
charley horse, 58–59
chase, a wild-goose, 306
cheapskate, 59
chew, to bite off more than you
    can, 28
chew the rag, to, 60
chicken feed, 60–61
chickens before they're hatched,
    don't count your, 93–94
chiffon, 61
chiffonier, 61
Chinaman's chance, not a, 61
china shop, like a bull in a, 44
chintz, 32
chip off the old block, a, 62
chowder/lasagna, 62–63
cinch, lead-pipe, 178–79
circle, vicious, 297–98
clichés, 186

clock, 63, 288
closet, a skeleton in the, 262
cloths, names of, 63–64
coach, 64–65
cobalt, 65
cobbler, stick to your last, 66
cobra, 66–67
coccus, 17
cock and bull story, 67
cocked hat, to be knocked into a,
    174
cockles of the heart, to warm the,
    300
cold-blood, 68
cold feet, to have, 68–69
cold shoulder, to give one the, 69
coleslaw, 69–70
cologne, 70
come to a head, to, 70–71
comfort, 71
congress, 72
conspicuous by his absence,
    72–73
contralto, 165
cook one's goose, to, 73
cool as a cucumber, 74
copper, 74
copulate, 72
corporation, 75
corset, 32
count your chickens before
    they're hatched, don't, 93–94
courtesan, 75–76
courtier, 75
cover, 7
craw, to stick in one's, 272
crazy bone, 120
creepers, jeepers, 167–68
crestfallen, 130

cretonne, 64
croissant, 76
crook, by hook or by, 50–51
crow, to eat, 100
cry wolf, 76–77
cuckold, 77–78
cuckoo, 77–78
cucumber, cool as a, 74
cue, 27
cup and lip, there's many a slip
  'twixt, 283
cut and dried, 78–79
cute, 79
cut no ice, 79–80
cut off one's nose to spite one's
  face, to, 80
cut the mustard, to, 80–81

dachshund, 92, 93
Dago, 103–04
Damocles, the sword of, 274–75
Damon and Pythias, 82
dance, St. Vitus's, 270–71
dandelion, 115
dark, to whistle in the, 304
dead as a doornail, 82–83
dead horse, to flog/beat a, 83
deadline, 84
debacle, 84–85
defend, 110
defender, 110
delicatessen, 85
delight, 85
delta, 86
derringer, 86
desperado, 87
Dickens, what the, 302
dictator, 87–88

diesel, 88–89
diet, 90
disaster, 85
discretion, the better part of valor
  is, 186
distaff, 270
doctor/physician, 90–91
dog, love me, love my, 190
dog, to put on the, 235
dog in the manger, 91
dogs, it's raining cats and,
  244–45
dogs, names of, 92–93
dogs lie, let sleeping, 181
dog's life, to lead a, 92
dollar, the almighty, 8
don't count your chickens before
  they're hatched, 93–94
don't look back, someone might
  be gaining on you, 94
don't swap horses in midstream,
  94
doornail, dead as a, 82–83
down, hands, 142–43
dried, cut and, 78–79
drop of a hat, at the, 95
drug on the market, 95
dry, high and, 147–48
Duce, 88
dukes, put up your, 237
dumb, 96
dumbbell, 96
Dutch uncle, 96
dwell, 97

eagle-eyed, 98
earmark, 98–99
ears, burning, 45

ears, even walls have, 299–300
earth, 99–100
eat crow, to, 100
eat high on the hog, to, 148
ecstasy, 101
egg, to lay an, 177–78
elephant, a white, 304–05
end of one's rope, at the, 101–02
enfranchise, 117
enough/galore, 102
enthusiasm, 102–03
eponym, 103
eponymous, 103
Eskimo, 156–57
essay/assay, 13
ethnic names, 103–04
eureka, 104
even-Steven, 105
even walls have ears, 299–300
evil, hear no, 145–46
exception proves the rule, the,
    105
eyed, eagle-, 98
eyelid, without batting an, 307
eyeteeth for, to give one's,
    128–29

fabrics, 106
face, to cut off one's nose to spite
    one's, 80
Fahrenheit/Celsius, 107
fair and square, 107–08
farm, 108
farrier, 30
fast, hard and, 148
fast and loose, to play, 227–28
fatal, 108–09
fatalism, 109

fateful, 109
fault, generous to a, 124
feast, a skeleton at the, 261
feather in one's cap, a, 109–10
feather one's nest, to, 110
feet, to have cold, 68–69
fence, 110
fend, 110
fender, 110
fiddle, fit as a, 112–13
file, 111
fingers/toes, 111–12
fire and water, to go through,
    134
fish, a fine kettle of, 172
fist, grease the, 166
fit as a fiddle, 112–13
flabbergast, 114
flammable, 161
flap, 113
flattery will get you nowhere,
    113–14
flog/beat a dead horse, to, 83
flowers, 114–15
fly in the ointment, a, 115
fool and his money are soon
    parted, a, 116
fool's paradise, a, 116
forty winks, 116–17
franchise, 117
frank, 117
franking privilege, 117
freeman, 182
freeman/slave, 117–18
from pillar to post, 118–19
from the sublime to the
    ridiculous, 119
fry, small, 264
fuchsia, 115

funny bone, 120
fury, 119–20

gab, gift of, 127
gabble, 126, 127
gadget, 121
gaff, 121–22
galore/enough, 102
game, 122
game leg, 122
gams, 122
gangplank, 123
gap, 150
gardenia, 114
gas, 123–24
gay, 151–52
generous to a fault, 124
geocentric, 99
geography, 99
geology, 99
geometry, 99
get one's goat, to, 124–25
get the sack, to, 125–26
gibberish, 126
giddy, 126–27
gift of gab, 127
gifts, beware of Greeks bearing, 135–36
giggle, 126
gild the lily, to, 127–28
gin, 128
give one's eyeteeth for, to, 128–29
give someone something to boot, to, 129
gizzard, 272
glad, 130
gladiolas, 115

glamour/grammar, 130–31
go against the grain, to, 131
goat, to get one's, 124–25
gobs, 132
God go I, there but for the grace of, 282–83
go haywire, to, 132–33
gonorrhea/syphilis, 133
good news, no news is, 210
goose, to cook one's, 73
goose barnacle, 19
goose chase, a wild-, 306
gorgeous/lavaliere, 177
go scot-free, to, 134
go the whole hog, 305–06
go through fire and water, to, 134
grace of God go I, there but for the, 282–83
grade, to make the, 195–96
grain, to go against the, 131
grain of salt, take with a, 278
grammar/glamour, 130–31
grass widow, 135
grease the palm or fist, 166
Greeks bearing gifts, beware of, 135–36
green-eyed monster, the, 136
greenhorn, 137
grin and bear it, 137
grog, 138
groggy, 138
grosgram, 138
guarantee/warranty, 138–39
guinea fowl, 291
Gumbo Limbo, 139

haberdashery, 140–41
hair, without turning a, 291

hairsbreadth, 141
hair stand on end, to make one's, 194
half a loaf is better than none, 141–42
Hamburg, 155
hand, a bird in the, 27–28
hand, to have the upper, 295
handkerchief, 142
hands down, 142–43
handwriting on the wall, the, 143
hard and fast, 148
hard as nails, 144
harp on one string, to, 144–45
hat, at the drop of a, 95
hat, to be knocked into a, 174
hatchet, to bury the, 46
hatter, mad as a, 191–92
have your cake and eat it, you can't, 145
haywire, to go, 132–33
head, to come to a, 70–71
head, to hit the nail on the, 148–49
head or tail, unable to make, 194
head over heels, to be, 146
hear no evil, 145–46
heart, to warm the cockles of the, 300
heart on one's sleeve, to wear one's, 300–01
heaven, to be in seventh, 258–59
heels, to be head over, 146
hen, mad as a, 193
hen parties, 119
herring, red, 246
he travels fastest who travels alone, 186
hidebound, 146–47

hide one's light under a bushel, to, 147
high and dry, 147–48
high horse, to be on one's, 214
high on the hog, to eat/live, 148
hit the nail on the head, to, 148–49
hitting below the belt, 149
hog, (go) the whole, 305–06
hog, to eat/live high on the, 148
hogwash, 149–50
hold at bay, to, 150
holiday, a busman's, 47
homage, 150–51
homosexual, 151–52
hook or by crook, by, 50–51
horns, to lock, 188
hors d'oeuvres, 152
horse, to be on one's high, 214
horse, to put the cart before the, 236
horse bay, 150
horse latitudes, 152–53
horselaugh, 154
horse of a different color, a, 153
horses in midstream, don't swap, 94
horse's mouth, straight from the, 119
hot-tempered, 68
housewife, 155
Hoyle, according to, 3–4
human kindness, the milk of, 199–200
humbug, 155–56
humerus, 120
hunch, 156
husky, 156–57
hussy, 154

ice, cut no, 79–80
ice, to break the, 38
icicle, 158
imp, 158–59
in a brown study, 41–42
in apple-pie order, 10
in a (pretty) pickle, to be, 159
index, 112
Indian, 160
Indian giver, 160
inflammable, 160–61
ingenuity, 128
inoculate, 161–62
in one's black book, 29–30
internecine, 162
in the nick of time, 207
in the same boat, to be, 163
Inuit, 156
inveigle, 163
iris, 244
iridescence, 243–44
irony, Socratic, 267
island, 164
isle, 164
isotopes, 294
is willin', Barkis, 19
Italian voices, 164–65
itching palm, to have an, 165–66
it's all over but the shouting, 7–8

jabber, 126
Jack Robinson, before you can
    say, 24–25
janitor, 167
January, 167
jeepers creepers, 167–68
jeopardy, 168
jersey, 64

jiminy crickets, 167–68
jingo, 168–69
jingoism, 169
Joe Miller, 169–70
jot/tittle, 169
jumbo, 170
jumbo, mumbo, 203

kaput, 171
karakul, 64
keep a stiff upper lip, to, 171–72
kettle of fish, a fine, 172
kibosh on, to put the, 236
kick the bucket, to, 173
kit and caboodle, 173–74
knocked into a cocked hat, to be,
    174
knock on wood, 175
know the ropes, to, 175–76

lamp, Aladdin's, 5
lasagna/chowder, 62–63
lascivious, 182
latitudes, horse, 152–53
laureate, 247
laurels, to rest on one's, 247
lavaliere/gorgeous, 177
lay an egg, to, 177–78
lay on, Macduff, 178
lead-pipe cinch, 178–79
leave in the lurch, to, 179
leave no stone unturned, to,
    179–80
led by the nose, to be, 180
leech, 112
left holding the bag, 225
leg, to pull someone's, 234

let her rip, 181
let sleeping dogs lie, 181
letters and numbers, 211–12
lewd, 182
liberal, 182
liberal arts, 182
lick and a promise, a, 183
lick into shape, to, 183–84
light fantastic, 186
like a bull in a china shop, 44
like a Dutch uncle, 96
Limbo, Gumbo, 139
limelight, 184
limerick, 184–85
line, toe the, 288
lion, to beard the, 21
lion's share, the, 185
lip, there's many a slip 'twixt cup and, 283
lip, to keep a stiff upper, 171–72
literary terms, 186
little bird told me, a, 186–87
little-man, 112
live high on the hog, to, 148
loaf is better than none, half a, 141–42
lobster Newburg, 187
lock horns, to, 188
lock, stock, and barrel, 188
log, to sleep like a, 262–63
loggerheads, 189
long-man, 112
longshoreman/stevedore, 272
loose ends, to be at, 189–90
Lothario, 55
love me, love my dog, 190
lurch, to leave in the, 178

macabre, 191
Macduff, lay on, 178
mad as a hatter, 191–92
mad as a hen, 193
mad as a march hare, 192–93
make a mountain out of a molehill, 193
make head or tail, unable to, 194
make no bones about it, to, 194
make one's hair stand on end, to, 195
make the grade, to, 195–96
manger, dog in the, 91
march hare, mad as a, 192–93
margarine, 196
mark, toe the, 288–89
masher, 196–97
master, 35
Mayday/May pole, 197
May pole/Mayday, 197
medicine, 91
Mediterranean, 100
Medusa, 198
Mercedes-Benz, 15
merrier, the more the, 202
mess, 198–99
milk of human kindness, the, 199
Miller, Joe, 169–70
minotaur, 4
mind your p's and q's, 200
mohair, 106
molehill, make a mountain out of a, 193
money, pin, 226
money are soon parted, a fool and his, 116
money burns a hole in his pocket, 200
money like water, to spend, 200

money run through your fingers, to let, 200
monkey, 216
monkey wrench, 201
monster, the green-eyed, 136
more the merrier, the, 202
mortgage, 201–02
mountain out of a molehill, make a, 193
mouth, butter won't melt in his, 8–49
mouth, straight from the horse's, 119
mud, his name is, 204–05
muff, 243
mumbo jumbo, 203
mushroom, 203
muslin, 64, 88
Mussolini, Benito, 88
mustard, to cut the, 80–81

nail on the head, to hit the, 148–49
nails, hard as, 144
naked, 204
naked truth, 204
name is mud, his, 204–05
narcissus, 205
nasturtium, 206
neck and neck, 209
necked, stiff-, 273
neck out, to stick one's, 273
Negro, 103
neither rhyme nor reason, 206
nest, to feather one's, 110
new broom sweeps clean, a, 206–07
Newfoundland, 92

news is good news, no, 210
nick of time, in the, 207
nine-day wonder, a, 208
nip and tuck, 208–09
nitrogen/oxygen, 218–19
Nobel laureate, 247
noisome, 211
non, 209–10
nonchalant, 209
nondescript, 209–10
no news is good news, 210
nonflammable, 161
nonplus, 210
nonsense, 149, 156
nose, to be led by the, 180
nose, to thumb the, 286
nose to spite one's face, to cut off one's, 80
no soap, 210–11
not a Chinaman's chance, 61
not turning a hair, 291
numbers and letters, 211–12

Ocean, Atlantic, 14–15
octopus, 213
ointment, a fly in the, 115
oleomargarine, 196
one, A-, 10
one string, to harp on, 144–45
one swallow does not make a summer, 215
onion, 213–14
on one's high horse, to be, 214
on tenterhooks, to be, 214
opossum, 228
orangutan, 215–16
orchid, 281–82
order, in apple-pie, 10

ordinary, 16
Orion, 216
ornery, 217
ounce, 217–18
over a barrel, 218
over but the shouting, it's all, 7–8
oxygen/nitrogen, 218–19
oyster, the world is my, 308

paddle your own canoe, to, 220
paisley, 64
pajamas, 221
palm, grease the, 166
palm, to have an itching, 165–66
par, up to, 294–95
paradise, a fool's, 116
parasite, 221
parting shot, a, 222
patter, 222–23
Pekingese, 92
penguin, 223
phaeton, 223–24
phalange, 112
phalanx, 112
physician/doctor, 90–91
physicist, 91
picayune, 224–25
pickle, to be in a (pretty), 159
pig in a poke, to buy a, 225
pigtail, 242
piker, 226–27
pillar of the church, 119
pillar to post, from, 118–19
pin money, 226
plain sailing, 227
play fast and loose, to, 227–28
play possum, to, 228
play the sedulous ape, to, 229

poet laureate, 247
Polack, 103
pole, wouldn't touch it with a
  ten-foot, 308
polka dot/polonaise, 229–30
polonaise/polka dot, 229–30
Pomeranian, 92
pompadour, 230
poplin, 230–31
porcelain, 231–32
porcupine, 231–32
Portland cement, 232
possum, to play, 228
post, from pillar to, 118–19
preposterous, 236
price, 233
private, 232
prize, 233
promise, a lick and a, 183
prostitute, 76
p's and q's, mind your, 200
psyche, 233–34
pull someone's leg, to, 234
pundit, 235
put on the dog, to, 235
put the cart before the horse, to,
  235
put the kibosh on, to, 236
put up your dukes, 237
Pygmalion, 237–38
Pythias, Damon and, 82
python, 238

quarantine, 117
quarry, 239
quarter, 240
queen, 240–41
queer, 241

queue, 241–42
quinsy, 242

rag, 61
rag, to chew the, 60
ragamuffin, 243
rainbow, 243–44
raining cats and dogs, it's,
    244–45
rankle, 245
rap, 22–23, 245–46
rap, to beat the, 22–23
rat, to smell a, 265
read the riot act, to, 248–49
reason, neither rhyme nor, 206
red herring, 246
reputation, 58
rest on one's laurels, to, 247
rhyme nor reason, neither, 206
ridiculous, from the sublime to
    the, 119–20
rigmarole, 248
riot act, to read the, 248–49
rip, let her, 181
robin, round, 250
Rome, do as the Roman do, when
    in, 303
rook, 249
rope, at the end of one's, 101–02
ropes, to know the, 175–76
roué, 249–50
round robin, 250
R's, the three, 285
rub, there's the, 283–84
Rubáiyát, 251
rug, snug as a bug in a, 267
rule, the exception proves the,
    105

rule of thumb, 251–52
ruminate, 252

sack, to get the, 125–26
sackcloth and ashes, to be in, 253
saga/sagacious, 253–54
sage, 254
sailing, plain, 227
sails, to take the wind out of
    someone's, 277
St. Vitus's dance, 270–71
salacious, 268
salad, 254
salad sauce, 254
salt, 254
salt, take with a grain of, 278
saltcellar, 254
Sam, Uncle, 293
sardine/tariff, 279–80
sardonic, 255
satin, 64
sauce, salad, 254
saucer, 254
sauté/somersault, 267–68
scenes, behind the, 26
schizophrenia, 255
schneider, 171
scot-free, to go, 134
scratch, to start from, 256
scratch one's back, 256
sedulous ape, to play the, 229
senator, 72
separate the wheat from the chaff,
    to, 256–57
serendipity, 257
sesquipedalian, 257–58
set one's cap for, to, 258
seven, 301

seventh heaven, to be in, 258–59

shantung, 64

ship comes in, when my, 303–04

short shrift, to give, 259

shot, a parting, 222

shot, big, 222

shot at, to have a, 222

shot his bolt, 259–60

shot in the arm, 222

shot wide of the mark, 222

shoulder, to give one the cold, 69

shouting, it's all over but the, 7–8

shrewd, 260

shrift, to give short, 259

sick bay, 150

silk purse out of a sow's ear, you can't make a, 310

six of one and half dozen of the other, 186

skate, 59

skeleton, 260–261

skeleton at the feast, 261

skeleton in the closet, a, 262

skin of one's teeth, by the, 51

Slav, 117

slave/freeman, 117–18

sleeping dogs lie, let, 181

sleep like a top/log, to, 263

sleeve, to wear one's heart on one's, 300–01

slip 'twixt cup and lip, there's many a, 283

slogan, 263–64

small fry, 264

smallpox, 264–65

smell a rat, to, 265

smithy, 30

sneeze, 266

snide, 266–67

snuff, up to, 294–95

snug as a bug in a rug, 267

Socratic irony, 267–68

soft soap, 114

someone might be gaining on you, don't look back, 94

somersault/sauté, 268

song, buy for a, 49–50

sop, 268–69

soprano, 165

sow's ear, you can't make a silk purse out of a, 310

spade a spade, to call a, 53–54

span, spick-and-, 269

spend money like a drunken sailor, to, 200

spend money like water, to, 200

spick-and-span, 269

spinster, 269–70

spirillum, 17

spitting image, the, 270

spleen, to vent one's, 297

square, fair and, 107–08

steal my thunder, to, 271–72

stevedore/longshoreman, 272

Steven, even-, 105

stick in one's craw, to, 272–73

stick one's neck out, to, 273

stick to your last, cobbler, 66

stiff-necked, 273–74

stock, and barrel, lock, 188

stone unturned, to leave no, 179–80

straight from the horse's mouth, 119

straw that broke the camel's back, the, 274

strength, tower of, 289–90

string, to harp on one, 144–45

stymied, to be, 274
sublime to the ridiculous, from the, 119–20
suede, 64
summer, one swallow does not make a, 215
swallow does not make a summer, one, 215
swap horses in midstream, don't, 94
sword of Damocles, the, 275
syphylis/gonorrhea, 133

T, to a, 276
T, to fit to a, 276
tail, unable to make head or, 194
take the cake, to, 277
take the wind out of someone's sails, to, 277
take with a grain of salt, 278
talk turkey, to, 278–79
tapering off, 54
tapers, 54
target, 279
tariff/sardine, 279–80
teapot, a tempest in a, 281
teddy bear, 280
tee, 276
teeth, by the skin of one's, 51
teetotaler, 280–81
tempest in a teapot, a, 281
ten-foot pole, wouldn't touch it with a, 308
tenor, 165
tenterhooks, to be on, 214
terrace, 99
terra firma, 99
terrestrial, 100

terrier, 92–93
territory, 99
testicle, 281–82
testimony, 281–82
the better part of valor is discretion, 186
the exception proves the rule, 105
the green-eyed monster, 136
the handwriting on the wall, 143
the milk of human kindness, 199–200
a new broom sweeps clean, 206–07
there but for the grace of God go I, 282–83
there's many a slip 'twixt cup and lip, 283
there's the rub, 283–84
thermometer, 107
the spitting image, 270
the straw that broke the camel's back, 273–74
the three R's, 285
the whole hog, (go), 305–06
the world is my oyster, 308
thick and thin, through, 285–86
thick as thieves, 284
thieves, thick as, 284
thin, through thick and, 285–86
third/three, 284–85
three R's, the, 285
three/third, 284–85
through thick and thin, 285–86
thumb, 111–12
thumb, rule of, 251–52
thumb the nose, to, 286
thunder, to steal my, 271
thunderstruck, 286–87
Thursday, 287

tilt at windmills, to, 287
time, in the nick of, 207
timepiece, 288
tittle/jot, 169
to a T, 276
to bark up the wrong tree, 18
to beard the lion, 21
to beat around the bush, 22
to be at loose ends, 189–90
to beat the rap, 22–23
to beef, 23–24
to be head over heels, 146
to be in a (pretty) pickle, 159
to be in sackcloth and ashes, 253
to be in seventh heaven, 258–59
to be in the same boat, 163
to be knocked into a cocked hat,
   174
to be led by the nose, 180
to be made a cat's paw, 57
to be on one's high horse, 214
to be on tenterhooks, 214
to be over a barrel, 218
to be stymied, 274
to bite off more than you can
   chew, 28
to bite the bullet, 28–29
to bite the dust, 29
to boot, to give someone
   something, 129
to break the ice, 38
to bring home the bacon, 39–40
to burn the candle at both ends,
   45–46
to bury the hatchet, 46–47
to buy a pig in a poke, 225
to call a spade a spade, 53–54
to chew the rag, 60
to come to a head, 70–71

to cook one's goose, 73
to cut off one's nose to spite
   one's face, 80
to cut the mustard, 80–81
to eat crow, 100
to eat/live high on the hog, 148
toes/fingers, 111–12
toe the line, 288
toe the mark, 288–89
to fit to a T, 276
to get one's goat, 124–25
to get the sack, 125–26
to give one's eyeteeth for, 128–29
to give one the cold shoulder, 69
to give short shrift, 259
to go haywire, 132–33
to go scot-free, 134
to go through fire and water, 134
to harp on one string, 144–45
to have a bee in one's bonnet, 23
to have an itching palm, 165–66
to have a shot at, 222
to have cold feet, 68–69
to hide one's light under a bushel,
   147
to hit the nail on the head,
   148–49
to hold at bay, 150
to keep a stiff upper lip, 171–72
to kick the bucket, 173
to know the ropes, 175–76
to lay an egg, 177–78
to lead a dog's life, 92
to leave in the lurch, 179
to leave no stone unturned,
   179–80
to let money run through your
   fingers, 200
to let the cat out of the bag, 225

to lick into shape, 183–84
to lock horns, 188
to make no bones about it, 194
to make one's hair stand on end, 195
to make the grade, 195–96
to paddle your own canoe, 220
to play fast and loose, 227–28
to play possum, 228
to play the sedulous ape, 229
to pull someone's leg, 234
to put on the dog, 235
to put the cart before the horse, 236
to put the kibosh on, 236
to read the riot act, 248–49
to rest on one's laurels, 247
top, to sleep like a, 262–63
tornado, 87
torpedo, 289
to separate the wheat from the chaff, 256–67
to set one's cap for, 258
to sleep like a top/a log, 262–63
to smell a rat, 265
to spend money like a drunken sailor, 200
to start from scratch, 256
to steal my thunder, 271
to stick in one's craw, 272
to stick one's neck out, 273
to take the cake, 277
to take the wind out of someone's sails, 277
to talk turkey, 278–79
to thumb the nose, 286
to tilt at windmills, 287
toucher, 112

to upset the applecart, 296
to walk on air, 299
to warm the cockles of the heart, 300
to wear one's heart on one's sleeve, 300–01
tower of strength, 289–90
to wet one's whistle, 302
to whistle in the dark, to, 305
travels fastest who travels alone, he, 186
tree, to bark up the wrong, 18
tree, up a, 18
Trojan horse, 136
tuck, nip and, 208–09
tumbler, 290
turkey, 290–91
turkey, to talk, 278–79
turning a hair, not/without, 291
turnpike, 226
turquoise, 291
turtle, 292
turtledove, 292
tweed, 106
typical, 16

unable to make head or tail, 194
unbowed, bloody but, 31
uncle, Dutch, 96
Uncle Sam, 293
unlettered, 182
up, all balled, 7
up a tree, 18
upper hand, to have the, 295
upset the applecart, to, 296
up the wrong tree, to bark, 18
up to snuff/par, 294–95

uranium, 99, 294
Uranus, 99, 294
usual, 16

venereal, 133
vent one's spleen, to, 297
vicious circle, 297–98
voices, Italian, 164–65

w, the letter, 212
walk on air, to, 299
wall, the handwriting on the, 143
walls have ears, even, 299–300
warm the cockles of the heart, to,
  300
warranty/guarantee, 138–39
watch, 288
water, to go through fire and, 134
wear one's heart on one's sleeve,
  to, 300–01
week, 301
wet one's whistle, to, 302
what the Dickens, 302
when in Rome, do as the Romans
  do, 303
when my ship comes in, 303–04
whistle, to wet one's, 302
whistle in the dark, to, 304
white elephant, a, 304–05
whole hog, (go) the, 305–06

who will bell the cat, 25–26
widow, grass, 135
wild-goose chase, a, 306
willin', Barkis is, 19
windmills, to tilt at, 287
wind out of someone's sails, to
  take the, 277
window, 307
winks, forty, 117
without batting an eyelid, 307
without turning a hair, 291
wolf, cry, 76–77
wonder, a nine-day, 208
wood, knock on, 175
Wop, 104
world is my oyster, the, 308
wouldn't touch it with a ten-foot
  pole, 308
wrench, monkey, 201
wrong tree, to bark up the, 18

X ray, 309

you can't make a silk purse out
  of a sow's ear, 310

z, the letter, 212
zest, 311
Zeus, 312

MERIDIAN

FROM A TO Z WITH EASE

☐ **HOW TO READ A POEM by Burton Raffel.** This book is not only a guide to understanding poetry, but a celebration of poetry as well. Raffel's discussion always focuses on specific poems. He includes more than 200 full-length poems, from Shakespeare to Marianne Moore, to help his readers appreciate what makes a poem memorable. (010330—$10.00)

☐ **THE STORY OF LANGUAGE By Mario Pei.** From the dawn of time to the mid-twentieth century . . . world-renowned linguist Mario Pei discusses the formation and development of language—the tool by which mankind has advanced from savagery to civilization. "A good book for both readings and reference."—*The New York Times* (008700—$14.00)

☐ **WORDS TO THE WISE** *The Wordwatcher's Guide to Contemporary Style and Usage* **by Morton S. Freeman.** Wise, witty, and enjoyable to read—an authoritative A-to-Z guide to word usage, grammar, punctuation and spelling. (010748—$9.95)

☐ **WORD FOR WORD** *A Cartoon History of Word Origins—From the Popular Associated Press Feature* **by Mike Atchison.** Frantic cartoon characters vividly and humorously reveal the histories of many of the words and phrases we use every day, helping us to discover not only why we say what we do, but how our culture influences our language and our lives. (266246—$6.95)

Prices slightly higher in Canada.
